MW00396451

Looking Ahead

Introduction to Academic Writing

SHARON L. CAVUSGIL

Georgia State University

SERIES EDITORS

PATRICIA BYRD
Georgia State University

JOY M. REID
University of Wyoming

Video notes in Instructor's Manual by
Elizabeth Mejia
Washington State University

Heinle & Heinle Publishers

I(T)P An International Thomson Publishing Company

Pacific Grove • Albany • Bonn • Boston • Cincinnati • Detroit • London
Madrid • Melbourne • Mexico City • New York • Paris
San Francisco • Tokyo • Toronto • Washington

The publication of *Looking Ahead: Introduction to Academic Writing* was directed by members of the Newbury House ESL/EFL at Heinle & Heinle:

Erik Gundersen, Editorial Director
Jonathan Boggs, Market Development Director
Kristin M. Thalheimer, Senior Production Services Coordinator
Nancy Mann Jordan, Senior Developmental Editor
Stanley J. Galek, Vice President and Publisher

Also participating in the publication of this program were:
Project Manager/Desktop Pagination: Thompson Steele, Inc.
Managing Developmental Editor: Amy Lawler
Manufacturing Coordinator: Mary Beth Hennebury
Associate Editor: Ken Pratt
Associate Market Development Director: Mary Sutton
Photo/video Specialist: Jonathan Stark
Media Services Coordinator: Jerry Christopher
Interior Designer: Sally Steele
Cover Designer: Ha Nguyen
Cover Artist: Katherine Stuart

For permission to use copyrighted material, grateful acknowledgment is made to the copyright holders on page 283, which are hereby made part of this copyright page.

Copyright ©1998 by Heinle & Heinle Publishers
All rights reserved. No part of this publication may be reproduced or transmitted in any form or by any means, electronic or mechanical, including photocopy, recording, or any information storage or retrieval system, without permission in writing from the publisher. Heinle & Heinle Publishers is a division of International Thomson Publishing, Inc. Manufactured in the United States of America.

Pre-recorded material supplied by CNN. ©1998 Cable News Network, Inc. All rights Reserved. ©1998 Turner Learning, Inc. All Rights Reserved.

ISBN 08384-7884-0
10 9 8 7 6 5 4 3 2 1

*T*hank You

The author and publisher would like to thank the following individuals who offered many helpful insights, ideas, and suggestions for change during the development of *Looking Ahead: Introduction to Academic Writing*.

Victoria Badalamenti, *LaGuardia Community College, New York*
Karen Batchelor, *City College of San Francisco*
Cheryl Benz, *Miami Dade Community College*
Pam Butterfield, *Palomar College, California*
Lisa Camp, *Hunter College, New York*
Marvin Coates, *El Paso Community College, Valle Verde Campus*
Carol Culver, *San Francisco State University*
Kathleen Flynn, *Glendale Community College, California*
Barbara Foley, *Union County College, New Jersey*
Byrun Hauser, *Miami Dade Community College*
Gayle Henrotte, *Mt. San Antonio Community College, California*
Mary Hill-Shinn, *El Paso Community College*
Cynthia Howe, *Seattle Central Community College*
Sheila McKee, *University of North Texas*
Lynne Nickerson, *DeKalb College, Georgia*
Norman Prange, *Cuyahoga Community College, Ohio*
Jennifer Ross, *LaGuardia Community College, New York*
Dawn Schmid, *California State University at San Marcos*
Catherine Sessions, *Hunter College, New York*
Bob Shiel, *St. Augustine College, Illinois*
Joe Starr, *Houston Community College*
Christine Tierney, *Houston Community College*
Patricia Weyland, *Ohio State University*

$\mathcal{C}$ontents

To the Teacher: xix

To the Student: xxi

Acknowledgments: xxv

• • • • • • • • •
Chapter 1: Introduction   2

Theme: The U.S. College or University Classroom   2

Goals   2

Sample Authentic College/University Assignments   3

GETTING READY   4

Grammar Preview   7

FOCUSING   8

Reading 1: Expectations and Habits in the U.S. Classroom   8

Writing About Course Expectations   11

Reading 2: Discover Your Learning Styles   13

Reading 3: Study Techniques and Learning Styles   16

Writing About the Study Habits of Your Classmates   20

Writing with General Ideas and Specific Details   21

Guidelines for a Memorandum   22

Writing a Memo   23

READING 5: Writing Habits Survey   25

Writing About Personal Writing Habits   27

PUTTING IT ALL TOGETHER   28

Final Writing Assignment: Your Writing Habits   29

Looking Ahead   31

Chapter 2: Collecting   32

THEME: CULTURE   32

GOALS: 32

SAMPLE AUTHENTIC COLLEGE/UNIVERSITY ASSIGNMENTS   33

GETTING READY   34

Introduction to Collecting   34

Grammar Preview   34

FOCUSING   35

READING 1: What Is Culture?   35

The Grammar of Persuasive Writing:
Opinion Structures   37

READING 2: Tamer's Lists   38

Guidelines for Listing   39

READING 3: Stereotypes   41

The Grammar of Persuasive Writing: Adverbs of Frequency,
Modal Auxiliaries, and Expressions of Quantity   42

Writing Accurate Generalizations   43

READING 4: My Experience with Young Americans   44

Writing Opinion Statements   45

Supporting Your Opinions   45

Charts and Graphs   46

READING 5: The One Thing Teens Want Most From Life   47

READING 6: The Single Worst Influence Facing
Today's Teens   48

Designing Your Own Graph   49

Connecting Ideas in Your Writing   50

Interviewing   52

READING 7: Youth in Vietnam   52

Differences Between Spoken and Written English   53

PUTTING IT ALL TOGETHER   55

Final Writing Assignment: Subcultures Within Societies   55

Looking Ahead   59

Chapter 3: Comparing and Contrasting   60

THEME: PERSONAL ECONOMICS   60

GOALS   60

SAMPLE AUTHENTIC COLLEGE/UNIVERSITY ASSIGNMENTS   61

GETTING READY   62

Introduction to Comparing and Contrasting   62

Grammar Preview   62

FOCUSING   63

Personal Economics   63

READING 1: Understanding Economics   64

Using Cohesion in Your Writing   65

The Grammar of Comparisons: Words of Differences 67

The Grammar of Comparisons: Words of Similarity 69

Writing Comparisons About Spending Habits 72

Extended Comparisons 73

READING 2: Igor's and Hector's Lifestyles 73

Organizing Your Ideas When Comparing and Contrasting 74

General Statements in Extended Comparisons 75

Using Logical Organizers for Cohesion 77

Writing an Extended Comparison 78

READING 3: Buying Versus Renting 79

The Grammar of Persuasive Writing: Conditional Sentences 81

Writing Conditional Sentences About Personal Economics 82

The Grammar of Comparisons: Comparatives 83

Writing Comparative Sentences to Make Housing Decisions 85

READING 4: Buying a Car 86

Writing Contrasting Sentences About Automobiles 88

READING 5: A Personal Letter 90

Guidelines for a Personal Letter 90

READING 6: An E-mail Message 92

Guidelines for an E-mail Message 93

PUTTING IT ALL TOGETHER 95

Final Writing Assignment: A Car Purchase 95

Looking Ahead 97

● ● ● ● ● ● ● ●
Chapter 4: Defining   98

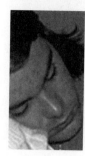

THEME: SLEEP AND DREAMS   98

GOALS   98

SAMPLE AUTHENTIC COLLEGE/UNIVERSITY ASSIGNMENTS   99

GETTING READY   100

Introduction to Defining   100

Grammar Preview   100

FOCUSING   101

READING 1: Dreaming   102

Analyzing the Format of Written Formal Definitions   104

The Grammar of Defining: Present Tense Verbs   105

The Grammar of Defining: Generic Articles and Nouns   106

The Grammar of Defining: Categorizing Nouns   108

The Grammar of Defining: Relative Clauses   110

Writing Formal Definitions   111

Other Definition Structures   112

READING 2: Stages of Sleep   112

Writing Definition Structures   115

READING 3: Sleep and Dreams Test   116

Writing Short Answer Responses   117

Extended Definitions   118

READING 4: Nightmares   118

The Parts of Extended Definitions   119

PUTTING IT ALL TOGETHER   122

Final Writing Assignment: Sleep Problems   122

Looking Ahead   125

Chapter 5: Developing   126

THEME: BLUE JEANS AND LEVI STRAUSS   126

GOALS   126

SAMPLE AUTHENTIC COLLEGE/UNIVERSITY ASSIGNMENTS   127

GETTING READY   128

Introduction to Developing   128

Grammar Preview   128

FOCUSING   129

Reading 1: Blue Jeans: Yesterday and Today   129

The Grammar of Past Time Narrative:
Chronological Organizers   131

The Grammar of Past Time Narrative:
Past Tense Verbs   132

READING 2: Passport to a New Life   135

Non-Restrictive Relative Clauses and Appositives: Giving
Information about People and Places   138

Developing Your Writing: Description   139

Using Description to Write About a Memorable Place   141

READING 3: Should Have Brought Pants   142

The Grammar of Past Time Narrative: Proper Nouns
and Personal Pronouns   144

Developing Your Writing: Personal Experience   145

Developing Your Writing: Examples   146

PUTTING IT ALL TOGETHER   149

Final Writing Assignment: Personal Success   149

Looking Ahead   151

Chapter 6: Classifying 152

THEME: PEOPLE AND PLACES 152

GOALS 152

SAMPLE AUTHENTIC COLLEGE/UNIVERSITY ASSIGNMENTS 153

GETTING READY 154

Introduction to Classifying 154

Grammar Preview 155

FOCUSING 155

READING 1: **What Is Geography?** 155

Organizing Your Ideas 156

Classification Sentences 158

READING 2: **The Subdivisions of Geography** 159

The Grammar of Informational Writing: Complex Noun Phrases and Prepositional Phrases 160

Punctuation in Classification Sentences 161

Developing Your Ideas 163

READING 3: **The Languages of Europe** 163

The Grammar of Informational Writing: Passive Sentences 165

Developing Ideas with Logical Organizers: Example Structures 165

Using Logical Organizers for Cohesion 167

READING 4: **A City** 168

Using Appropriate Logical Organizers for Classification 169

Parallelism in Your Writing   170

READING 5: Migration   173

PUTTING IT ALL TOGETHER   177

**Final Writing Assignment: Migrating to
Your Community   177**

Looking Ahead   179

Chapter 7: Discovering   180

THEME: CONSUMER BEHAVIOR   180

GOALS   180

SAMPLE AUTHENTIC COLLEGE/UNIVERSITY ASSIGNMENTS   181

GETTING READY   182

Introduction to Discovering   182

Grammar Preview   183

FOCUSING   183

READING 1: Understanding Consumer Behavior   184

**The Grammar of Interactive Communication in
Writing:** *You, We,* **and** *I* **Pronouns   185**

READING 2: The "Typical" American Consumer   187

Designing a Table About the Typical Student   189

READING 3: A Survey   190

Survey Information   192

READING 4: Planning Survey Questions   193

**Turning Spoken Language
into Written English   194**

Designing Your Own Survey 195

READING 5: Video and Music Preferences 198

Developing and Analyzing a Tally Sheet 199

PUTTING IT ALL TOGETHER 202

Final Writing Assignment: Survey
and Data Collection 202

Looking Ahead 205

GRAMMAR AND LANGUAGE REFERENCE 206

APPENDICES 275

CREDITS 283

INDEX 285

*W*ill your students be ready to meet the academic writing expectations of their instructors and professors when they leave your ESL program?

*T*hey will if they use *Looking Ahead,* Heinle & Heinle's new 4-level academic writing/grammar series.

SUCCESSFUL WRITING . . . WITH *LOOKING AHEAD*!

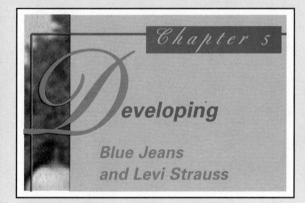

Chapter 5

*D*eveloping

Blue Jeans
and Levi Strauss

Will your students be ready . . . to perform various types of academic writing?

  Looking Ahead focuses on the various types of writing that successful students must learn to employ: *collecting, comparing, defining, developing, classifying,* and others. In practicing these various forms of academic writing, students call upon a host of rhetorical modes such as *definition* and *classification* to support their ideas and opinions. They also develop facility in using a variety of academic writing formats such as *paragraphs, memos, and surveys.*

Will your students be ready . . . to understand and meet challenging academic expectations?
Each chapter begins with authentic academic assignments from across the disciplines (e.g. sociology, history) for students to analyze and discuss. These assignments show how writing tasks are used in the "real world" of academic course work.

GOALS

WRITING
♦ learn different ways to collect ideas for your writing

GRAMMAR
♦ practice the grammar of informational writing, persuasive writing, and interactive communication in writing

CONTENT
♦ learn about different cultures, customs, and values

Will your students be ready . . . to apply their own writing skills to academic situations?
Each chapter contains several short writing activities and most contain at least one longer writing assignment designed to prepare students for the writing tasks they will encounter in college classes. Throughout the chapters, students practice writing activities that are appropriate for a specific academic setting (e.g. writing short answer responses). The writing activities in each chapter end with a writing assignment that guides students step-by-step through the process.

PUTTING IT ALL TOGETHER

FINAL WRITING ASSIGNMENT: SURVEY AND DATA COLLECTION

  Write two or more paragraphs about your survey and data collection. Because you and your group members have already given an oral presentation about your survey, much of your planning for this paper is complete. You will, however, need to change your ideas and spoken English from your presentation into written English for this paper. In addition, attach a copy of your group's survey, the tally sheet, and the chart/graph to your paper.

Activity 7-14   Designing Your Own Survey

With a small group of classmates, design a survey about one of the following. You will give your survey to respondents *not* in this class. If possible, design your survey on the computer.

- preferred restaurants and/or meals
- favorite recreational and entertainment activities
- preferred stores, products, and/or brand names
- popular majors, classes, and/or professors
- (ask your teacher about other ideas you might have)

1. To help you design your own survey, review the *Video and Music Preferences* survey on page 191 and the format/grammar ideas for a survey (Activity 7-11) on page 192.

2. With your group members, decide what you will survey. Discuss possible questions or statements for your respondents and take notes about your ideas.

3. Write four or five questions/statements for your survey. There should be just one idea for each item, and your items should give people choices to make (*yes/no, always/usually/never*).

4. Include a statement to explain the purpose of your survey, brief directions for completing the survey, and a statement to thank the respondent.

5. When you finish, make a copy of the survey for each member of your group.

Will your students be ready . . . to exercise key vocabulary acquisition skills?

Special focus is given to developing vocabulary acquisition skills necessary for success in a variety of academic fields. Students gain strategies for learning new vocabulary and the relevant grammar associated with these vocabulary items.

LEARNER'S NOTEBOOK

Family Customs and Traditions

A custom or tradition is a usual practice or habit. In your learner's notebook, write about a custom or tradition in your family. You may choose to write about a holiday, a special occasion, or even family roles and responsibilities. For example, does your family celebrate a wedding or graduation from school in a special way? Or, you might write about who usually prepares the family meals or cleans the house. Explain one of your family's customs or traditions.

Will your students be ready . . . to look ahead to their academic future?

Chapters end as they begin--with information about authentic academic tasks and assignments. Students can analyze these tasks and assignments to learn more about the work that will be required of them when they enter degree programs. These sample tasks and assignments motivate students by showing them that they will apply the skills they are learning with their work in *Looking Ahead*.

Will your students be ready . . . to exploit a variety of academic skills in writing?

Being a successful student means being a successful academic writer. In *Looking Ahead*, students learn essential academic writing skills like *brainstorming, seeking* and *using input from peers, gathering ideas from various sources,* and *editing*.

FOCUSING

Consumer Behavior

Activity 7-1   Pre-reading Vocabulary

The following words are *italicized* in the next reading. Find the italicized words, and read the sentences. Then, match each definition to the appropriate word. One answer is provided.

1. _____ consumer
2. _____ typical
3. _____ marketing
4. _____ product
5. _a_ service
6. _____ hobby
7. _____ commercial
8. _____ data

a. anything a business does to meet customers' needs
b. radio or television advertisement
c. activity done for pleasure
d. person who buys and uses goods and services
e. facts, information
f. showing the more common characteristics of a particular group
g. activities by which goods or services are advertised and sold

---

Will your students be ready . . . to apply the reflective skills necessary for fluency in academic writing?

Each chapter contains several *Learner's Notebook* activities that accomplish two purposes. First, *Notebook* activities give students an opportunity to gain fluency through reflective writing that will not be evaluated. Second, this type of free-writing helps students generate ideas for the academic writing tasks to come later in the chapter.

PUTTING IT ALL TOGETHER   59

In your academic classes, you will often need to collect information for your assignments. You can collect information in many ways, including

reading	discussing ideas with classmates
listing	asking questions and interviewing
studying or developing charts or graphs	checking the WWW
thinking about opinions or personal experiences	

Read the following assignments from different academic classes. On the lines provided, write how you could collect information for these assignments. There may be more than one correct answer. The first answer is provided.

American Literature

Name the twentieth century American author whom you like the best. Explain why you like this person's writing.

thinking about opinions and personal experiences

SUCCESSFUL GRAMMAR ACQUISITION
WITH *LOOKING AHEAD*!

Will your students be ready ... to recognize the different discourse types found in academic writing?
Authentic readings and writing assignments in *Looking Ahead* were selected based on the academic discourse types that students most often need to read and produce in academic settings. These authentic materials give students opportunities to see and analyze how English grammar and rhetoric "work."

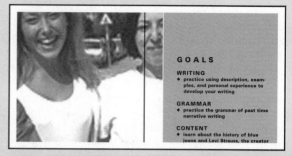

GOALS

WRITING
♦ practice using description, examples, and personal experience to develop your writing

GRAMMAR
♦ practice the grammar of past time narrative writing

CONTENT
♦ learn about the history of blue jeans and Levi Strauss, the creator

---

Grammar Preview

In this chapter, you will practice the *grammar of informational writing* and of *persuasive writing*. Generally, when you write statements of fact or habit, you use the grammar of informational writing. This chapter focuses on the following aspects of this grammar: *present tense verbs, subject-verb agreement*, and *logical organizers*.

When you wish to persuade or convince your readers to support your ideas in your writing, you use the grammar of persuasive writing. In addition to structures to control the strength of your generalizations, you will practice *conditional sentences*.

Will your students be ready ... to apply the grammar of academic writing?
Recent research has shown that specific grammar structures appear in clusters within types of discourse. By concentrating on different grammar clusters in each chapter, *Looking Ahead* focuses only on the grammar that is essential for the writing typical of a specific discourse type.

Will your students be ready ... to easily access important academic grammar information?
The *Grammar and Language Reference* (*GLR*) section at the back of the book pulls together all of the grammar explanations and authentic examples for easy student access. Additional activities are also provided. An icon (GLR) tells students when to refer to the *GLR*.

5C   Structures to Control the Strength of Generalizations: Adverbs of Frequency

always 100%	usually	often/frequently	sometimes	seldom/rarely	never 0%

Adverbs of frequency tell how often something happens. Adverbs of frequency range from *always* (100%) to *never* (0%).	Culture **always** influences the way we live.
Adverbs of frequency have positive and negative meanings. *Always, usually, often, frequently,* and *sometimes* have positive meanings. *Seldom, rarely,* and *never* have negative meanings.	People from the same culture **often** speak, dress, eat, think, and act in similar ways. People from different cultural groups **seldom** have identical customs.

SUCCESSFUL ACADEMIC READING
WITH *LOOKING AHEAD*!

Will your students be ready ... to apply essential reading skills for successful writing preparation?
Simply stated, effective reading skills are essential for success as an academic writer. Academic writing requires that you draw on reading sources in a variety of ways—to get ideas for writing, to get background information on a topic, and to use the information you find to support your ideas. Given this, each chapter in *Looking Ahead* has a "reading theme," which allows students to become familiar with the vocabulary, ideas, and issues within that topic. In both content and style, readings reflect the types of selections that students encounter in their academic classes.

FOCUSING

People and Places

READING 1   WHAT IS GEOGRAPHY? (GEOGRAPHY TEXTBOOK)

Read this excerpt to learn more about the field of geography.

WHAT IS GEOGRAPHY?

The term *geography* comes from two Greek words—"geo" for *earth* and "graphia" for *write about*. Geographers study physical and cultural features on or near the surface of the earth. **Physical features** are those that occur naturally, such as mountains, rivers, and oceans. **Cultural features** are those created by people, such as boundaries, towns, and roads. Geographers also look at living things—plants, animals, and people. They want to know how people shape and are shaped by their **environment**—all the things that surround us.

Geography, then, is the study of the earth in a way that shows the relationship between humans and their environment. That makes geography a story of people, places, and relationships.

CNN Video
with
Looking Ahead!

Will your students be ready . . . to use a variety of authentic media to prepare for their academic future?
Each chapter in the *Looking Ahead* series has a CNN video clip related to the chapter theme and designed to further stimulate authentic discussion and writing. Appealing to the learning style preferences of auditory and visual students, the videos connect the content of *Looking Ahead* to the real world. An introduction to video use in the ESL classroom by Elizabeth Mejia (see the Instructor's Manual) provides the foundation for sound teaching strategies with video.

The CNN videos are provided free of charge for teachers who adopt one or more of the *Looking Ahead* textbooks for their classes.

The World Wide Web
with
Looking Ahead!

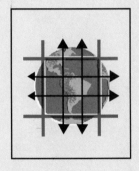

Are you ready . . . to provide all you can for your students' academic preparation?
The authors and editors of *Looking Ahead* have created an on-line system of support for teachers using the series. At **http://lookingahead.heinle.com**, teachers can find expanded versions of the Instructor's Manuals, lesson plans provided by teachers who are using the books, additional materials to supplement the books, and other support materials. In addition, the site includes opportunities to communicate with the editors and authors—to ask questions, share ideas, and make suggestions for improvements in the *Looking Ahead* series and its support materials.

Get Ready
with
Looking Ahead!

The four textbooks in the *Looking Ahead* series are designed to prepare students to be successful in their academic courses in U.S. colleges and universities. Specifically, *Looking Ahead* teaches students to read academic texts and materials, understand academic assignments, apply effective study skills, and respond appropriately to writing assignments. Each book "looks ahead" to the next in the series, and together as a group they look ahead to the writing students will do in their degree programs.

To the Teacher

Looking Ahead: Introduction to Academic Writing is a low-intermediate level writing and grammar textbook for ESL students. Each chapter is organized into the following sections.

Goals: Writing, grammar, and content objectives help teachers and students recognize the goals of the chapter.

Sample Authentic Academic Assignments: A list of assignments from content-area college and university courses illustrate typical writing required in academic courses.

Getting Ready:
   Chapter Introductions: Introductory statements explain both the writing and the grammar featured in the chapter.
   Warm-Up Activity: Various activities introduce students to the writing, grammar, or content focus of the chapter. A common activity is the learner's notebook, a journal where students reflect on what they already know or get ideas for their writing.

Focusing:
   Readings: Authentic readings develop background knowledge and model academic writing and grammar.
   Writing Assignments: Numerous learner's notebook activities develop background knowledge and fluency. Guided writing assignments, at the sentence and paragraph level, allow students to focus on accuracy.

Grammar Activities: The chapter focuses on different types of academic writing and the grammatical features used in that writing. Explanations, examples, and activities that help students recognize and produce those grammatical features are provided.

Putting It All Together:
Final Writing Assignment: A final writing assignment asks students to implement what they have learned in previous sections and chapters. It takes students through the steps of gathering information, organizing and developing ideas, self-editing, peer response, and revision. Assignments are paragraph length, with the exception of the last chapter, where students are asked to write a two-paragraph essay. This prepares students for the writing of *Looking Ahead: Learning About Academic Writing.*

Looking Ahead: This activity illustrates how the skills studied in the chapter are used in academic courses.

The Grammar and Language Reference: The GLR 🔘 is a quick and easy reference that supplies additional explanations, examples, and activities of the grammar features discussed in the chapters. The GLR is a good way to individualize grammar instruction for students who need extra work on particular structures.

Appendices: Appendices provide useful grammar and writing lists (Linking Verbs, Common Prepositions, Adjectives, Irregular Verbs, and Example Structures). Additional information can also be found on the *Looking Ahead* Web Site: http://lookingahead.heinle.com.

To the Student

Are You "Looking Ahead"?

What are your goals for the future? Are you looking ahead to a college degree and a profession? If you want to get a college education in English, then you need to write well. Writing is required in many forms in college: tests, research papers, business letters, and more. Improving your writing will help you to complete college and reach your goals.

How Can This Book Help You?

For many ESL students, writing is a challenge. It is often difficult to put ideas onto paper and to remember grammar rules when you write. This book will help you develop fluency. *Fluency* means being able to easily understand and use a language. The best way to develop fluency is to practice writing. This book gives you many opportunities to write. You will practice many different types of academic writing. This book will also help you build accuracy in your writing. *Accuracy* means that you apply the rules of English grammar when you write. Grammar is a major part of this book. You will learn how the grammar of academic writing works.

What Will You Find Inside?

Each chapter includes real assignments from college and university courses. These assignments show that the writing in the chapters is typical of academic courses.

The **Getting Ready** section introduces the writing and grammar points of the chapter. This section may also ask you to "get ready" for the chapter by writing in a learner's notebook. In a learner's notebook, you write to reflect on what you already know and to get ideas for writing.

In *Focusing,* you learn about writing skills like Collecting, Defining, and Developing. You also learn to recognize and practice the grammar of academic writing, such as informational writing (writing that informs) or past time narrative writing (writing that tells a past story). This section includes many different writing activities.

The *Putting It All Together* section contains a final writing assignment and activities like those you will do in academic courses.

How Do You Get More Help in Grammar?

The **Grammar and Language Reference** (GLR) section contains explanations, real examples, and activities of the grammar of academic writing. This section is a good reference if you have any questions about the grammar of written English. In addition, **appendices** provide useful grammar and writing lists.

*A*cknowledgments

Several people deserve special thanks for their assistance with this text. I want to thank Dr. Patricia Byrd and Dr. Joy Reid, the editors of the series, for their support, encouragement, and invaluable advice. I have learned a great deal from Pat and Joy while developing and refining this text and truly appreciate all that they have done. I also wish to thank my students at Georgia State University, who participated in field testing many of my materials. Their ideas and questions helped me to improve directions and activities, and their model writings are an excellent addition to the text. Lastly, I wish to thank my husband Alper and daughters, Peri and Sera. Without their support, I could not have completed this text. I look forward to comments from teachers and students who use this text.

Sharon L. Cavusgil
Georgia State University
Atlanta, Georgia
scavusgil@gsu.edu

Chapter 1

Introduction

The U.S. College or University Classroom

GOALS

WRITING
◆ practice organizing ideas from general to specific

GRAMMAR
◆ practice the grammar of writing complete sentences and the grammar of informational writing
◆ become familiar with the Grammar and Language Reference section of this book

CONTENT
◆ learn about the U.S. classroom and about your own learning styles and techniques

Sample Authentic College/University Assignments

At the beginning of Chapters 2–7, you will find samples of *real* writing assignments from college and university courses. These samples will give you an idea of the types of writing found in academic courses. You may wish to discuss the assignments with your teacher and classmates.

 CNN video support is available for this chapter.

GETTING READY

Warm-up Activity

Study the photos of the different U.S. classroom environments on these pages. Then, with your classmates, make a list of words and phrases that explain these photos. Write your ideas in the space near each photo. Some ideas are already listed.

small group work
use of computers

student presentation

LEARNER'S NOTEBOOK

Classroom Environments

During this course, you will write in a learner's notebook. In this notebook, write your feelings, thoughts, and opinions. Do not worry about *how* you are writing (for example, your organization, grammar, or spelling). Instead, focus on *what* you are writing (that is, your ideas). In a learner's notebook, there are never any wrong ideas. A learner's notebook gives you good writing practice, and it helps you put your ideas onto paper. Later, you can read your ideas again and use some in assignments.

In your learner's notebook, respond to some of these questions. Use words and phrases from the Warm-up Activity.

- What different classroom environments have you been in? Discuss the different class sizes, room arrangements, and activities you have experienced.
- What do you think are the advantages or disadvantages of the different environments?
- In your opinion, which environment is the best way to learn? Why?

An example of a learner's notebook entry follows on the next page. Notice the format of this student writing.

(continued)

Classroom Environments (continued)

Student Writing Model

Indent each paragraph   one main idea in each paragraph: student's background

    I studied in a small classroom with only four to eight people in my class. There were enough desks and materials for everyone. The teachers had enough time to explain and correct mistakes of each student. My classmates worked in groups, and we exchanged ideas and opinions.

Indent   one main idea: student's opinions

    I think the best way to learn well is in a classroom with only a few students. In this case, the teachers have more time to explain things to their students. Also, the students can understand or practice more easily. Because they work in groups, their classmates can help them, too. They share their ideas, opinions, and answers to find the better solution to problems.

Barry Abdourahamane
Guinea, West Africa

Grammar Preview

    Academic writing is the type of writing used in colleges and universities. In this chapter, you will practice *writing complete sentences* as required in academic writing. You will also practice using the *grammar of informational writing*. Generally, you use the grammar of informational writing when you write statements of fact or habit. This chapter focuses on *present tense verbs, subject-verb agreement,* and *logical organizers.*

The Grammar and Language Reference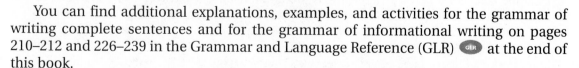

    You can find additional explanations, examples, and activities for the grammar of writing complete sentences and for the grammar of informational writing on pages 210–212 and 226–239 in the Grammar and Language Reference (GLR) GLR at the end of this book.

    Turn to page 207, and spend some time becoming familiar with the GLR. See how it is organized and what it includes. Throughout this textbook, you can refer to the GLR to get further grammar information for each chapter.

FOCUSING

Teachers' Classroom Expectations

| Activity 1-1   Chapter Vocabulary |

The following words are in the readings and activities of this chapter. Read the definitions, and then find the word that *best* matches each definition. One answer is provided.

1. ___ homework
2. ___ effective
3. ___ habits
4. ___ attendance
5. ___ flexible
6. ___ survey
7. ___ to lecture
8. _a_ expectations
9. ___ to permit
10. ___ opinions
11. ___ environment
12. ___ to socialize

a. future desires, wants, and goals
b. a list of questions or statements to be filled out
c. to present ideas or lessons
d. to spend time in a friendly way
e. to allow, let
f. being present in class
g. usual actions, behaviors, or styles
h. willing to change or adapt
i. ideas or thoughts on an issue
j. successful
k. assignments completed outside of class
l. living, working, or study conditions

READING 1   EXPECTATIONS AND HABITS IN THE U.S. CLASSROOM

Read this paragraph about different teaching styles. Notice that it is indented. It also contains one main idea: Teachers have their own classroom expectations and habits.

EXPECTATIONS AND HABITS IN THE U.S. CLASSROOM

Teachers have their own teaching habits or styles. One teacher may feel comfortable lecturing from notes. Another teacher may prefer to organize students into small discussion groups. In addition, some teachers want students to call them by their first name—Paul or Natasha. Other teachers expect students to use their title and family name such as Dr. Park, Ms. Larson, or Professor Rodriguez. Finally, some teachers may be very flexible about   5
homework and attendance, but other teachers might be very strict. To succeed in the U.S. classroom, you must learn the expectations and styles of your teachers.

Activity 1-2   Completing a Survey

Teachers often use surveys in the classroom. Surveys are a way to get information about students and their opinions. Surveys can provide discussion ideas for the classroom. Read and complete the following survey about the U.S. classroom.

THE U.S. CLASSROOM

Directions: Read each statement, and decide if the statement is true or false. Write T (true) or F (false) on the line next to each statement. Answer the way you think is correct *for the U.S. classroom.* Be ready to explain your answers to your teacher and your classmates. Different teachers may have different opinions about the answers.

_____   **1.**   You should complete all your homework before class.

_____   **2.**   Group work is common in the U.S. classroom.

_____   **3.**   Your teacher wants you to write notes and answers in your textbook.

_____   **4.**   Most college or university teachers socialize with their students during class time.

_____   **5.**   Sharing test answers with a classmate is okay.

_____   **6.**   If you are late for class, knock on the classroom door before you enter.

_____   **7.**   Your teacher permits students to eat and drink in the classroom.

_____   **8.**   When your teacher calls on you to answer a question, you should stand up.

_____   **9.**   Copying a classmate's homework answers is okay.

_____   **10.**   You must be good friends with your discussion group members. If you are not friends, you will not learn anything.

_____   **11.**   College or university teachers want you to call them by their first name.

_____   **12.**   An effective student asks questions when he or she doesn't understand.

_____   **13.**   Students should not talk or whisper during a test.

_____   **14.**   If you need to miss class, you should tell your teacher.

_____ **15.** Your teacher doesn't care if you leave the classroom to get a drink or use the restroom.

_____ **16.** You can share your ideas and opinions even when they are not like everyone else's.

_____ **17.** Your teacher permits you to submit your homework late.

_____ **18.** If you are absent on a test day, you can take the test later.

Source: Adapted from Becky Bodnar and Sharon Cavusgil, "Classroom Management Techniques," Annual Georgia TESOL Conference, Atlanta, Georgia, March 9, 1996. Reproduced by permission.

Pair and Small Group Discussions

Your teacher will often have you discuss your ideas and assignments with another classmate or in small groups. This activity lets you share your ideas and opinions. It gives you practice with your English. It also allows you to learn from your classmates. You do not always have to agree with your partner or group members, but you should always listen and try to share your ideas and opinions.

Activity 1-3   Small Group Discussion

Form small groups, and share your responses to "The U.S. Classroom" survey, page 9. If your group members disagree with you, explain your answers. Your teacher will then share her or his expectations of your class. Remember that different teachers may have different opinions. Effective students must learn the individual expectations of their teachers.

Activity 1-4   Identifying Sentence Parts

Read the following sentences from "The U.S. Classroom" survey. Notice that each sentence begins with a capital letter and ends with a period. For each sentence, underline the complete subject with one line. Underline the complete verb with a double line (two lines). Circle any direct objects or complements. Place parentheses around adverbials.

> **GLR**   See page 210 in the GLR for more information on basic sentence structure.

EXAMPLE

You can take (the test)(later).

1. You should complete all your homework before class.

2. Group work is common in the U.S. classroom.

3. Your teacher accepts late homework.

4. You must be good friends with your discussion group members.

5. An effective student asks questions.

6. Students should not talk or whisper during a test.

7. You can share your ideas and opinions.

Activity 1-5   Writing About Course Expectations

Most teachers want you to understand their expectations for their classes. To show your teacher that you understand, write sentences to describe her or his expectations. If you do not understand the expectations, ask your teacher to explain them again. When you write, use complete sentences like those required for academic writing. Use some of the sentences from the survey on page 9, and write some of your own. Two examples are given.

1. **Homework Expectations**

    a. _____ My teacher does not accept late homework. _____

    b. _____

    c. _____

2. **Attendance Expectations**

    a. _____

    b. _____

    c. _____

3. **Test or Quiz Expectations**

    a. _____

    b. _____

    c. _____

4. **Basic Classroom Expectations**

    a. _____ Small group work is common in this writing class. _____

    b. _____

    c. _____

Activity 1-6   Self-editing

1. Read your sentences again. Is the information accurate? Do your sentences say what you want them to say? Make any changes needed to improve the meaning of your writing.

2. Edit your sentences for the grammar of writing complete sentences. For each sentence, complete the following, and correct any errors that you find. After you have edited for these features, check (✓) the box.

    a. edit for complete sentences

        ☐ underline the complete subject once

        ☐ underline the complete verb twice

        ☐ circle the direct object or complement

        ☐ place parentheses around adverbials

b. edit for capitalization and punctuation

    ☐ capitalize the first word of your sentence

    ☐ use punctuation to end your sentence

LEARNER'S NOTEBOOK

Surprising Expectations

In your learner's notebook, list two or three surprising things you learned about your teacher's expectations and/or the U.S. classroom. Explain to your teacher why these things surprise you.

Learning Styles

Activity 1-7   Pre-reading Vocabulary

The following words are *italicized* in the next reading. With a small group of students, find each word in the reading, read the sentence, and guess the word's meaning. Then, write a brief definition.

1. discover _____

2. prefer _____

3. ability (abilities) _____

4. participate _____

5. dialogs _____

6. methods _____

7. practice _____

8. unique _____

READING 2   DISCOVER YOUR LEARNING STYLES
(LEARNING STYLES TEXTBOOK)

Read the following excerpt about learning styles.

DISCOVER YOUR LEARNING STYLES

People study and learn in different ways. Some students work alone (individual learners). They learn better by themselves. Other students study best with a partner (pair learners) or with several classmates (small group learners). They can learn from their classmates. In the college or university classroom, you will *participate* in many different learning activities, both alone and with your classmates. 5

People are often *unique* in how they learn. Some students learn more easily when they can read (visual learners) and think silently about the material. Others are effective learners when they listen to the teacher talk about the material (auditory learners). Many engineering and science students like to learn with their hands (tactile learners). For example, they learn by building models, doing experiments, and taking notes. Some other students *prefer* 10 to learn with their whole bodies (kinesthetic learners). For instance, athletes, dancers, and musicians improve their *abilities* by practicing physical movements. Language students increase their language skills when they present role-plays and *dialogs* with their whole bodies.

Most students use more than one way to learn new things. These students are flexible 15 learners. However, some students are not flexible. They use only one or two learning styles. To be successful in the classroom, you should *practice* several styles of learning. This will help you learn from teachers who use different *methods* in the classroom, such as giving a lecture, showing a video, or organizing a group activity. If you *practice* several styles of learning, you can learn more easily. 20

Students can become more effective learners if they understand how they learn best. Then, they can increase their *ability* to understand information and to remember it. Students can also *discover* ways they do not learn well, and they can work to increase their *ability* in those areas.

Source: Joy M. Reid, Ed., *Learning Styles in the ESL/EFL Classroom*
(Heinle & Heinle Publishers, 1995). Reproduced by permission.

Activity 1-8   Using Vocabulary

Check your understanding of the learning styles vocabulary. Use these words from the previous reading to complete the following sentences. Use each word only once. The first answer is provided.

pair	small group	individual	visual
auditory	tactile	kinesthetic	flexible

1. Omid and Carlos like to study in several ways. They are called _____flexible_____ learners.

2. Paul prefers to learn English by studying alone. Paul is a(n) _____ learner.

3. Peri likes to work with one friend. Peri is a(n) _____ learner.

4. Some students take notes while the teacher lectures. These students are visual, auditory, and _____ learners.

5. I am more successful when I study with several classmates. I am called a(n) _____ learner.

6. Minh learns English by listening to audiotapes, so he is a(n) _____ learner.

7. Yoko and Ana like to learn English by presenting dialogs in class. Yoko and Ana are _____ learners.

8. If you learn best by watching television and videotapes, you are both an auditory and a(n) _____ learner.

Textbook Features

Authors of U.S. textbooks use many different features to help you identify important ideas and information in books. These features include different print styles, photographs, boxes, charts, and so on. Many U.S. textbooks also contain appendices. When authors want to provide additional useful information, they often put it in an appendix. Appendices are located at the end of a book.

Activity 1-9   Identifying Textbook Features

1. Use the visual learning style to look through this textbook and find examples of the following features. Write the page number(s) where you find the features. Share your findings with your class.

   a. **boldfaced print**, pages _____

   b. *italicized print*, pages _____

   c. underlined print, pages _____

   d. large print, pages _____

   e. boxes , pages _____

   f. tables or charts, pages _____

   g. illustrations or photographs, pages _____

2. Find the appendices in this textbook. Then, use auditory and small group learning styles to discuss the usefulness of appendices with your teacher and classmates.

3. Look through your textbooks from other courses or textbooks your teacher brings to class. How do the authors identify important ideas and information? Do the textbooks

have appendices? What information is included in the appendices? Use the tactile learning style to write your ideas in your learner's notebook. Then, share your findings with your class.

Writing in Your Textbook

Sometimes, you will learn best when you combine learning styles. Visual and tactile learning styles are used when authors (and teachers) ask you to read and then write in your textbooks. Authors and teachers may ask you to write notes or questions in the margins of your books. They may also ask you to highlight or underline important ideas in your books. Authors may even leave space for you to write your answers and ideas in the book.

Activity 1-10   Writing in Your Textbook

1. Look through this textbook, and find places where the author wants you to write in it. Write the page numbers here, and share your findings with your class.

_____

_____

_____

2. With a few classmates, practice auditory and small group learning styles by discussing your experiences and feelings about writing in your books.

   a. In your former schools, did you write in your books? Why or why not?

   b. Do you like to write in your books? Why or why not?

   c. How can writing in your books help you with your studies?

Study Techniques and Learning Styles

READING 3   STUDY TECHNIQUES AND LEARNING STYLES (CHART)

When we study, we often use special techniques to help us learn. These techniques reveal information about our preferred learning styles. Read the following study techniques used by the students in Ms. Larson's class. Determine the learning styles that they use, and write the styles on the lines provided. Some students may use more than one learning style. An example is included.

MS. LARSON'S CLASS

Name of Student(s)	Study Technique	Learning Style(s)
Carlos	write and rewrite information	tactile
Boris	learn new vocabulary with flashcards	_____
Ana and Tuyen	highlight important ideas in the book	_____
Erin	practice dialogs with classmates	_____
Sera	take notes in the margins of assignments	_____
Yoko and Omid	discuss the class materials	_____
Joon	read new ideas several times	_____
Tam and Minh	tape lectures and listen to them at home	_____

Activity 1-11   Writing About the Study Habits of Ms. Larson's Students

When you write sentences about habits, use the grammar of informational writing. This means you should write in complete sentences, use the simple present tense, and use subject-verb agreement.

GLR   See page 210 of the GLR for more information on basic sentence structure and pages 233–237 for more information on present tense verbs and subject-verb agreement.

For each student or pair of students in the previous chart, write a complete sentence about the learning styles. Some students may use more than one learning style. In this case, choose one style, and write a statement about it. There may be more than one correct answer. An example is provided.

1. **Tactile Learning Style**

   a. _____ Carlos writes and rewrites information in his notebook. _____

   b. _____

   c. _____

2. **Visual Learning Style**

   a. _____

   b. _____

3. **Auditory Learning Style**

   a. _____

   b. _____

4. **Kinesthetic Learning Style**

   a. _____

   b. _____

Activity 1-12   Self-editing

1. Read your sentences again. Is the information accurate? Do your sentences say what you want them to say? Make any changes needed to improve the meaning of your writing.

2. Edit your sentences for the grammar of informational writing. Correct any errors that you find. After you have edited for these features, check (✓) the box.

   ☐ complete sentences

   ☐ present tense verbs

   ☐ subject-verb agreement

   ☐ capitalization and punctuation to end your sentences

Activity 1-13   Small Group Activity

It is important to understand how you learn best. When you understand your own learning styles, you can use effective study techniques to help you learn. You should also try new learning styles and study techniques to improve the way you learn.

1. Think about your own study techniques. Write your name, your study technique(s), and your learning style(s) in the following chart. Write notes only, not complete sentences. An example is provided.

TECHNIQUES AND STYLES		
Name of Student	Study Technique(s)	Learning Style(s)
EXAMPLE Peri	discuss ideas with friends	auditory
a.		
b.		
c.		
d.		
e.		

2. Then, ask two to four classmates about their study techniques and learning styles. Write the information in the chart above. Again, write notes only, not complete sentences.

Activity 1-14   Writing About the Study Habits of Your Classmates

Write complete sentences about your habits and the habits of some of your classmates (from the previous activity). For each item, your first sentence should describe the learning style and your second sentence should identify the study technique. Because this writing is about habits, you need to use the grammar of informational writing. An example is provided.

learning style   study technique

Example   Peri is an auditory learner. She likes to discuss her ideas with friends.

1. _____

   _____

2. _____

   _____

3. _____

   _____

4. _____

   _____

5. _____

   _____

Activity 1-15   Self-editing

1. Read your sentences again. Do your sentences clearly state the learning style? Do they identify a study technique? Make any changes needed to improve the meaning of your writing.

2. Edit your sentences for the grammar of informational writing. Correct any errors that you find. After you have edited for these features, check (✓) the box.

   ☐ complete sentences

   ☐ present tense verbs

   ☐ subject-verb agreement

   ☐ capitalization and punctuation to end your sentences

Writing with General Ideas and Specific Details

In English, we often begin by writing or saying something *general*. We then provide some *specific details* that support or prove our general statement. In this paragraph from Reading 2, the writer begins with a *general statement*. The writer then provides *specific details*. The details may become more specific as the paragraph develops. Study the development of this paragraph.

DISCOVER YOUR LEARNING STYLES

general statement   specific details

People are often unique in how they learn. Some students learn more easily when they can read (visual learners) and think silently about the material. Others are effective learners when they listen to the teacher talk about the material (auditory learners). Many engineering and science students like to learn with their hands (tactile learners). For example, they learn by building models, doing experiments, and taking notes. Some other students prefer to learn with their whole bodies (kinesthetic learners). For instance, athletes, dancers, and musicians improve their abilities by practicing physical movements.

Activity 1-16   Analyzing the Use of General to Specific

1. Read the following sentences, and notice the general statements and specific details.

    EXAMPLES

    general statement   specific details
    I am a visual learner. For instance, I improve my vocabulary by reading the new words several times.

    general statement   specific details
    Boris is a visual and an auditory learner. For example, he reads his notes, and he repeats the ideas aloud.

2. Sometimes, a logical organizer joins (connects) the general statement and the specific details. Study the examples above to answer these questions.

    a. What words often connect general statements and specific details? _____

    _____

    b. What punctuation is often used after these logical organizers? _____

> **GLR**   See pages 230–231 of the GLR for more information on logical organizers.

For more information on *for instance* and *for example*, see Appendix E: Example Structures.

Activity 1-17   Completing Sentences

The following informational sentences move from general statements to specific details. Logical organizers join many of the sentences. Complete these sentences with an appropriate answer from your own experience.

1. I am a(n) _____ learner. For example, _____

   _____ .

2. I also use other learning styles, especially _____ and

   _____ . I use a combination of these learning styles when I

   _____ .

3. My most important learning style is _____ . For instance,

   _____ .

4. I am not a good _____ learner. For instance,

   _____ .

5. _____ is a learning style that I need to

   practice. For example, _____ .

Guidelines for a Memorandum

A memorandum (memo) is a written message. People in companies or schools use memos to communicate with each other. Memos might ask for information, give information, announce meetings, and so on. A memo has a heading and a message. The heading has four lines. Study the following guidelines for a memo.

MEMORANDUM

TO: The person to receive the memo.

FROM: The writer of the memo.

DATE: When the memo was written.

SUBJECT: What the memo is about. This line should be short but informative. For example, "UPCOMING MEETING" for a memo can announce a meeting.

You should begin your message with a general statement that explains the purpose of your memo. The other lines should be specific details about that purpose. Because memos are often used in formal situations, such as work, write in complete sentences and use accurate spelling and punctuation.

Memos are typed messages. You do not indent your paragraphs in a memo. Instead, leave a blank line between each paragraph.

Activity 1-18   Writing a Memo

Use some of your sentences from Activity 1-17 to write a memo to your teacher. The purpose of the memo is to describe your learning styles and study techniques. In the following memo, a general statement is already provided. Include specific details by describing two or three of your most important learning styles. Be sure to give examples (study techniques) to show how you use those learning styles. This is an informational memo, so use the grammar of informational writing. If possible, use computer word processing to prepare your memo.

MEMORANDUM

TO: _____

FROM: _____

DATE: _____

SUBJECT: MY LEARNING STYLES AND STUDY TECHNIQUES

The following statements explain my learning styles and study techniques. I hope that my statements help you understand how I learn most effectively. _____

_____

_____

_____

_____

_____

_____

_____

_____

_____

_____

_____

_____

_____

Activity 1-19   Self-editing

1. Read your memo again. Does it say what you want it to say? Is it organized in the best way for this particular writing task? Do you move from general ideas to specific details? Make any changes needed to improve the meaning of your writing.

2. This is a memo about habits, so edit your sentences for the grammar of informational writing. Correct any errors that you find. After you have edited for these features, check (✓) the box.

☐ complete sentences
☐ correct verb tense
☐ subject-verb agreement
☐ appropriate logical organizers (*for example, for instance*) and punctuation
☐ capitalization and punctuation to end your sentences

3. Rewrite your memo. Make the corrections that you decided on during editing.

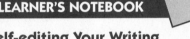

LEARNER'S NOTEBOOK

Self-editing Your Writing

Write about the self-editing process for your memo. For example, what changes did you make in your writing? In what ways did those changes improve your writing?

Personal Writing Habits

READING 4 WRITING HABITS SURVEY (LEARNING STYLES TEXTBOOK)

In addition to our own special learning styles and study techniques, we all have unique writing habits. To discover more about your own habits, read and complete the following survey.

WRITING HABITS SURVEY

Directions: Circle the answer that helps you feel most comfortable when you complete writing assignments for your classes.

1. **Place:** formal (desk, straight-backed chair, at the library)

   informal (bed, pillows, soft chair, on the floor)

   not important

2. **Surroundings:** clean   messy   not important

3. **Time:** early morning   late morning   early afternoon

    late afternoon   evening   late evening

    not important

4. **Tools:** pencil   pen   highlighter

    notebook   dictionary   computer

    other(s): _____

5. **Light:** bright   soft   dark   not important

6. **Temperature:** warm   cool   not important

7. **Sound:** quiet   noisy   music   television

    other(s): _____

    not important

8. **Rewards:** Do you promise yourself rewards for beginning your work?

    If so, what? _____

    Do you promise yourself rewards for finishing your work?

    If so, what? _____

    not important

9. **Other:** List additional habits you follow when you do your assignments. (Examples could include clothing habits or eating/drinking habits.)

    _____

    _____

    _____

Source: Joy M. Reid, Ed., *Learning Styles in the ESL/EFL Classroom* (Heinle & Heinle Publishers, 1995, 218–219). Reproduced by permission.

Activity 1-20   Small Group Discussion

With a small group of classmates, discuss your survey results. Try to answer the following questions. Take notes on the lines to help you remember.

1. In what ways are you similar to your classmates? _____
    _____
    _____

2. In what ways are you different? _____
    _____
    _____

3. What do your classmates do that surprises you? Why? _____
    _____
    _____

4. What do your classmates do that does not surprise you? Why? _____
    _____
    _____

LEARNER'S NOTEBOOK

Best Learning Environment

In your learner's notebook, describe the environment in which you learn and write best. Use your answers from the "Writing Habits Survey" on pages 25 and 26.

Activity 1-21   Writing About Personal Writing Habits

Use your answers on the "Writing Habits Survey" (pages 25 and 26) and the previous learner's notebook, "Best Learning Environment," to write three general statements about your writing habits. Be sure to include (1) specific details to support those statements and (2) logical organizers to join the general statements and specific details. Because this writing is about habits, use the grammar of informational writing. Examples follow.

EXAMPLES

general statement   logical organizer   specific details

I prefer to study in the early morning. For instance, I study best between 5 a.m. and 7 a.m.

general statement   logical organizer   specific details
I use many tools when I study. For example, I use a dictionary, a notebook, and a pen.

Activity 1-22   Self-editing

1. Read your sentences again. Do they say what you want them to say? Are your ideas organized in the best way for this particular writing task? Do you move from general ideas to specific details? Make any changes needed to improve the meaning of your writing.

2. You wrote about personal habits, so edit your sentences for the grammar of informational writing. Correct any errors that you find. After you have edited for these features, check (✓) the box.

    ☐ complete sentences

    ☐ correct verb tense

    ☐ subject-verb agreement

    ☐ appropriate logical organizers (*for example, for instance*) and punctuation

    ☐ capitalization and punctuation to end your sentences

3. Rewrite your sentences. Make the corrections that you decided on during editing.

PUTTING IT ALL TOGETHER

LEARNER'S NOTEBOOK

Your Writing Habits

Collect ideas about your writing habits by describing the different assignments you have had in the past (in this class or in another, in your first language or in English). Then, respond to some of the following questions in your learner's notebook. Use a different paragraph for each main idea.

1. How do you usually prepare for your writing assignments? For example: Do you talk to a friend or to yourself? Do you read a lot about the topic? Do you take notes or make lists of ideas?

2. Where and when do you prefer to write your assignments? For example, do you write in the library, on the floor, late at night?

3. How do you usually complete your assignments? For instance: Do you listen to music? Do you reward yourself at different stages of the writing process? Do you write the assignment in advance or shortly before the due date?

4. What tools do you use to complete your assignments? For instance, do you use a computer, paper and pencils, a dictionary, and so on?

FINAL WRITING ASSIGNMENT: YOUR WRITING HABITS

Use ideas from your learner's notebook to write a memo to your teacher. The purpose of your memo is to explain your writing habits. You may want to include statements about your study techniques, your writing environment, and the strategies you use to make your writing easier. Because this is a memo about habits, use the correct memo format and the grammar of informational writing. If possible, use computer word processing. Two student writing models follow.

Student Writing Model 1

MEMORANDUM

TO: Mrs. Cavusgil

FROM: Li-Jen Chen (Republic of China)

DATE:

SUBJECT: MY WRITING HABITS

I believe that a suitable environment can make me feel better, and that is quite important for my writing. My own habit is to find a sofa, a soft light, some paper, and some pencils. I also make myself tea. My clothing is important, too. For instance, I dress in simple clothes to help me relax. I usually work in my bedroom; in that way, whenever I cannot think about what to write, I just lie down and take a rest.

Student Writing Model 2

MEMORANDUM

TO: Mrs. Cavusgil

FROM: Fumiko Suzuki (Japan)

DATE:

SUBJECT: MY WRITING PROFILE

I do many things before I start to write. For example, I clean the surface of my desk a little bit. I make a space for writing because my desk is always messy. Then, I make my favorite tea (green tea, red tea, or other kind of tea). I turn off the music or TV or any kind of sounds because I like a quiet environment for studying. I then make a plan in my mind, and I pick the examples to support my topic. After I do this thinking, I make an outline about these thoughts, and I start writing. But sometimes I change my ideas. For instance, I add a new example or delete an idea. Therefore, although it's necessary for me to make a rough outline, I can change some details. For me, my outline is necessary but flexible.

Editing Your Writing

1. Read your memo again. Does it clearly explain your writing habits to your teacher? Are your ideas organized in the best way for this particular writing task? Do you move from general ideas to specific details? Did you use the memo format? Make any changes needed to improve the meaning of your writing.

2. You wrote about personal habits, so edit your sentences for the grammar of informational writing. Correct any errors that you find. After you have edited for these features, check (✓) the box.

    ☐ complete sentences

    ☐ correct verb tense

    ☐ subject-verb agreement

    ☐ appropriate logical organizers (*for example, for instance*) and punctuation

    ☐ capitalization and punctuation to end your sentences

Providing Peer Support

Exchange papers with a partner, and read your partner's memo.

1. On your partner's paper, <u>underline</u> the example you like best.

2. Explain why you like that example. In the margin of the memo, write a statement such as:

    I like the vocabulary you used.   This habit was surprising to me.

    This example made me smile.   I use this learning style, too!

    This example is interesting.   I'm going to try this strategy, too.

3. Give one suggestion to make the writing better. In the margin of the memo, write one question such as:

    What other details can you add about your writing?

    Can you use another example here?

    Do you use any other strategies when you write?

    What does this word mean?

Revising Your Writing

1. With your partner, discuss her or his ideas and suggestions for your writing.

2. Make two or three changes to improve your writing.

Finalizing Your Writing

1. Make the corrections that you decided on during the self-editing and peer-support processes. You may want to refer to the previous check list on page 30 again.

2. Rewrite your memo to submit to your teacher.

• •

Understanding your individual learning styles can help you become a better student. Read the following paragraph from a student who used her knowledge of learning styles to improve her studies. Then, with your classmates, discuss your ideas on how understanding learning styles can help you and your classmates.

Student Writing

My friend is a visual learner. He always reads and studies the textbook materials before he listens to his professor's lectures. He says that he must see the new information before he can understand the lectures. I am also a visual learner, so I have used my friend's advice. This strategy has helped me become more successful in my college classes.

Berrin Er
Turkey

Chapter 2

Collecting
Culture

GOALS

WRITING
◆ learn different ways to collect
ideas for your writing

GRAMMAR
◆ practice the grammar of informational writing, persuasive writing,
and interactive communication in
writing

CONTENT
◆ learn about different cultures,
customs, and values

ACADEMIC FIELDS
Anthropology
Sociology

Sample Authentic College/University Collecting Assignments

In your academic classes, you will use the skills you learn in this chapter to complete activities like the students in these photos.

These students are enrolled in a sociology class. Their assignment is to write about the habits and values of teenagers around the world. Study the photos, and read the sentences that explain how the students are collecting information for the assignment.

Sam explores ideas in his learner's notebook.

Carlos learns from his own personal experience and observation.

Sera interviews an international student.

Erin reads her sociology textbook.

Peri discusses ideas with her classmates.

 CNN video support is available for this chapter. Turner Le@rning

GETTING READY

Introduction to Collecting

Collecting means bringing or gathering together. Some people collect stamps or coins. Others like to collect music CDs and tapes. Elvis Presley was a collector of automobiles.

Writers collect ideas and information. Before you begin any writing assignment, it is important to collect (gather) ideas and information. When you think about an assignment and then write in your learner's notebook, you are gathering your ideas about a topic. Planning or discussing an assignment with group members is also a way to collect information. There are other ways to collect, too. When you read a book or article or study and understand a graph, you are collecting information. In addition, you can collect information on the World Wide Web (WWW) or by asking or interviewing people about their knowledge or opinions.

Warm-up Activity

Think about the ways *you* learn new information and collect ideas in your classes. What is your favorite way to learn new things? Why is this your favorite? Discuss your ideas with your classmates.

Grammar Preview

In this chapter, you will practice the *grammar of informational writing* (*present tense verbs, subject-verb agreement,* and *logical organizers*). You use informational writing when you write statements of fact or habit.

When you make a generalization and you wish to convince your reader to support those ideas, you use the *grammar of persuasive writing*. You can use various grammar structures to persuade your reader to support your generalizations. These structures (*opinion structures, adverbs of frequency, modal auxiliaries,* and *expressions of quantity*) will be practiced in this chapter.

Finally, you will practice the *grammar of interactive communication in writing*. This writing includes features of conversational grammar. This chapter focuses on one of those features: *question asking*.

GLR See pages 226–237 and 255–261 of the GLR for more information about the grammar of informational writing and interactive communication in writing.

FOCUSING

Culture

LEARNER'S NOTEBOOK

Family Customs and Traditions

A custom or tradition is a usual practice or habit. In your learner's notebook, write about a custom or tradition in your family. You may choose to write about a holiday, a special occasion, or even family roles and responsibilities. For example, does your family celebrate a wedding or graduation from school in a special way? Or, you might write about who usually prepares the family meals or cleans the house. Explain one of your family's customs or traditions.

Activity 2-1   Pre-reading Vocabulary

These words are *italicized* in the next reading. Find the italicized words, and read the sentences. Then, match each definition to the appropriate word. One answer is provided.

1. _____ humans
2. _____ similar
3. _____ behavior
4. _____ strange
5. _a_ culture
6. _____ anthropologist
7. _____ society
8. _____ artifact

a. beliefs, values, and habits
b. the way that a person acts
c. a person who studies humans
d. odd, unusual
e. people, mankind
f. anything made by man
g. like, the same
h. a group of people with shared customs and laws

READING 1   WHAT IS CULTURE? (ANTHROPOLOGY TEXTBOOK)

Reading is a good way to collect information. To collect information about culture, read the following excerpt from an anthropology textbook.

WHAT IS CULTURE?

When *humans* live in groups, they develop and share *similar* ways of *behavior*. We call this *culture*. *Culture* includes all the ways that *humans* live in the environment and with each other. Culture also includes all the ways that a group of people thinks and behaves.

Culture is many things. One anthropologist, Edward Tylor, stated that culture includes knowledge, beliefs, art, law, customs, and any other habits of man in a *society*. Physical   5 items (food, clothing, houses, and tools) are a part of culture. You can see, touch, and handle these things. They are what *anthropologists* call *artifacts*. But human life is more than just objects. Culture includes your ideas of what is right and wrong, good and bad, or beautiful and ugly. All of these together make up our culture.

All humans have culture. It is reflected in their customs. Culture makes us *human*. And   10 each human group—a family, a tribe, or a nation—has its own culture. Most members of the same cultural group usually share *similar* customs and values. For example, they often speak, dress, eat, think, and act in *similar* ways. Most people think that their customs are natural, right, and good. They believe their way of life is the best way. But these customs may seem *strange* to others.   15

Source: Adapted from H. Leon Abrams, Jr., *Inquiry into Anthropology* (Globe Fearon, Simon & Schuster Education Group, 1987). Reproduced by permission of Globe Fearon.

Activity 2-2   Showing Your Understanding

Answer these questions about culture and customs.

1. List three physical things that are a part of culture.

    _____

    _____

    _____

2. List three nonphysical things that are a part of culture.

    _____

    _____

    _____

3. List two customs that are normal to you but that may be strange to another person.

    _____

    _____

    _____

Making Accurate Generalization Structures in Persuasive Writing

Academic writers avoid "overgeneralizing." For example, writers avoid making statements like "Americans always use credit cards" or "All Americans love football" because these statements are not true for everyone. In the following paragraph from Reading 1, the writer did not overgeneralize about people and culture. Instead, the writer used various grammar structures to make the generalizations more accurate and to persuade the reader to support those generalizations. For example, the writer used opinion structures, adverbs of frequency, modal auxiliaries, and expressions of quantity. Read the paragraph again, and notice the structures that make generalizations more accurate.

All humans have culture. It is reflected in their customs. Culture makes us

human. And each human group—a family, a tribe, or a nation—has its own culture.

expression of quantity   adverb of frequency

<u>Most members</u> of the same cultural group <u>usually</u> share similar customs and

                    adverb of frequency

values. For example, they <u>often</u> speak, dress, eat, think, and act in similar ways.

expression
of quantity   opinion structure   opinion structure

<u>Most</u> <u>people think that</u> their customs are natural, right, and good. <u>They believe</u>

                                   modal auxiliary

their way of life is the best way. But these customs <u>may</u> seem strange to others.

The Grammar of Persuasive Writing: Opinion Structures

One way to persuade your readers to agree with your generalizations is to use an opinion structure. The following structures are often used to introduce opinions.

Opinion Structures	Examples
In my opinion, I believe (that) I think (that) I feel (that)	*In my opinion*, most people share the same values. *They believe* their way of life is the best way. *Most people think that* their customs are natural, right, and good. *Most U.S. teenagers feel that* they are not ready for marriage.

GLR   See page 246 in the GLR for more information on opinion structures.

Activity 2-3   Using Opinion Structures in Small Group Discussions

1. You can collect ideas by *discussing* things with your classmates. With a small group
    of classmates, collect ideas and opinions about the U.S. culture. Read the following
    list of words. Do they describe the U.S. culture? Use various opinion structures *(in
    my opinion, I believe,* etc.) to share your opinions and move from general opinions
    to specific details. Examples of two students' work are provided.

hunger	soccer	freedom
independence	automobiles	crime

Student Model 1

general opinion   specific details
***I believe** hunger describes the U.S. culture* because many people in the downtown
area are hungry and don't have a place to live.

Azam Jourabchi
Iran

Student Model 2

general opinion   specific details
***In my opinion,** soccer does not describe the U.S. culture.* *I don't think* many people in
the U.S. play or like the sport.

Tamer Adel Soliman
Egypt

2. Write down two or three of your group's most interesting opinions to share with your
    class. Each statement should have an opinion structure, a general opinion, and spe-
    cific details (examples and/or reasons).

Collecting Ideas with Lists

READING 2   TAMER'S LIST (STUDENT'S LISTS)

Listing is another way to collect information. Read and study the following lists to
see how Tamer, a student from Turkey, collects ideas.

TAMER'S LIST

1. Tamer wants to write about the culture of his native country. Before Tamer writes, he
    quickly makes a list of words and groups of words that describe the culture of Turkey.

First List

mosques	casual dressers
family-oriented	play soccer
friendly	drink tea
interested in politics	speak Turkish, some Arabic
enjoy feta cheese and olives	Turkish baths
hospitable	hardworking

2. Tamer looks through his list of ideas and combines ideas that are similar. For example, he sees that two of his ideas (*mosques* and *Turkish baths*) relate to the general category of *important places.* Study the following to see how Tamer organizes his ideas in his second list.

Second List with General Categories

<u>behaviors</u>

casual dressers
play soccer
speak Turkish, some Arabic

<u>important places</u>

mosques
Turkish baths

<u>food and drink</u>

drink tea
enjoy feta cheese and olives

<u>values</u>

family-oriented
interested in politics
hospitable
hardworking
friendly

3. Tamer reviews his list again. He sees that he has the most ideas about *values.* He decides to write about the Turkish people and their values because he can think of many examples and personal experiences that will interest his audience (his readers).

Guidelines for Listing

Study the following guidelines for using lists to collect ideas.

LISTING

When you make your first list:

- write all ideas that come to mind
- write as quickly as possible
- write words and groups of words
- do not judge ideas as good or bad, right or wrong
- do not worry about spelling or grammar
- do not worry about sentence structure

When you make your second list:

- identify general categories
- list specific details under your general categories (sometimes the same detail may come under several categories)
- determine which category has the best or most interesting information
- choose one category to write about

GLR   See page 240 of the GLR for activities on writing general categories and grouping similar ideas.

Activity 2-4   Collecting Your Own Ideas Through Listing

1. On another piece of paper, make a list of words and ideas to describe the culture of the United States or another country.

2. Write your ideas on the board, or share them with a small group. Then, with your classmates, list your ideas in categories, and give each category a general heading. Finally, decide which category has the best or most interesting information.

LEARNER'S NOTEBOOK

Opinions on Listing

In your learner's notebook, write about your opinions about *listing*. What are some advantages to this collecting strategy? What are some disadvantages? Then, share your opinions with your classmates.

Stereotypes

LEARNER'S NOTEBOOK

Changing Opinions

We often have opinions about people who are different from us, but after we learn more about those people, our opinions may change. Write about an opinion you have about someone. Has your opinion changed? Why or why not?

READING 3   STEREOTYPES (INTERCULTURAL COMMUNICATIONS TEXTBOOK)

Read the following paragraph to collect some information about stereotypes.

STEREOTYPES

We often form opinions about others and later discover that those opinions are incorrect. We might form these opinions because of stereotypes. Stereotypes are exaggerated beliefs about people. These beliefs may be positive or negative, but they are often untrue because they overgeneralize about all members of a group. Stereotypes frequently occur when we know very little about someone or about a group of people. We may see one person from a group behave a certain way. Then, we might believe that *all* people from that group behave the same way. For example, a person may see several people acting similarly and say, "They are all like that" or "That's what they always do." These comments are stereotypes. Members of all cultural groups make such comments, usually about members of other cultural groups.

5

10

Activity 2-5   Pair Discussion

With a partner, share and discuss your learner's notebook entry, "Changing Opinions" (see page 40). Do you think your opinion is or was based on a stereotype? Discuss this with your partner.

The Grammar of Persuasive Writing: Adverbs of Frequency, Modal Auxiliaries Expressions of Quantity

One way to express accurate generalizations and to persuade your readers to support your generalizations is to use opinion structures. Writers can also control the strength of generalizations by using the following structures:

Adverbs of Frequency	Modal Auxiliaries	Expressions of Quantity
usually often/frequently sometimes seldom/rarely	might may	a number of many several a lot of most some
EXAMPLES		

adverb of frequency
Teenagers *often* have part-time jobs in the United States.

modal auxiliary
People from another culture *might* have problems adjusting to life in the United States.

expression of quantity
Most Americans are friendly.

GLR   See pages 247, 250, and 252 in the GLR for more information on adverbs of frequency, modal auxiliaries, and expressions of quantity.

Activity 2-6   Recognizing Accurate Generalization Structures in Persuasive Writing

The following sentences are from Readings 1 and 2. Compare the sentences in both columns. Then, underline the structures in the second column that control the strength of the generalizations and make the generalizations more accurate. The first answer is provided.

Overgeneralizations

1. We form opinions about others.

2. We form these opinions because of stereotypes.

3. These beliefs are untrue.

4. We see one person behave a certain way, and we believe that all people behave the same way.

More Accurate Generalizations

1. We <u>often</u> form opinions about others.

2. We might form these opinions because of stereotypes.

3. The beliefs are often untrue.

4. We may see one person behave a certain way, and we might believe that all people behave the same way.

Overgeneralizations	More Accurate Generalizations
5. These customs seem strange to others.	**5.** These customs may seem strange to others.
6. Members of the same cultural group share similar customs and values.	**6.** Most members of the same culture group usually share similar customs and values.

Activity 2-7   Writing Accurate Generalizations

The following sentences are stereotypes about Americans. Rewrite these stereotypes to make the generalizations more accurate and to persuade your readers to agree with the generalizations. In your sentences, underline the structures that you use.

EXAMPLES

All Americans like to wear casual clothes.   Americans <u>often</u> like to wear casual clothes.
American teens start socializing too early.   <u>In my opinion</u>, American teens <u>may</u> start socializing too early.

1. Americans eat junk food more than healthy meals.

_____

2. All Americans are rich.

_____

3. All Americans have blonde hair and blue eyes.

_____

4. Americans never express their feelings.

_____

5. Americans always eat at fast-food restaurants.

_____

6. Americans love watching sports like football and basketball.

_____

7. All Americans use credit cards for their purchases.

_____

8. Americans love cats and dogs.

_____

9. All American women work outside the home.

_____

10. All Americans have jobs.

_____

Youth in the United States

READING 4   MY EXPERIENCE WITH YOUNG AMERICANS (STUDENT WRITING)

You have studied several ways to collect and develop ideas, such as reading and list-ing. Sometimes you can use *personal experience* to develop ideas in your writing. In the following paragraph, this student has used her own experience to explain her opinion about young Americans. This student has used the grammar of informational writing. She has also used the grammar of persuasive writing to make accurate generalizations.

MY EXPERIENCE WITH YOUNG AMERICANS

In my opinion, many young Americans are disrespectful. I have a 15-year-old daughter in high school. In the evenings, she tells me about her school day. Her classmates often talk and laugh during class. Sometimes the noise is so loud that she cannot hear her teacher. Some students are frequently late to class, and often students might not complete their homework. My daughter and I feel that these actions are disrespectful.   5

Maria Cervantes
Mexico

Activity 2-8   Recognizing the Grammar of Informational Writing and Persuasive Writing

Review the grammar of informational writing and persuasive writing by doing these tasks in the previous student writing.

1. With one line, underline all subjects.

2. With two lines, underline all present tense verbs.

3. Circle opinion structures (*I believe that, in my opinion*).

4. Place parentheses around adverbs of frequency (*often, frequently*).

5. Place a box around the modal auxiliaries *may* and *might*.

6. Circle expressions of quantity (*most, many*).

Activity 2-9   Writing Opinion Statements

1. In small groups, make a list of four to six opinions about American youth. Include your ideas about education, work, family, clothing, interests, beliefs, and behaviors.

    EXAMPLES

    informal dressers
    interested in world issues
    independent

2. Select three opinions from your list. For each opinion, write a sentence that begins with an opinion structure. In addition, be sure to make accurate generalizations by using adverbs of frequency, modal auxiliaries, and/or expressions of quantity.

    EXAMPLES

    I believe most young Americans like to dress informally.
    In my opinion, young Americans are *usually* interested in world issues.
    I feel that American youth are *often* independent.

Activity 2-10   Supporting Your Opinions

You can use your opinions when you write, but you should explain them. This will make your opinions stronger and more interesting. One way to explain opinions is to use personal experience. Rewrite your three opinions from the previous activity. Then, write one to two complete sentences from your personal experience to explain each opinion. Use a different paragraph for each opinion. An example follows.

EXAMPLE

| opinion | personal experience |
| (general statement) | (specific details) |

    I believe most young Americans like to dress informally. For example, my class-mates usually wear jeans and T-shirts to school. My co-workers often dress in casual clothes, too.

Activity 2-11   Self-editing

1. Read your paragraphs again. Do they say what you want them to say? Are they orga-nized from general opinions to specific details? Make any changes needed to improve the meaning of your writing.

2. Because you wrote about general opinions and you want those generalizations to be accurate, edit for the grammar of informational writing and persuasive writing. Correct any errors that you find. After you have edited each sentence for these fea-tures, check (✓) the box.

- ☐ complete sentences

- ☐ correct verb tense

- ☐ subject-verb agreement

- ☐ structures for accurate generalizations

        opinion structures (*I believe, in my opinion*)

        adverbs of frequency (*usually, often*)

        modal auxiliaries (*might, may*)

        expressions of quantity (*most, some*)

- ☐ appropriate logical organizers (*for example, for instance*) and punctuation

- ☐ capitalization and punctuation to end your sentences

3. Rewrite your paragraphs. Make the corrections that you decided on during editing.

Charts and Graphs

    When you do not have personal experience to include in your writing, you can col-lect information in other ways, such as from *charts and graphs.* First, you must know how to read charts and graphs. A survey, *The Mood of American Youth,* was mailed to 1,500 American teens, aged 13 to 17. Nine hundred and thirty-eight (938) teens com-pleted the survey. They answered questions about their cultural beliefs about family, school, social concerns, and the government. The following graph and chart provide information about American youth and that survey.

READING 5   THE ONE THING TEENS WANT MOST FROM LIFE (BAR GRAPH)

1. Study this bar graph. It shows what teens want most from life.

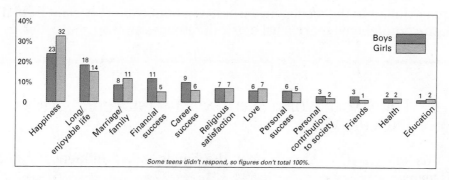

Source: Adapted from a survey sponsored by the Horatio Alger Association for Distinguished Americans, Inc., in partnership with the National Association of Secondary School Principals and reported by Dianne Hales in "How Teenagers See Things," *Parade* Magazine, August 18, 1996, 4–5. Reprinted with permission from *Parade,* copyright ©1996, the Horatio Alger Association, and Dianne Hales.

2.   Answer the following questions.

a. Why is this graph called a "bar graph"? _____

_____

b. What do young Americans in the United States value the most?

_____

c. Do more teenagers want an enjoyable life or financial success?

_____

d. What percentage of boys value personal success the most?

_____

_____

e. Who values marriage and family the most—boys or girls?

_____

LEARNER'S NOTEBOOK

Wants and Values

When you value something or someone, that thing or person is important to you. List several things that you value in life. In what ways are your values different from or similar to the teenagers' responses about what they want from life? In your learner's notebook, make a list of the differences and/or similarities.

READING 6   THE SINGLE WORST INFLUENCE FACING TODAY'S TEENS (PIE CHART)

1. Study this pie chart. It shows what the single worst influence is that faces today's teens.

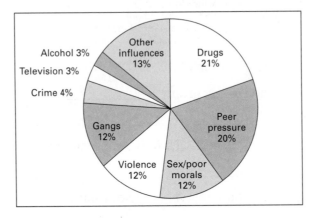

Source: Adapted from a survey sponsored by the Horatio Alger Association for Distinguished Americans, Inc., in partnership with the National Association of Secondary School Principals and reported by Dianne Hales in "How Teenagers See Things," *Parade* Magazine, August 18, 1996, 4–5. Reprinted with permission from *Parade*, copyright ©1996, the Horatio ALger Association, and Dianne Hales.

2. Answer the following questions.

    a. Why is this chart called a "pie chart"? _____

    _____

    b. What negatively influences teens the most? _____

    _____

    c. What percentage of teens are influenced by violence? _____

    _____

d. Are more teens negatively influenced by peer pressure or by sex?

_____

e. What negatively influences young Americans the least? _____

_____

f. In your opinion, what other things might influence teenagers?

_____

Activity 2-12 Writing General Opinions and Specific Details

Do you agree or disagree with the teenagers' opinions about the most negative influences today? Write a paragraph to share your opinions with your teacher and classmates. Your paragraph should begin with a general opinion of agreement or disagreement. Then, write one to three sentences to explain your opinion. Use the grammar of informational writing and persuasive writing to make your generalizations accurate.

Activity 2-13 Designing Your Own Graph

The following information is also from *The Mood of American Youth* survey. With a partner, use this information to design your own bar graph. If possible, design your graph on a computer. Title your graph. Then, share your graph with your class.

- 83% believe that the government should increase spending on AIDS research.
- 81% feel that the government should provide a national health plan for citizens.
- 79% think the government is dishonest.
- 67% feel the government should reduce legal immigration to the United States.
- 55% believe that being rich is necessary for governmental election.

Source: Adapted from a survey sponsored by the Horatio Alger Association for Distinguished Americans, Inc., in partnership with the National Association of Secondary School Principals and reported by Dianne Hales in "How Teenagers See Things," *Parade* Magazine, August 18, 1996, 4–5. Reprinted with permission from *Parade,* copyright ©1996 the Horatio Alger Association, and Dianne Hales.

Activity 2-14 Writing Statements

Before you studied the information about American youth, you may have had some stereotypes about young Americans. Now that you have collected knowledge and information about American youth, what are your thoughts and opinions? Write sentences to share your opinions with your teacher and classmates. Complete the following sentences, and give reasons for your opinions.

1. It surprises me that _____

_____

_____

2. It does not surprise me that _____

_____

_____

3. I am impressed that _____

_____

_____

Connecting Ideas in Your Writing

Good writers sometimes connect ideas and statements in their writing. You can connect two sentences with words like *and, but,* and *so.* Writing some connected sentences in your paragraphs makes your writing more interesting and easy to read. When you connect two complete sentences, a comma is used before the logical organizers *and, but,* and *so.*

LOGICAL ORGANIZERS
and   *additional information*   EXAMPLE   Americans usually smile at strangers. Americans often say hello.   Americans usually smile at strangers, **and** they often say hello.
but   *contrasting information*   EXAMPLE   The United States is a multi-cultural country. Most Americans speak only English.   The United States is a multi-cultural country, **but** most Americans speak only English.
so   *resulting information*   EXAMPLE   Americans often enjoy driving expensive cars. Many people think that Americans are rich.   Americans often enjoy driving expensive cars, **so** many people think that Americans are rich.

GLR   See page 230 in the GLR for more information on logical organizers.

Activity 2-15 Using the Logical Organizers *And, But,* and *So*

The following sentences contain information from *The Mood of American Youth* survey. Read the sentences. On another piece of paper, combine these sentences using *and, but,* or *so*. More than one answer may be correct. An example is provided.

EXAMPLE

12% of teens say they see abuse at home. 17% of teens say their parents use drugs.

12% of teens say they see abuse at home, ***and*** 17% of teens say their parents use drugs.

1. Teenagers say they admire their parents.

    Teenagers say they will use different parenting styles.

2. Teens expect to marry in their late 20s.

    Teens expect to have two children.

3. Many teens believe smoking and drinking are unhealthy.

    Many teens choose not to smoke and drink.

4. Teenagers have little confidence in the government.

    79% of teenagers say people in the government are dishonest.

5. A college degree helps young people get a job.

    67% of girls and 54% of boys plan to go to college.

6. 11% of boys greatly value financial success.

    Only 5% of girls greatly value financial success.

Source: Adapted from a survey sponsored by the Horatio Alger Association for Distinguished Americans, Inc., in partnership with the National Association of Secondary School Principals and reported by Dianne Hales in "How Teenagers See Things," *Parade* Magazine, August 18, 1996, 4–5. Reprinted with permission from *Parade,* copyright ©1996, the Horatio ALger Association, and Dianne Hales.

Activity 2-16 Writing General Statements and Specific Details

Tell your teacher three things that you value and believe are important. Write a general statement for the things that you value, and then explain your statement with specific details (examples and/or reasons). Begin a new paragraph for each main idea. Combine some of the sentences in your paragraphs with *and, but,* and *so.*

Interviewing

Activity 2-17   Listing Questions

What questions did you ask yesterday that helped you gather information? For example, you may have asked the following questions: *How are you? What? When is this assignment due?* On another piece of paper, list all the questions you can remember.

READING 7   YOUTH IN VIETNAM (INTERVIEW)

Asking questions is a common way to gather information. Through questions, you learn and collect information that will help you be successful in your academic work. When you *interview* people, you ask their ideas and opinions about a topic.

The following reading is part of an informal interview. In this interview, one person is collecting information about young people in Vietnam. Read the interview silently. Then, read it again with a partner, each reading one of the parts.

YOUTH IN VIETNAM

S: I'm interested in learning about young people in Vietnam—their interests and values. Umm, can you talk about what young people do after school? For example, what'd you do for fun?

T: Oh, my friends and I went skating or played soccer ... things like that. But usually after we finished school, we just stayed home and did homework.   5

S: Really?!

T: Uh huh, I studied a lot. Never had a job in high school.

S: Wow! That's different from many students in the United States.

T: Yeah, just a few young people go to work. Because they can't find a job easily ... not enough jobs. You need a college education.   10

S: Hmm, that's interesting. (pause) Ah, in high school, do young people date?

T: Yeah (laugh). Yeah, they do.

S: What kinds of things do they do? Where do they go when it's nice outside?

T: They go to some ... ah movies, for coffee, to a park. Oh, the beach when it's nice out-side.   15

S: And what about the age? Because I know my dad didn't want me to date. Not until I was 15.

T: Fifteen? Umm, in my country, from what I remember, people, umm, they ... they were about 18. But ... now I think they're 16 or 15.

S: So it's getting younger (laugh).   20

T: Yeah (laugh).

S: Mmm. Okay. Well, I have another question. Can you tell me what young people value? You know, what ... what's important to them? A good education, a lot of money, or to be popular ... ?

T: Umm. Well, I know a lot of young people, they … (pause). Like my friend, his father 25
works for the government and has a lot of money. My friend can take his father's money
and go anywhere. He doesn't need a job. Ya know, most young people in Vietnam don't
plan for the future. If they have $5, they spend $5. In my opinion, they don't think about
tomorrow.

S: I think that's often a problem everywhere. 30

T: Yeah.

Thong Phan
Vietnam

Activity 2-18 Differences Between Spoken and Written English

1. Our spoken language is usually different from our academic writing. For example, we
often speak in fragments (incomplete sentences), but in written academic English,
incomplete sentences are very seldom used. In addition, in conversations, we use
filler words like "well" and "umm," but these words do not usually appear in academic writing. With a partner, find fragments and other characteristics of spoken language in the previous interview. Write down the line number of an example of each.

> **GLR**   See page 266 in the GLR for more information on fragments.

_____ fragment (incomplete sentence)

_____ repetition of words (*we … we*)

_____ laughter

_____ conversational "filler" (*ah, umm*)

_____ informal vocabulary (*yeah* instead of *yes*)

_____ contractions (*that's* instead of *that is*)

2. With your classmates, discuss how written English is different from spoken English.

Activity 2-19 Giving an Interview

Interview a classmate to find out her or his ideas and opinions about youth in another
culture.

1. Plan your interview. Write two or three yes/no questions and two or three information questions about youth in another culture. Place the questions in the first column of the following chart. When you write your questions, you do not need to

identify the culture. You can fill that in when you select your partner and begin your interview. Examples of yes/no and information questions are provided in the first column.

GLR   See page 256 in the GLR for more information on question formation.

Questions	Spoken Answers	Written Statements
Yes/No In high school, do young people date?	Yeah. Yeah, they do.	In Vietnam, young people usually date in high school.
a.		
b.		
c.		
Information Where do people go on a date?	They go to some . . . ah movies, for coffe, to a park. Oh, the beach when it's nice outside.	On a date, many teenagers go to the movies, to a park, or to the beach. They might also go for coffee.
a.		
b.		
c.		

2. Interview your partner about her or his ideas and opinions, and record your partner's spoken answers in column two of the chart. Ask your partner to repeat answers if necessary.

Activity 2-20   Turning Spoken Language into Written English

1. Spoken language is very different from written language. In the third column of the previous chart, change your partner's spoken answers into written statements. Be sure to use the grammar of informational writing and persuasive writing to make accurate generalizations.

2. Share your written statements with your partner. Ask your partner to identify any necessary changes. Together, rewrite any overgeneralizations to make them more accurate.

LEARNER'S NOTEBOOK

Interesting Responses

Review the written statements from your interview about youth in another culture. In your opinion, what is the most interesting information you collected? Why? Respond in your learner's notebook.

PUTTING IT ALL TOGETHER

In the United States, like most countries, there are subcultures within societies. For example, people from the East Coast (e.g., Washington, D.C.) may have different beliefs and customs from people from the West Coast (e.g., Los Angeles, California). In New York City, Hispanic Americans may have different beliefs and customs from Asian Americans. Other examples of subcultures in the United States are American farmers, African Americans, working mothers, older Americans, homeless people, and teenagers.

FINAL WRITING ASSIGNMENT: SUBCULTURES WITHIN SOCIETIES

Select a subculture that you have personal experience with or are familiar with, and write about that subculture's customs. Your purpose is to describe or explain that subculture to an audience (reader) that may know very little about it.

Collecting Ideas: Listing

To begin, collect ideas for your assignment by making a list of words that define or explain your chosen subculture. Include ideas about customs, habits, beliefs, clothing, food, music, and so on. When you finish your first list, make a second list and combine your ideas into general categories. If you do not have enough ideas, interview someone from that subculture, and add ideas to your list.

Here is an example of how one student approached this assignment.

First List

many women in Somalia

enjoy family	usually tired	hardworking
care for family	work on farm	no school
difficult life	get up early	make breakfast
collect firewood	do cooking, cleaning	illiterate
intelligent		

Second List with General Categories

education

no school
illiterate
intelligent

daily routines

make breakfast
do cooking, cleaning
collect firewood
get up early
work on farm
care for family

characteristics

intelligent
usually tired
hardworking

family life

enjoy family
care for family
difficult life

Writing from General to Specific

Select several ideas from your list, and write sentences that state your general ideas and opinions. Then, use personal experiences to explain each idea and opinion. Be sure to begin a new paragraph for each main idea. In addition, because you are writing about generalizations, use the grammar of informational writing and persuasive writing.

EXAMPLE

In Somalia, many women do not work outside the home. A lot of these women might not be able to read and write. This doesn't mean they aren't intelligent. It does mean that it is difficult for them to change their lives. In some villages, there are no schools. Women do not always have the chance to go to school. Most of these women have a difficult life. They often get up at 4:00 a.m. They prepare breakfast. They do other household chores. Then, they might walk half an hour or more to work on a farm. These women also do most of the domestic work. They often collect firewood and water. They do the cooking, cleaning, and washing. They take care of the family.

Using Logical Organizers

To make your writing easier to understand, combine some of your supporting statements with *and, but, so, for example*, and *for instance.*

EXAMPLE

In Somalia, many women do not work outside the home. A lot of these women might not be able to read and write. This doesn't mean they aren't intelligent, *but* it does mean that it is difficult for them to change their lives. In some villages, there are no schools, *so* women do not always have the chance to go to school. Most of these women have a difficult life. *For instance,* they often get up at 4:00 a.m. They prepare breakfast, *and* they do other household chores. Then, they might walk half an hour or more to work on a farm. These women also do most of the domestic work. *For example,* they often collect firewood and water. They do the cooking, cleaning, and washing, *and* they take care of the family.

Safia Sheikh
Somalia

Editing Your Writing

1. Read your paper again. Do you clearly explain the customs of your chosen subculture? Should you provide more details to help your audience understand that subculture? Are your ideas organized from general ideas to specific details? Make any changes needed to improve the meaning of your writing.

2. You wrote about generalizations of a subculture, so edit your sentences for the grammar of informational writing and persuasive writing. Correct any errors that you find. After you have edited for these features, check (✓) the box.

    ❏ complete sentences

    ❏ correct verb tense

    ❏ subject-verb agreement

☐ structures for accurate generalizations

opinion structures (*I believe, in my opinion*)

adverbs of frequency (*usually, often*)

modal auxiliaries (*might, may*)

expressions of quantity (*most, some*)

☐ appropriate logical organizers (*and, but, for example*) and punctuation

☐ capitalization and punctuation to end your sentences

Providing Peer Support

Exchange papers with a partner, and read each other's ideas.

1. On your partner's paper, <u>underline</u> the example or personal experience you like best.

2. Explain why you like that example or personal experience. In the margin of the paper, write a statement such as:

Great detail!	I had an experience just like this.
I smiled when I read this example.	I was amazed that this happened.
I like the vocabulary you used.	I learned from this example.

3. Give one suggestion to make the writing better. In the margin of the paper, write a question such as:

I don't understand. Can you use another example to help me?

What happened after this?

Could you please give more details here?

How can you make this generalization more accurate?

Revising Your Writing

1. With your partner, discuss her or his ideas and suggestions for your writing.

2. Make two or three changes to improve your writing.

Finalizing Your Writing

1. Make the corrections that you decided on during the self-editing and peer-support processes. You may want to refer to the checklist which begins on page 57 again.

2. Rewrite your paper to submit to your teacher.

• •

In your academic classes, you will often need to collect information for your assignments. You can collect information in many ways, including

reading

listing

studying or developing charts or graphs

thinking about opinions or personal
    experiences

discussing ideas with classmates

asking questions and interviewing

checking the WWW

Read the following assignments from different academic classes. On the lines provided, write how you could collect information for these assignments. There may be more than one correct answer. The first answer is provided.

American Literature

Name the twentieth century American author whom you like the best. Explain why you like this person's writing.

thinking about opinions and personal experiences

Economics

Develop a graph to show this year's unemployment numbers by race, age, and gender.

_____

Marketing

In what ways do advertisements influence consumers?

_____

Psychology

What childhood experience influenced you the most? Why?

_____

Criminal Justice

Discuss the U.S. crime rates for the last five years. Explain why crime is increasing (or decreasing) in America.

_____

U.S. History

What changes, if any, should be made in the current immigration laws?

_____

Chapter 3

Comparing and Contrasting

Personal Economics

GOALS

WRITING
◆ practice comparing and
   contrasting ideas and things

GRAMMAR
◆ practice the grammar of
   informational writing
   and persuasive writing

CONTENT
◆ learn about consumer issues like
   personal budgeting and car buying

ACADEMIC FIELD
Consumer Economics

Sample Authentic College/University Comparing and Contrasting Assignments

In your academic classes, you will use the skills you learn in this chapter to complete assignments and exam questions like these:

Economics

Define socialism. How does it differ from capitalism?

Sociology

Compare the jobs of a janitor and a partner at an accounting firm. Answer these questions: How much skill is required? What rewards go with the job? What are the advantages and disadvantages of each job? Explain.

Marketing

What are the major differences in the marketing strategies of companies that produce goods and those that produce services?

Anthropology

Compare the Baganda people's attitudes toward the dead with your own attitudes. How are they similar? How are they different?

CNN video support is available for this chapter. Turner Le@rning

GETTING READY

Introduction to Comparing and Contrasting

In academic writing, you often need to explain how two or more things are different or similar. When you explain differences, you are *contrasting*. When you explain similarities, you are *comparing*. However, when teachers ask you to compare, they often want you to look at *both* differences and similarities. Comparing/contrasting is one of the most common and most useful skills for students to learn.

LEARNER'S NOTEBOOK

Warm-up Writing

Think about your spending habits for transportation, housing, entertainment, education, and food. How did you spend your money five years ago? How do you spend your money today? Are there differences? Why or why not? Write your responses in your learner's notebook.

Grammar Preview

In this chapter, you will practice the *grammar of informational writing* and *of persuasive writing*. Generally, when you write statements of fact or habit, you use the grammar of informational writing. This chapter focuses on the following aspects of this grammar: *present tense verbs, subject-verb agreement,* and *logical organizers.*

When you wish to persuade or convince your readers to support your ideas in your writing, you use the grammar of persuasive writing. In addition to structures to control the strength of your generalizations, you will practice *conditional sentences.*

GLR   See pages 226–237 and 246–254 in the GLR for more information on the grammar of informational writing and of persuasive writing.

FOCUSING

Personal Economics

Activity 3-1   Pre-reading Vocabulary

The following sentences contain *italicized* words from this chapter. Read each sentence, and then match a definition to each italicized word. The first answer is provided.

1. __b__ Economics is the study of how a society uses *resources*, such as money, labor, and materials.

2. ____ Economics is a *broad* subject, so you cannot learn everything about it in a single textbook.

3. ____ Individuals and families who want to spend and save their money effectively should develop a *budget*.

4. ____ His *income* increased when he got a different job. He now earns $35,000 a year.

5. ____ Companies do research to determine what *consumers* think of their products.

6. ____ The *expense* of the trip was more than we could pay. We had to cancel our vacation.

7. ____ She wants to *invest* in an ice cream shop. She is certain she will become rich.

8. ____ This morning, we had a *productive* class and learned a great deal about the subject of economics.

   a. producing valuable results

   b. things that have a value or use, like money or land

   c. cost or price

   d. to put money into a business with the hope of making money

   e. money earned by working

   f. persons who buy and use goods and services

   g. a plan of expected income and expenses

   h. covering many topics

READING 1   UNDERSTANDING ECONOMICS (ECONOMICS TEXTBOOK)

Read the following introduction to economics.

UNDERSTANDING ECONOMICS

Economics is the study of how a society uses resources, such as money, labor, and materials. Economics is a broad subject. You cannot cover everything about economics in a single chapter, or even a single textbook or course. However, the more you learn about economics, the better you can make intelligent decisions as a consumer and as a citizen. For example, your understanding of economics will help you decide how to save, invest, or   5
spend your money. These decisions will affect you, your family, and others around you.

This chapter focuses on personal economics, an area of economics that deals with consumer issues and topics such as developing a personal budget, renting an apartment, and buying a car. Understanding personal economics can help you make better decisions about economic matters. It can also help you live a more productive and enjoyable life.   10

Source: Adapted from Allen W. Smith, *Understanding Economics* (Random House, Inc., 1986, xxiii–xxvi).

Activity 3-2   Checking Your Comprehension and Identifying Grammar

Use the previous reading to respond to the following tasks.

1. What does the field of economics study? _____

_____

_____

2. List reasons why understanding economics is important.

_____

_____

_____

3. What is personal economics?

_____

_____

4. List reasons why understanding personal economics is important.

_____

_____

_____

_____

5. Reading 1 provides basic information about economics, so the writer used the grammar of informational writing. Review this grammar by:

   a. underlining the present tense verbs

   b. studying the subject-verb agreement of those verbs

   c. circling the logical organizers (*and, so, for instance*) that show the reader how ideas and sentences are related.

Using Cohesion in Your Writing

Good writers are coherent in their writing when they make their ideas easy to read and understand. Cohesion devices, like logical organizers, show readers that your ideas and sentences are related to each other. There are several ways to use cohesion in your writing.

COHESION DEVICES
Repetition of key words and phrases   *Economics* is the study of how a society uses resources, such as money, labor, and materials. *Economics* is a broad subject. (Repetition of *economics*.)
Logical organizers   The more you learn about economics, the better you can make intelligent decisions as a consumer *and* as a citizen. *For example,* your understanding of economics will help you decide how to save, invest, *and* spend your money. (*For example* shows example; *and* shows additional idea.)
Pronouns   *Understanding personal economics* can help you make better decisions about economic matters. *It* can also help you live a more productive and enjoyable life. (*It* refers to *understanding personal economics.*
Different forms of a word   Your understanding of economics will help you *decide* how to save, invest, or spend your money. *These decisions* will affect you, your family, and others around you. (Same word family: *decide*—verb, *decisions*—noun.)

Activity 3-3   Identifying Cohesion

Return to Reading 1 on page 64. With a partner, find and highlight examples of cohesion. Be ready to discuss your examples with your teacher and classmates.

A Personal Budget

A budget is a plan of expected income and expenses. When you use and follow this plan, you are budgeting. Businesses and governments use budgets to guide them in their spending. Similarly, individuals and families who want to spend and save their money effectively should develop a budget.

In Sera's economics class, she is learning about a personal budget plan. Professor Green asked Sera's class to compare the spending habits of two students. Study the following table, which outlines the monthly spending patterns and income of Igor and Hector.

PERSONAL MONTHLY BUDGET

	Igor	Hector

Food
    Groceries
    Eating Out
	$135
	20
		$30
		110

Housing
    Rent Payment
    Utilities
	$800
	120
		$0
		0

Transportation
    Auto Payment
    Gas and Oil
    Public Transportation
	$0
	0
	48
		$250
		80
		0

Education
    Tuition
    Texts and Supplies
	$960 (nonresident fees)
	35
		$265 (resident fees)
		35

Recreation/Entertainment	$20	$100
Miscellaneous Expenses	$40	$40

Total Monthly Income
(including loans, etc.)
  − Total Monthly Expenses
  = Total Monthly Savings
	$2,250
	
	2,183
	67
		$1,000
		
		895
		105

Activity 3-4   Writing About Spending Habits

Sera's class studied the previous table and observed many differences between Igor's and Hector's spending habits. Study and complete this list of differences. Because this writing is about spending habits, use the grammar of informational writing.

EXAMPLE   *Food*
Igor spends $135 on groceries each month.
Hector spends $30 on groceries each month.

1. *Housing*

   Igor _____

   Hector _____

2. *Transportation*

   Igor _____

   Hector _____

3. *Education*

   Igor _____

   Hector _____

4. *Recreation/Entertainment*

   Igor _____

   Hector _____

5. *Monthly Savings*

   Igor _____

   Hector _____

The Grammar of Comparisons: Words of Difference

Four common logical organizers that show difference are *but, however, on the other hand,* and *in contrast.* These words show that two things or ideas are not similar. Study the following chart for the correct usage and punctuation of these logical organizers.

LOGICAL ORGANIZERS: WORDS OF DIFFERENCE

but	I didn't pay college tuition five years ago, *but* now I pay $795 per term.
however	I rode public transportation five years ago; *however,* I now own a car. I rode public transportation five years ago. *However,* I now own a car.
on the other hand	I didn't pay rent five years ago; *on the other hand,* I pay $770 for rent now. I didn't pay rent five years ago. *On the other hand,* I pay $770 for rent now.
in contrast	I had $10 in my savings account five years ago; *in contrast,* I now have $850 saved. I had $10 in my savings account five years ago. *In contrast,* I now have $850 saved.

GLR   See pages 212 and 230 of the GLR for more information about comparisons and logical organizers.

Activity 3-5   Writing Sentences Using Words of Difference

Use the logical organizers *but, however, on the other hand,* and *in contrast* to show your ideas about the differences between Igor's and Hector's spending habits. Write on a separate piece of paper. Be sure to use the grammar of informational writing and correct punctuation with your logical organizers. An example is provided.

EXAMPLE   Food (however)

Each month, Igor spends $135 on groceries; **however,** Hector spends only $30 on groceries.

1. Housing (but)

2. Transportation (on the other hand)

3. Education (however)

4. Recreation/Entertainment (but)

5. Monthly Savings (in contrast)

Activity 3-6 Self-editing

1. Read your sentences again. Do they say what you want them to say? Is the information accurate? Make any changes needed to improve the meaning of your writing.

2. You wrote about spending habits, so edit your sentences for the grammar of informational writing. Correct any errors that you find. After you have edited for these features, check (✓) the box.

   ☐ complete sentences

   ☐ correct verb tense

   ☐ subject-verb agreement

   ☐ appropriate logical organizers (*but, however*) and punctuation

   ☐ capitalization and punctuation to end your sentences

LEARNER'S NOTEBOOK

Spending Money

    We all have opinions about spending money. For example, one person might value having a new car to drive to work and school. However, another person might want to save money and ride the bus instead. What different opinions do you and your friends or family members have about spending money? Describe those differences in your learner's notebook. Use personal experiences and examples to explain your ideas, and begin a new paragraph for each main idea.

The Grammar of Comparisons: Words of Similarity

    Sometimes when you compare two things or ideas, you want to focus only on their likenesses or similarities. Three common logical organizers that show similarity are *both, also,* and *too.* Study the following chart for the correct usage and punctuation of these logical organizers.

LOGICAL ORGANIZERS: WORDS OF SIMILARITY

both	*Both* Sera and John study economics with Dr. Green.
	Sera and John *both* study economics with Dr. Green.
also	Sera studies economics with Dr. Green. John *also* studies economics with Dr. Green.
	Sera studies economics with Dr. Green. John studies economics with Dr. Green *also*.
too	Sera studies economics with Dr. Green. John studies economics with Dr. Green, *too*.

GLR   See pages 212 and 230 of the GLR for more information about comparisons and logical organizers.

Activity 3-7   Writing Sentences Using Words of Similarity

Some of Igor's and Hector's spending habits are similar (see the Personal Monthly Budget on page 66). Using the logical organizers *both, also,* and *too*, write sentences to explain their likenesses. Because this writing is about spending habits, use the grammar of informational writing. Use correct punctuation with your logical organizers. One sample answer is provided.

EXAMPLE   Igor and Hector *both* spend $40 on miscellaneous expenses each month.

1. (both) _____

   _____

2. (too) _____

   _____

3. (also) _____

   _____

LEARNER'S NOTEBOOK

Favorite Places

Select two of your favorite restaurants or stores, and write about them in your learner's notebook. Why do you enjoy those places? What are their differences and/or similarities? For example, you might enjoy eating at a local Chinese restaurant and a local Mexican restaurant because they both are inexpensive and near your home. Before you begin to write, develop a chart like the following.

Topic: Chinese and Mexican Restaurants in my City

Differences	**Similarities**
variety of entrees that the	inexpensive
restaurants serve	close to my apartment

Activity 3-8   Completing a Personal Budget

1. Many economists believe that developing a personal budget plan is very important. Complete the following budget for your personal expenses. Write your expenses in the "Self" column.

PERSONAL MONTHLY BUDGET

	Self	**Partner**
Food		
Groceries		
Eating Out		
Housing		
Rent or Mortgage Payment		
Utilities		
Transportation		
Auto Payment		
Gas and Oil		
Public Transportation		

PERSONAL MONTHLY BUDGET *(continued)*

	Self	Partner
Education 　Tuition 　Materials and Supplies		
Recreation/Entertainment		
Miscellaneous Expenses		

2. Compare your spending habits with a partner, and then complete your partner's column in the Personal Monthly Budget table.

Activity 3-9   Writing Comparisons About Spending Habits

Write about two differences and two similarities between your partner's spending habits and your own. Include a variety of logical organizers that show difference and similarity. Because you are writing about habits, use the grammar of informational writing. In addition, use the grammar of persuasive writing to express accurate generalizations.

EXAMPLE

I often spend $100 on groceries each month. On the other hand, my partner usually spends $150 on groceries.

Activity 3-10   Self-editing

1. Read your sentences again. Do they say what you want them to say? Is the information accurate? Make any changes needed to improve the meaning of your writing.

2. You wrote about spending habits, so edit your sentences for the grammar of informational writing. In addition, because you want your generalizations to be accurate,

edit for the grammar of persuasive writing. Correct any errors that you find. After you have edited for these features, check (✓) the box.

- ☐ complete sentences
- ☐ correct verb tense
- ☐ subject-verb agreement
- ☐ appropriate logical organizers (*but, however*) and punctuation
- ☐ structures that express accurate generalizations (adverbs of frequency like *usually, often, frequently*)
- ☐ capitalization and punctuation to end your sentences

LEARNER'S NOTEBOOK

Personal Spending Habits

What are your opinions about your personal spending habits? For example, do you think that you budget your money carefully or carelessly? What ideas do you have for improving your spending habits? Support your opinions and ideas with examples.

Extended Comparisons

READING 2   IGOR'S AND HECTOR'S LIFESTYLES (PARAGRAPHS)

Read these paragraphs that show organizational formats. They are extended (longer) comparisons of two things. These extended comparisons show two ways to explain the differences between Igor and Hector.

IGOR'S AND HECTOR'S LIFESTYLES

Plan A

Igor's and Hector's lifestyles and spending habits are different for three main reasons. First, Igor usually buys groceries and cooks meals at home. Second, he rarely spends money on recreational activities. Lastly, most of Igor's income goes to housing and tuition. For example, he spends $800 per month on rent and $120 on utilities. He is a nonresident and pays $960 a month for tuition. On the other hand, Hector usually goes out to eat. He might   5 spend a total of $110 at restaurants each month. In addition, he spends a lot of his money on entertainment. Also, Hector lives with his parents, so he doesn't pay for housing. He pays less for tuition, too—only $265 a month.

Plan B

Igor's lifestyles and spending habits are different from Hector's for three main reasons. 10
First, Igor usually buys groceries and cooks meals at home, but Hector usually goes out to eat. In fact, Hector might spend a total of $100 at restaurants each month. Second, Igor rarely spends money on recreational activities; however, Hector spends a lot of his money on entertainment. Lastly, most of Igor's income goes to housing and tuition. For example, he spends $800 per month on rent and $120 on utilities. He is a nonresident and pays $960 15
a month for tuition. On the other hand, Hector lives with his parents, so he doesn't pay for housing. He pays less for tuition, too—only $265 a month.

Organizing Your Ideas When Comparing and Contrasting

There are two basic ways to organize your ideas when you compare or contrast information. Study the two organizational formats outlined in the following chart.

Plan A	**Plan B**
General Statement	General Statement
I. Discuss all of Subject A, idea by idea	I. Discuss one idea of both Subjects A and B
a. Idea 1	a. Subject A, Idea 1
b. Idea 2	b. Subject B, Idea 1
II. Discuss all of Subject B, idea by idea	II. Discuss another idea of Subjects A and B
a. Idea 1	a. Subject A, Idea 2
b. Idea 2	b. Subject B, Idea 2

Activity 3-11   Understanding the Organization of Extended Comparisons

1. Compare the following outlines to the extended comparisons that begin on page 73.

<table>
<tr><td align="center">**Plan A**</td><td align="center">**Plan B**</td></tr>
<tr><td>*Differences between Igor and Hector*</td><td>*Differences between Igor and Hector*</td></tr>
<tr><td>I. *Igor*</td><td>I. *Food*</td></tr>
<tr><td> a. Food</td><td> a. Igor</td></tr>
<tr><td> b. Recreation</td><td> b. Hector</td></tr>
<tr><td> c. Housing</td><td>II. *Recreation*</td></tr>
<tr><td> d. Tuition</td><td> a. Igor</td></tr>
<tr><td>II. *Hector*</td><td> b. Hector</td></tr>
<tr><td> a. Food</td><td>III. *Housing*</td></tr>
<tr><td> b. Recreation</td><td> a. Igor</td></tr>
<tr><td> c. Housing</td><td> b. Hector</td></tr>
<tr><td> d. Tuition</td><td>IV. *Tuition*</td></tr>
<tr><td></td><td> a. Igor</td></tr>
<tr><td></td><td> b. Hector</td></tr>
</table>

2. Look at the two extended comparisons again, but this time circle the logical organizers that show *difference.*

General Statements in Extended Comparisons

When you write an extended comparison of two things, you begin with a general statement. This general statement explains (1) *what you are comparing or contrasting* and (2) *what you are focusing on* (the similarities or the differences). The general statement often includes (3) *how many ideas will be compared or contrasted.*

EXAMPLE

Igor's lifestyles and spending habits *are different from* Hector's for three main reasons.

There are many ways to write a general statement in an extended comparison. Examples follow.

COMPARING

A and B *are similar* in several ways.
A and B *are alike* in several ways.
A *is similar to* B in several ways.

A *is like* B in several ways.

A *is the same as* B in several ways.

There are several similarities between A and B.

CONTRASTING

A and B *are different* in many ways.

A *differs from* B in many ways.

A *is different from* B in many ways.

A and B *have many differences.*

A and B *differ* in many ways.

There are many differences between A and B.

Activity 3-12   Writing General Statements in Extended Comparisons

Use a variety of comparing and contrasting structures to write general statements for the following items. Include one or more reasons for some of your general statements. Use the grammar of informational writing. Because you want to persuade your readers to agree with you, also use the grammar of persuasive writing.

> EXAMPLE   a Florida vacation and a California vacation
>
> In my opinion, a Florida vacation and a California vacation are similar because both places have warm climates and are on the ocean coast.

1. the tuition costs for resident and nonresident students

2. buying used versus new textbooks

3. eating at two different fast-food restaurants

4. driving or owning a car versus using public transportation

5. living in an apartment or in a dormitory

Activity 3-13   Self-editing

1. Read your sentences again. Do they say what you want them to say? Do you begin with a general statement of comparing or contrasting? Do you include specific details (reasons)? Make any changes needed to improve the meaning of your writing.

2. Edit your sentences for the grammar of informational writing and persuasive writing. Correct any errors that you find. After you have edited for these features, check (✓) the box.

☐ complete sentences

☐ correct verb tense

☐ subject-verb agreement

☐ appropriate logical organizers (*also, but, however*) and punctuation

☐ structures that express accurate generalizations

opinion structures (*I believe, in my opinion*)

adverbs of frequency (*usually, often*)

modal auxiliaries (*might, may*)

expressions of quantity (*most, some*)

☐ capitalization and punctuation to end your sentences

Using Logical Organizers for Cohesion

As you have studied, logical organizers provide cohesion in your writing. In other words, logical organizers show how ideas are related. They also help the reader understand the organization of your writing.

When you compare or contrast several points in an extended comparison, logical organizers tell your reader when you are moving to the next point. The following logical organizers are often used in extended comparisons to help the reader move from one comparison to the next.

LOGICAL ORGANIZERS IN EXTENDED COMPARISONS	
First, ... (Second/Third, ...) Next, ... (Then, ...) Finally, ... (Lastly, ...)	Another *noun phrase + verb* ... In addition, ... Also, ...

Commas are usually used after these logical organizers, except for *another*. Discuss the use of *another* with your teacher and classmates.

GLR   See page 230 in the GLR for more information about logical organizers.

Activity 3-14   Recognizing the Parts of an Extended Comparison

1. In the following extended comparison, complete these tasks.

   a. Underline the general statement.

   b. Highlight the logical organizers that help the reader move from one comparison to the next (*first, second, in addition,* etc.).

   > Igor's lifestyles and spending habits are different from Hector's for three main reasons. First, Igor usually buys groceries and cooks meals at home, but Hector usually goes out to eat. In fact, Hector might spend a total of $100 at restaurants each month. Second, Igor rarely spends money on recreational activities; however, Hector spends a lot of his money on entertainment. Lastly, most of Igor's income goes to housing and tuition. For example, he spends $800 per month on rent and $120 on utilities. He is a nonresident and pays $960 a month for tuition. On the other hand, Hector lives with his parents, so he doesn't pay for housing. He pays less for tuition, too—only $265 a month.

2. Review the grammar of informational writing and persuasive writing by completing the following tasks in the previous paragraph.

   a. Underline all present tense verbs.

   b. Place parentheses around structures that express accurate generalizations.

   c. You have already highlighted the logical organizers of extended comparisons. Now circle additional examples of cohesion (other logical organizers, repetition of key words/phrases, pronouns, different forms of the same word).

Activity 3-15   Writing an Extended Comparison

Write an extended comparison of your spending habits and a classmate's.

1. To begin, review Activity 3-8 (your Personal Monthly Budget) and Activity 3-9 (your comparison sentences).

2. Then, use either Plan A or Plan B to make an outline of your ideas to include in an extended comparison. (For a review of the plans, see page 74.)

3. Write a general statement for your extended comparison.

4. Develop the ideas from your outline, and connect your ideas with appropriate logical organizers. Begin a new paragraph for each main idea.

Activity 3-16   Self-editing

1. Read your extended comparison again. Does it say what you want it to say? Are your ideas organized in the best way for this particular writing task? Do you move from general ideas to specific details? What cohesion devices did you use to relate ideas and sentences to each other? Make any changes needed to improve the meaning of your writing.

2. Edit your sentences for the grammar of informational writing and persuasive writing. Correct any errors that you find. After you have edited for these features, check (✓) the box.

☐ complete sentences

☐ correct verb tense

☐ subject-verb agreement

☐ appropriate logical organizers (*also, but, for instance*) and punctuation

☐ structures that express accurate generalizations

opinion structures (*I believe, in my opinion*)

adverbs of frequency (*usually, often*)

modal auxiliaries (*might, may*)

expressions of quantity (*most, some*)

☐ capitalization and punctuation to end your sentences

Consumer Housing

As consumers in the United States, we spend a lot of our money on housing. Decisions about our housing are important. These decisions include where we want to live, how much we want to spend, and who we want to live with. One housing decision many Americans make is whether to buy or to rent.

READING 3   BUYING VERSUS RENTING (HOUSING OPTIONS)

Read the following excerpt about buying and renting homes.

BUYING VERSUS RENTING

Owning a home is a popular dream for many Americans, but home ownership has both advantages and disadvantages. The first advantage is that houses are usually bigger than apartments. Houses may have more space and larger rooms than apartments do. Second, houses often have yards between the house and the neighbor's house, so houses are often more private than apartments. However, owning a home also has several disadvantages. For   5
example, home ownership is more expensive than apartment renting. Houses demand a large down payment and require more maintenance than an apartment. If something breaks, the homeowner is responsible for it. This costs the owner time and money. Finally, houses offer less flexibility. If owners need to move because of work or for personal reasons, they cannot easily do so. They must first find a buyer for their house.   10

Home ownership is a common American dream. However, because of the cost and commitment of home buying, many people still prefer to rent.

Activity 3-17   Check Your Comprehension and Identify Grammar

Use the previous reading to complete the following tasks.

1. List the advantages and disadvantages to owning a home.

Advantages	Disadvantages

2. Underline all present tense verbs.

3. Place parentheses around structures that express accurate generalizations.

4. Circle the logical organizers that help the reader move from one comparison to the next.

5. Highlight additional examples of cohesion devices (other logical organizers, repetition of key words/phrases, pronouns, different forms of the same word).

LEARNER'S NOTEBOOK

Housing Options

Do you prefer to own or rent your home? Why? In your learner's notebook, write a memo to your teacher to explain your opinion about housing. Use the memo format (see Chapter 1, page 22 for a review).

The Grammar of Persuasive Writing: Conditional Sentences

Academic writers often use conditional sentences in persuasive writing. Conditional sentences show a cause and a result. Look at these examples from Reading 3.

Cause	**Result**
If something breaks,	the homeowner is responsible for it.
If owners need to move because of work or for personal reasons,	they cannot easily do so.

Writers use conditional sentences to try to convince readers that a cause-result relationship exists between two ideas or situations. To be as accurate as possible, writers may also use structures (like adverbs of frequency or modal auxiliaries) to reduce the strength of the generalizations in their conditional sentences.

EXAMPLE

Young married couples are *frequently* renters instead of home owners. If the couple does not have enough money for a down payment on a house, they *might* not have any other choice.

GLR   See page 254 in the GLR for more information on conditional sentences.

Activity 3-18   Writing Conditional Sentences About Personal Economics

Based on the readings in this chapter, complete the following conditional sentences. Write your sentences on a separate piece of paper. There may be more than one appropriate answer.

EXAMPLE

If you want to learn more about how a society uses resources, ___you should study___
___economics.___

1. If you understand personal economics, _____
2. If you want to spend and save your money effectively, _____
3. _____, you should buy a house.
4. _____, you should rent an apartment.

Activity 3-19   Analyzing the Meaning and Purpose of Conditional Sentences in Academic Writing

1. The following paragraph is from Chapter 1, Reading 2, "Discover Your Learning Styles." The writer of this paragraph uses a conditional sentence. Read the paragraph, and underline the conditional sentence. Then, write the cause-result in the following chart.

> Most students use more than one way to learn new things. These students are flexible learners. However, some students are not flexible. They use only one or two learning styles. To be successful in the classroom, you should practice several styles of learning. This will help you learn from teachers who use different methods in the classroom, such as giving a lecture, showing a video, or organizing a group activity. If you practice several styles of learning, you can learn more easily.

Cause	Result

2. What is the writer trying to persuade or convince the reader to believe? Do you agree with this argument? Why or why not? Discuss your opinions with your teacher and classmates.

The Grammar of Comparisons: Comparatives

When we show the difference between two things, we often use *comparatives*. Words like *faster, friendlier*, or *more convenient* are comparatives.

> **GLR**   See page 214 in the GLR for more information on comparatives.

Activity 3-20   Using Comparatives to Make Housing Decisions

1. Return to Reading 3 on page 80. Draw a box around the comparatives, and discuss their use with your teacher and classmates.

2. Practice using comparative structures. With a partner, use the list on page 84 to discuss additional differences between buying and renting. Be sure to use complete sentences.

    EXAMPLE

    Buying a house is a better investment than renting.

    or

    Renting is a poorer investment than buying a house.

BUYING VERSUS RENTING

Buying	Renting
better investment than	poorer investment than
often quieter than	often less quiet than
more storage space than	less storage space than
more yard work than	less yard work than
less time for fun	more time for fun
greater/more opportunities to meet people	fewer opportunities to meet people
fewer amenities (washer-dryer, swimming pool, etc.)	more amenities

Activity 3-21   Looking for an Apartment

When you look for an apartment, you should carefully compare two or more places. This will help you make the best decision for you and your needs. Study these rental ads from the newspaper.

ADVERTISEMENT 1

Wood Hill Complex

Suwanee, Georgia
(30 miles north of Atlanta, off I-85)

770-813-8000

476 one-, two-, and three-bedroom apartments

Includes pool, tennis courts, and weight room; washer/dryer connection; fireplace; covered parking. No pets allowed.

One-bedroom unit	Two-bedroom unit	Three-bedroom unit
715 sq ft $580	980 sq ft $660	1,289 sq ft $795

Security deposit $150

ADVERTISEMENT 2

Lexington Apartments

Downtown Atlanta, Georgia

404-439-8672

390 brand-new apartments

Fireplace, washer/dryer hookup, secured entrance, alarm system, walk-in closets. Close to public transportation. Pets under 25 lbs. permitted (limit 1/unit).

One-bedroom unit	Two-bedroom unit
873 sq ft $670	1,219 sq ft $720

Security deposit $300
Pet fee $350, $150 refundable

Activity 3-22   Writing Comparative Sentences to Make Housing Decisions

Write four sentences of contrast about these apartment buildings. Use a variety of comparatives like *farther, closer*, and *more expensive*. In addition, use the grammar of informational writing.

EXAMPLE

Wood Hill Complex is *farther* from downtown Atlanta *than* Lexington Apartments.

Activity 3-23   Self-editing

1. Read your sentences again. Do they say what you want them to say? Do they clearly explain the differences between the two apartment buildings? Make any changes needed to improve the meaning of your writing.

2. Edit your sentences for the grammar of informational writing. Correct any errors that you find. After you have edited for these features, check (✓) the box.

   ☐ complete sentences

   ☐ correct verb tense

   ☐ subject-verb agreement

   ☐ correct use of comparatives

LEARNER'S NOTEBOOK

Apartment Hunting

Review the rental ads and your comparative sentences. Which apartment building would you choose? Why? In your learner's notebook, write a memo to your teacher to explain your decision. Use the memo format and a variety of comparatives. Use the grammar of informational writing and persuasive writing.

Consumers and Transportation

Activity 3-24   Pre-reading Vocabulary

These words are *italicized* in the next reading. Find the italicized words and read the sentences. Then, match each definition to the appropriate word. One answer is provided.

1. ____ dealer
2. ____ model (car)
3. ____ test drive
4. _a_ rate
5. ____ durable
6. ____ option

a. measure the value by comparing to others
b. particular type of vehicle, like Honda or Ford
c. something chosen or offered for choice
d. drive a vehicle to see if you like it
e. long-wearing, sturdy
f. people who sell cars; the place where cars are sold

READING 4   BUYING A CAR (EXCERPT FROM A BUYING GUIDE)

Read the following excerpt about car buying.

BUYING A CAR

Buying a new car is usually the second most expensive purchase many consumers make, after the purchase of their home. Because a car is such an expensive purchase, you want to make the best decision possible.

Before you visit a *dealer*, it helps to know what car *model* and *options* you want and how much you are willing to spend. That way, you are less likely to feel pressured into making a quick or expensive decision and you are more likely to get a better deal.   5

To help you with your decision, first gather information about car features and prices. Check consumer magazines, such as <u>Consumer Reports</u>, at your local library or bookstore.

Consumer magazines discuss things like product cost, safety, and *durability*. You can also check the WWW for useful information. Gathering information will help you *rate* the 10 different cars available.

Then, visit several dealers and compare models and prices. *Test drive* the cars that you like most. Try not to make a decision until you have made several comparisons.

Consider ordering your new car if you do not see the car you want on the *dealer's* lot. This usually takes time, but cars on the lot frequently have *options* you do not want—which 15 add considerably to the cost.

Source: Adapted from *Facts for Consumers: New Car Buying Guide*, Federal Trade Commission, March 1992.

Model name	Dealer price range		
	INVOICE	TARGET	MS
Cadillac DeVille	$35,183	$35,183	$38
Chevrolet Blazer 4-door	22,510	22,510	24,8
Chevrolet Cavalier 4-door	12,927	12,927	13,7
Chevrolet Tahoe LS	28,189	29,189	32,1
Chevrolet Truck K1500 Ext. Cab	20,535	20,885	23,4
Dodge Grand Caravan LE	23,936	23,936	26,4
Dodge Intrepid ES	21,608	21,608	23,
Dodge Ram BR 1500	22,366	22,866	25
Ford Contour GL	14,334	14,334	15,
Ford Escort ZX2 (1998)	14,655	14,655	15,7
Ford Explorer XLT	25,118	25,218	27,8
Ford Ranger XL	18,229	18,229	20,3
Ford Taurus GL	18,644	18,644	20,3
Ford Truck F-150 XL Super Cab	21,426	21,626	24,5
Ford Windstar LX (1998)	25,236	25,236	28.0
Honda Accord LX	20,277	20,277	22,8
Honda Civic LX	14,011	14,511	15,
Jeep Grand Cherokee Laredo	25,448	25,448	28,
Lincoln Town Car	34,222	34,222	38,
Nissan Altima GXE	18,329	18,329	20,4
Nissan Maxima GXE	21,734	21,734	24,2
Saturn SL1 (1998)	13,895	15,905	15,9
Toyota Camry LE	19,689	20,689	22,65
Toyota Corolla DX	15,346	15,346	17,24

Activity 3-25   Checking Your Comprehension and Understanding of Cohesion

Use the previous reading to complete the following tasks.

1. List two places you can get accurate car information, such as safety and cost.

_____

_____

2. In addition to gathering information, list at least two other things you should do when shopping for a car.

_____

_____

3. Find and circle cohesion devices that show how ideas and sentences are related to each other (logical organizers, repetition of key words/phrases, pronouns, different forms of the same word).

Activity 3-26   Shopping for a Used Car

Study the following newspaper ads for used automobiles.

ADVERTISEMENT 1

1994 foreign sports car (manual). Only 40,000 miles; $30,000. Accessories include AM/FM stereo, CD player, speakers, power windows, and AC. 608-752-7053

ADVERTISEMENT 2

Family car at a great price: just $9,000. 1995 automatic, American-made car. 70,000 miles. Has stereo AM/FM, cassette player, and air conditioning. 608-751-3939 before 9 p.m.

Activity 3-27   Writing Contrasting Sentences About Automobiles

Write four sentences of contrast about the automobiles in the newspaper ads. Use a variety of comparatives and logical organizers that show difference. Use the grammar of informational writing.

Activity 3-28   Self-editing

1. Read your sentences again. Do they say what you want them to say? Do you clearly explain the differences between the two automobiles? Make any changes needed to improve the meaning of your writing.

2. Edit for the grammar of informational writing. Correct any errors that you find. After you have edited for these features, check (✓) the box.

    ☐ complete sentences

    ☐ correct verb tense

    ☐ subject-verb agreement

    ☐ comparatives and logical organizers that show difference

    ☐ capitalization and punctuation to end your sentences

LEARNER'S NOTEBOOK

Car Shopping

In your learner's notebook, compare buying a new car with buying a used car. To begin, make a list of the advantages and disadvantages of both. Use a chart like the one that follows. Then, write a paragraph to explain which car is the better choice. In other words, would you purchase a new or a used car? Why?

Buying a New Car		Buying a Used Car	
Advantages	Disadvantages	Advantages	Disadvantages

Personal Letters and E-mail Messages

READING 5   A PERSONAL LETTER

A personal letter is a letter to a friend or family member. Read the following example.

PERSONAL LETTER

July 4, 199___

Dear Peri,

    I recently moved into a new apartment, and I wanted to send you my new address:

    2780 Factor Walk Boulevard   5
    Suwanee, GA 30174

    My new place is a lot bigger than my old apartment. It has a large bedroom, a kitchen, a nice living room, and one bathroom. Also, this apartment is less expensive. I'm saving the extra money to take a vacation to Turkey this summer! On the other hand, this place is 10 farther from school than my former apartment. Can you believe that it sometimes takes 40 minutes to get to class? However, when I drive to school and work, I listen to music and try to enjoy the time alone.

    If you can visit, I'd enjoy seeing you again. My phone number is the same, so call me.   15

Love,

Alper

Guidelines for a Personal Letter

A personal letter has these four parts:

1. *Heading*: Write the date in the top right-hand corner. Sometimes, people put their address above the date.

2. *Greeting*. Use the greeting "Dear _____," (including the comma).

3. *Body*. Begin your message by explaining the purpose of the letter. This is your general statement. The other sentences in your letter provide the specific details, or information, about your general statement. In the body of your letter, use complete sentences and correct spelling, capitalization, and punctuation. Begin a new paragraph for each main idea, and indent your paragraphs.

4. *Closing.* Use a closing like *Love, Warmly, Sincerely,* or *Best regards* followed by a comma. You should sign your name at the bottom.

Activity 3-29   Identifying the Parts of a Personal Letter

Return to the personal letter in Reading 5, and write the four parts of the letter on the lines provided.

Activity 3-30   Writing a Personal Letter About a Purchase

Write a letter to a friend or family member. Tell her or him about a product that you want to purchase (computer, motorcycle, jacket, and so on). Compare and/or contrast that product to another one (e.g., two different motorcycles). Explain your preference to your friend or family member. In other words, why do you prefer one product over the other? Use the grammar of informational writing and persuasive writing. Also, use the format of a personal letter.

Activity 3-31   Self-editing

1. Read your letter again. Does it say what you want it to say? Have you compared the two products? Have you explained your preference? Do you move from general ideas to specific details? Make any changes needed to improve the meaning of your writing.

2. Edit for the grammar of informational writing and persuasive writing. Correct any error(s) that you find. After you have edited for these features, check (✓) the box.

   ☐ complete sentences
   ☐ correct verb tense
   ☐ subject-verb agreement
   ☐ comparatives and logical organizers that show differences and/or similarities
   ☐ structures that express accurate generalizations
   >   opinion structures (*I believe, in my opinion*)
   >   adverbs of frequency (*usually, often*)
   >   modal auxiliaries (*might, may*)
   >   expressions of quantity (*most, some*)
   ☐ conditional sentences
   ☐ cohesion devices (other logical organizers, repetition of key words/phrases, pronouns, different forms of the same word)
   ☐ capitalization and punctuation to end your sentences

READING 6   AN E-MAIL MESSAGE

An electronic mail (e-mail) message is sent through a computer system. An e-mail message to a friend or family member is personal. Messages to co-workers can also be personal, but they are used more often to communicate messages about work situations. For example, an e-mail message might announce a future meeting or a new policy at work. Nowadays, many teachers use e-mail in the classroom. They might send homework assignments or messages to students or ask students to complete activities like journals or discussions through e-mail. In any case, you should realize that your e-mail messages can be read by other people. If your message isn't appropriate for others to read, don't send it that way.

Read this e-mail message between two co-workers.

Date: Mon, 05 May 199- 15:36:32

From: Sharon L. Cavusgil <scavusgil@mmm.edu>

To: Debra Snell <dsnell@mmm.edu>

Subject : Meeting Reminder

—— Message Text ——   5

Debra,

Just a reminder that we'll be meeting this Friday to

discuss the ESL reading clases. there are several

things I want to discuss: 1) textbook selection for

next term, 2) use of reading notes during exams, and   10

3) the final exm schedule.

Is there anything I've missed? Let me know if you can't

makeit. thanks.

Sharon L. Cavusgil

scavusgil@mmm.edu   15

Guidelines for an E-mail Message

An e-mail message has the same parts as a personal letter, but the format is different. An e-mail message uses the format of a memorandum. Here are the four parts of an e-mail message:

1. *Heading.* Your heading includes TO, FROM, DATE, and SUBJECT lines. You should include a short but informative subject line in your message. For example, if you are telling a friend you moved, your subject line could be "New Apartment." If you are telling your co-worker about a meeting, your subject line could be "Meeting Time."

2. *Greeting.* Writers often use the reader's first name as a greeting (followed by a comma). The greeting "Dear" is usually not used.

3. *Body.* Begin your message by explaining its purpose or by writing a brief summary of the topic you are writing about. This is your general statement, and it helps your reader understand the context easily. The other sentences in your message provide the specific details, or information, about your general statement. E-mail messages are similar to conversations, and writers might use phrases and incomplete sentences. In addition, there is often less attention paid to spelling, capitalization, and punctuation than in other written documents. You do not indent your paragraphs in an e-mail message. Instead, you leave a blank line between paragraphs.

4. *Closing.* A formal closing (like *Sincerely* or *Love*) is usually not used, but the writer should type her or his name at the end of the message. The writer often includes her or his e-mail ID, too.

Activity 3-32   Identifying Parts of an E-mail Message

Return to the e-mail message in Reading 6, and write the four parts of an e-mail message on the lines provided.

Activity 3-33   Writing Sentences That Compare Personal Letters and E-mail Messages

Write about two differences and two similarities between a personal letter and an e-mail message. Use the guidelines on pages 90 and 93 to help. Include a variety of comparison structures (logical organizers that show differences/similarities and comparatives). In addition, use the grammar of informational writing and persuasive writing.

Activity 3-34   Self-editing

1. Read your sentences again. Do they say what you want them to say? Do your sentences clearly state the differences and similarities between personal letters and e-mail messages? Make any changes needed to improve the meaning of your writing.

2. Edit for the grammar of informational writing. Correct any errors that you find. After you have edited for these features, check (✓) the box.

   ☐ complete sentences

   ☐ correct verb tense

   ☐ subject-verb agreement

   ☐ comparatives and logical organizers that show differences and similarities

   ☐ structures that express accurate generalizations

   > opinion structures (*I believe, in my opinion*)

   > adverbs of frequency (*usually, often*)

   > modal auxiliaries (*might, may*)

   > expressions of quantity (*most, some*)

   ☐ conditional sentences

   ☐ cohesion devices (other logical organizers, repetition of key words/phrases, pronouns, different forms of the same word)

   ☐ capitalization and punctuation to end your sentences

PUTTING IT ALL TOGETHER

FINAL WRITING ASSIGNMENT: A CAR PURCHASE

Review the newspaper advertisements for automobiles on page 88. Select the car you want to buy, and write a letter (or, if you have computer access, an E-mail message) to a friend. The purpose of your letter is to tell your friend about the two cars and about the one you want. Explain your decision. In other words, why do you choose that car? Be sure to use the correct format of a personal letter (or E-mail message). Use the grammar of informational writing. In addition, because you want your friend to understand and perhaps agree with your choice, use the grammar of persuasive writing.

Editing Your Writing

1. Read your letter again. Have you clearly explained your car decision? Should you provide more details to help your friend understand your decision? Do you move from general ideas to specific details? Make any changes needed to improve the meaning of your writing.

2. Edit for the grammar of informational writing and persuasive writing. Correct any errors that you find. After you have edited for these features, check (✓) the box.

☐ correct use of the personal letter (or E-mail message) format

☐ complete sentences

☐ correct verb tense

☐ subject-verb agreement

☐ structures for accurate generalizations

    opinion structures (*I believe, in my opinion*)

    adverbs of frequency (*usually, often*)

    modal auxiliaries (*might, may*)

    expressions of quantity (*most, some*)

☐ conditional sentences

☐ appropriate comparison structures (words of difference, words of similarity, comparatives)

☐ cohesion devices (other logical organizers, repetition of key words/phrases, pronouns, different forms of the same word)

☐ capitalization and punctuation to end your sentences

Providing Peer Support

Exchange letters with a partner, and read each other's ideas.

1. On your partner's paper, label the parts of a personal letter (see page 90 for an
example) or e-mail message (see page 92).

2. Place an X next to the detail/reason you like best.

3. Explain why you like that detail/reason. In the margin of the paper, write a statement such as:

> I smiled when I read this.
> I chose this same car, too!
> Your reasons for choosing this car are very interesting.

4. Give one suggestion to make the writing better. In the margin of the paper, write a
question such as:

> Where is your heading?
> Could you please give more details here?
> Why do you feel this way? Can you give a reason?

Revising Your Writing

1. With your partner, discuss her or his ideas and suggestions for your writing.

2. Make several changes to improve your writing.

Finalizing Your Writing

1. Make the corrections that you decided on during the self-editing and peer-support
processes. You may want to refer to the check list on page 95 again.

2. Rewrite your letter to submit to your teacher.

L
O
O
K
I
N
G

A
H
E
A
D

Before you register for your academic classes, you need to compare different classes to make the best choice for you. When you compare, you might look at the textbooks, the number of exams, or the professors' reputations.

With your classmates, list other things you might want to compare and consider when you select your classes.

Chapter 4

Defining

Sleep and Dreams

GOALS

WRITING
◆ practice writing definitions

GRAMMAR
◆ practice the grammar of written
definitions and persuasive writing

CONTENT
◆ learn about dream research and
common sleep problems

ACADEMIC FIELD
Psychology

Sample Authentic
College/University
Defining Assignments

In your academic classes, you will use the skills you learn in this chapter to complete assignments and exam questions like these:

Economics

What does *foreign exchange* mean? What are foreign exchange markets?

Marketing

Explain "word-of-mouth publicity." Why is it important?

Hospitality Management

Define service as it relates to the hospitality industry.

Sociology

Stereotypes are made about all cultural groups. Write a paragraph explaining what a stereotype is. Provide an example of a stereotype about your culture.

 CNN video support is available for this chapter.

GETTING READY

Introduction to Defining

In this chapter, you will learn how to use defining in your writing. *Defining* is an important part of your academic learning process. Every day you read, hear, and write about new terms and ideas. These terms and ideas often need to be defined or explained.

When you read academic materials, you can find definitions and explanations of important terms and concepts in the readings. The definitions and explanations help you understand the material. In addition, as you write academic assignments, you often need to define important terms and concepts. Definitions can help you explain your ideas to your readers, usually your teachers. They can also add detail to your writing. Finally, when you take exams, your teachers often ask you to define or explain terms and concepts. Definitions can show your knowledge of the material.

Warm-up Activity

You learned several terms in Chapters 1, 2, and 3, including

- learner's notebooks
- learning styles
- appendix
- collecting
- extended comparison

With a classmate, define and explain each of these terms. Take turns explaining and listening.

Grammar Preview

Academic writing includes many definitions for words that you need to understand and use in your own writing. Written definitions are a part of informational writing. This chapter focuses on the *grammar of written definitions*. This grammar includes *present tense verbs, generic articles and nouns, categorizing nouns,* and *relative clauses.*

In addition, you will practice persuasive writing in this chapter. When you wish to persuade or convince your readers to support your ideas in your writing, use the *grammar of persuasive writing.* This includes using structures to control the strength of a generalization (*opinion structures, adverbs of frequency, modal auxiliaries,* and *expressions of quantity*) and *conditional sentences.*

> **GLR**   See pages 238 and 246 in the GLR for more information on the grammar of written definitions and persuasive writing.

FOCUSING

Sleep and Dreams

> **LEARNER'S NOTEBOOK**
>
> ### Exploring Your Ideas and Questions About Dreams
> What do you feel is most surprising or interesting about dreams? What questions do you have about dreams? Write your ideas and questions in your learner's notebook.

Activity 4-1   Pre-reading Vocabulary

These words are *italicized* in the reading on the next page. Find the italicized words, and read the sentences. Then, match each definition to the appropriate word. One answer is provided.

1. ____ mental   a. of or relating to material things

2. ____ react   b. usual, typical

3. ____ claim   c. of the mind

4. ____ approximately   d. segment of time with a beginning and an end

5. ____ average   e. act in response to

6. ____ recall   f. state or say as the truth

7. ____ period   g. remember

8. _a_ physical   h. about, almost

READING 1   DREAMING (ENCYCLOPEDIA)

Read this excerpt about dreaming from the encyclopedia, *The New Book of Knowledge.*

> ### DREAMING
>
> A dream is one kind of *mental* experience. It often seems as real as something that actu-
> ally happens. In a dream, many dreamers believe that they act and *react*, but during dreams,
> the body is asleep. However, the thinking part of the brain is more active during dreams
> than it sometimes is when the body is awake.
>
> Some people *claim* they never dream, but research shows that all people dream *approx-*   5
> *imately* the same amount. During eight hours of sleep, the *average* person dreams a total of
> about one to two hours. In fact, the *average* person has about five dream *periods*. Some
> people simply cannot remember their dreams. People who wake up quickly may *recall* their
> dreams better than those who awaken slowly. In other words, if you are slow to wake up,
> you may not remember your dreams.   10
>
> Scientists learn about dreams by studying the actual *physical* process of dreaming.
> They do this with a machine called an electroencephalograph. Electroencephalographs are
> machines that record activity in the brain. Researchers study recordings of the brain activ-
> ity (like the one in Diagram A) to learn more about sleep and dreams.

Source: Adapted from "Dreaming," *The New Book of Knowledge*, Vol. 4D
(Grolier, Inc., 1991, 317). Reproduced by permission.

Diagram A

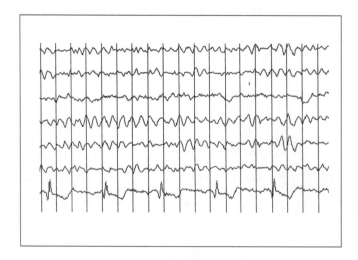

Activity 4-2 Checking Your Comprehension

Are these statements true or false? Write T (true) or F (false) on the line next to each statement.

_____ **1.** A dream happens in the mind.

_____ **2.** Our brain is not very active when we sleep.

_____ **3.** Everyone dreams.

_____ **4.** We all dream approximately one to two hours each night.

_____ **5.** If you wake up quickly, you will probably remember your dreams.

LEARNER'S NOTEBOOK

Dream Experiences

Describe your dream experiences to your teacher. In your learner's notebook, answer these questions. Begin a paragraph for each new idea.

1. How often do you remember your dreams?
2. Do you dream more at certain times than others (for example, after you eat a big meal, when you are stressed, if you watch a scary movie)? Explain.
3. Do you usually enjoy your dreams? Why or why not?

Activity 4-3 Identifying the Grammar of Informational Writing and Persuasive Writing

Reading 1 on page 102 uses the grammar of informational writing and persuasive writing. Study and review this grammar by completing the following tasks in the excerpt:

1. Underline present tense verbs.

2. Highlight logical organizers (*and, for instance*).

3. Circle structures that control the generalizations:

   opinion structures (*he believes that, in my opinion*)

   adverbs of frequency (*often, frequently*)

   modal auxiliaries *may* or *might*

   expressions of quantity (*most, many*)

4. Place a box around conditional sentences.

5. Find and highlight additional cohesion devices (repetition of key words/phrases, pronouns, different forms of the same word).

Activity 4-4   Analyzing the Format of Written Formal Definitions

1. With a partner, return again to Reading 1 on page 102, and discuss the meaning of the word *electroencephalograph*. Do not use a dictionary. Instead, discuss how the definition is given in the reading.

2. In Reading 1, the word *electroencephalograph* is defined using a *formal definition*. Study the format of a formal definition in the examples below.

FORMAL DEFINITIONS			
TERM	**is/are**	**CATEGORY**	**DEFINING DETAILS**
Electroencephalographs	are	machines	that record brain activity.
Encephalo	is	the Greek word	for brain.
A nightmare	is	a long and frightening dream.	(long and frightening)

The formal definition of a noun has four parts:

a. the term to be defined

b. the verb (often the verb *to be*: *is/are*)

c. the category that the term belongs to

d. the details that separate the term from other terms in the same category

3. Dictionaries often use the formal definition format. In each of these dictionary definitions of nouns (*n*), underline the category for each noun. Circle the defining details. The first answer is provided.

a. *dream*   (*n*) <u>thoughts and images</u> (that are experienced during sleep)

b. *sleep*   (*n*) a period of natural rest of the body

c. *science*   (*n*) knowledge that depends on testing facts and stating natural laws

d. *scientists*   (*n*) people who work in a field of science

e. *laboratory*   (*n*) a building or a room for scientific research

Formal Definitions: A Closer Look

Writing formal definitions requires the use of present tense verbs, generic articles and nouns, categorizing nouns, and defining details (often relative clauses). Each of these parts of a formal definition are explained separately in the following pages.

The Grammar of Defining: Present Tense Verbs

The grammar of defining includes complete sentences with subjects and verbs. The verb form in the definition is usually the simple present tense, often the verb *to be*. The examples below show the use of the simple present tense.

EXAMPLES

A dream *is* one kind of mental experience.
Electroencephalographs *are* machines that record activity in the brain.
Parasomnia *includes* sleep problems like sleepwalking, night terrors, and sleep eating.

> GLR   See page 239 in the GLR for more information on present tense verbs.

Activity 4-5   Using the Simple Present Tense in Written Definitions

These sentences are definitions of terms related to sleep and dreams. For each sentence, circle the term being defined. Then, write the correct form of the verb on the line. Notice that the verb in a written definition is often, but not always, the verb *to be*.

EXAMPLE

(*be*) (An electroencephalograph) <u>is</u> an instrument that measures activity in the brain.

1. (*be*) The alpha state _____ the time before sleep when people often have great thoughts and ideas.

2. (*mean*) The term *narcolepsy* _____ a sleep disorder where people fall asleep while talking, eating, or even riding a bike.

3. (*be*) Researchers _____ people who study a subject to learn new facts.

4. (*refer to*) Insomnia _____ a person's inability to sleep well for several nights.

5. (*be*) Sleep apnea _____ a disorder where the sleeper briefly stops breathing.

6. (*be*) A sleepwalker _____ a person who walks around while asleep.

7. (*help*) Sleeping pills _____ a person to sleep.

8. (*be*) Night terrors _____ periods of sleep where the sleeper appears terrified or very frightened.

The Grammar of Defining: Generic Articles and Nouns

When you write a definition of a noun, you are often communicating about groups of people or categories of things, not about particular people or things. For instance, in the following example, the writer is not defining a particular sleep laboratory. Instead, the writer is defining sleep laboratories in general.

EXAMPLE

A sleep laboratory is a place where researchers study sleep and dreams.

When we define groups of people or categories of things, we communicate with generic articles and nouns. All articles (*a, an, the,* or no article) and all types of nouns (singular, plural, and noncount) can be used for generic meaning.

When you write a definition of a noun, you need to decide if the noun is singular, plural, or noncount. This will determine your article usage. Study the following examples and their use of generic articles and nouns.

GENERIC ARTICLES AND NOUNS IN WRITTEN DEFINITIONS

singular noun (a/an article)

EXAMPLE

> *A sleep laboratory* is a place where researchers study sleep and dreams.

plural noun (no article)

EXAMPLE

> *Sleeping pills* help a person to sleep.

noncount noun (no article)

EXAMPLE

> *Insomnia* refers to a person's inability to sleep well for several nights.

> **GLR**   See page 229 in the GLR for more information on generic articles and nouns.

Activity 4-6   Identifying Nouns

1. Before you can determine the use of generic articles in your definitions, you need to know if the nouns are singular, plural, or noncount. Mark each of the following nouns as being singular (S), plural (P), or noncount/uncount (U). Use a dictionary, such as the *Newbury House Dictionary of American English*, to determine noncount nouns. (Note: Most dictionaries use the letter *U* for noncount/uncount nouns.) The first answer is provided.

   a. __U__ data   i. ____ equipment

   b. ____ computer   j. ____ professors

   c. ____ dreams   k. ____ education

   d. ____ information   l. ____ laboratory

   e. ____ instrument   m. ____ homework

   f. ____ assignment   n. ____ students

   g. ____ sleep   o. ____ book

   h. ____ pencil   p. ____ answer

2. For each of the singular nouns in the previous section, insert the article *a* or *an*.

   EXAMPLE   *a* computer   *an* instrument

| **Activity 4-7   Building Definitions with Generic Articles and Nouns** |

In these definitions of nouns, underline all noun phrases. Write S (singular), P (plural), or U (noncount/uncount) above each noun phrase. Then, if necessary, insert the correct generic article before the noun phrases. In addition, for each sentence, capitalize the first word, and put a period at the end.

EXAMPLE

A laboratory is a building or a room for scientific research.

1. sleeping   pill   is   pill   that   contains   medicine   to   help   people   sleep

2. dream   is   fantasy   that   person   experiences   while   asleep

3. nightmares   are   frightening   dreams   or   terrible   experiences

4. electroencephalograph   machine   helps   scientists perform   dream research

5. during   lucid dreams,   sleepers   are   aware   that   they   are   dreaming

The Grammar of Defining: Categorizing Nouns

When you write a formal definition of a noun, you put the noun into a category. The noun (term) that you are defining is *detailed and exact.* The categorizing noun is *general and broad.*

EXAMPLES

TERM	**is/are**	**CATEGORY**	**DEFINING DETAILS**
detailed and exact A sleepwalker	is	general and broad a person	who walks around while asleep.
detailed and exact Sleep apnea	is	general and broad a disorder	where the sleeper briefly stops breathing.

GLR   See page 240 in the GLR for more information on categorizing nouns.

| **Activity 4-8   Identifying the Grammar of Written Definitions** |

1. Read the following formal definitions found in textbooks from other courses.

   a. A constitution is a set of basic principles and laws of a group. (*U.S. history*)

   b. Comparative advertising refers to a strategy where a message compares two or more brands or products. (*consumer behavior*)

c. Delinquents are young people who disobey authority, violate laws, or behave in ways that endanger the safety of the community. (*sociology*)

d. Puberty is the developmental period in young people during which many physical changes occur. (*child development*)

e. Emotions are feelings that include joy, resentment, and anger. (*psychology*)

2. With a partner, complete the following tasks for each of the previous definitions. See the example below.

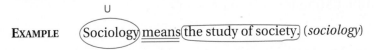

EXAMPLE   (Sociology) means (the study of society.) (*sociology*)

a. Circle the term being defined.

b. Label the term as singular (S), plural (P), or noncount/uncount (U). (A dictionary can help you determine noncount nouns.) Then, study the generic article being used with that term.

c. Underline the simple present tense verb twice.

d. Draw a box around the general category.

Activity 4-9   Writing Sentences with General Categories

With a small group of classmates, determine a general category that each term belongs to. Then, use the grammar of written definitions to write complete sentences with the general categories. There may be more than one correct answer.

EXAMPLE   ear   An ear is a body part.

a. necklace _____

b. taxi drivers _____

c. New York City _____

d. toothache _____

e. diamonds _____

f. Valentine's Day _____

g. potatoes _____

h. soccer _____

i. police officer _____

j. winter _____

Activity 4-10   Self-editing

Edit your sentences for the grammar of written definitions. Correct any errors that you find. After you have edited for these features, check (✓) the box.

- ☐ the term being defined
- ☐ simple present tense verbs (with subject-verb agreement)
- ☐ appropriate generic articles with nouns
- ☐ the general category that the term belongs to
- ☐ capitalization and punctuation to end your sentences

The Grammar of Defining: Relative Clauses

Adjectives are words that add more information or details about nouns. For example, in the sentence "He had a terrible nightmare," *terrible* is the adjective. It adds more information to the noun, *nightmare*. Similarly, relative clauses (also called adjective clauses) give more information about nouns: "He had a nightmare that was terrible."

EXAMPLES

adjective
The scientists made an *interesting* discovery.

relative/adjective clause
The scientists made a discovery *that was interesting.*

Relative clauses often provide the defining details for a formal definition of a noun. These details separate the term you are defining from other terms in the same category. The following chart illustrates the use of relative clauses in formal definitions of nouns.

	Term	**Verb**	**Category**	**Defining details = Relative clause**			
				relative pronoun	**subject**	**verb**	**specific details**
1.	A ring	is	a piece of jewelry	that	a person	wears	on her finger.
2.	Daydreams	are	thoughts	which		are	pleasant but not real.
3.	Composers	are	people	who		write	music.
4.	A camp	is	a place	where	people	sleep	outdoors in tents.
5.	Bedtime	is	a time	when	people	go	to sleep.

The relative pronoun *who* and sometimes the relative pronouns *that* and *which* are the subject of your relative clause (defining details).

GLR   See page 217 in the GLR for more information on relative clauses.

Activity 4-11   Using Relative Clauses in Written Definitions

1. Complete each sentence below with an appropriate relative pronoun from the following list. You may use each pronoun more than once, and there may be more than one correct answer.

    that   which   who   where   when

    EXAMPLE   Encephalo is a Greek word _____that/which_____ **means brain.**

    a. A researcher is a person _____ **studies a subject to learn new facts**.

    b. A sleep lab is a place _____ **sleep habits are tested.**

    c. The 1940s and 1950s was a time _____ **sleep research became important.**

    d. If you are a patient at a sleep lab, you get ready for bed in a room _____ **looks like a hotel room.**

    e. A person _____ **is 75 years old** has had approximately five years of dreams.

2. The relative clause in each sentence, which includes the relative pronoun, is **bold-faced**. Place brackets [ ] around the relative clause, and draw an arrow to the term it is describing.

    EXAMPLE   Encephalo is a Greek word [_____that/which_____ **means brain.**]

Activity 4-12   Writing Formal Definitions

Return to Activity 4-9, page 109, on writing categories for terms. Work in small groups to add defining details to your sentences. Your defining details should separate the term from other terms in the same category. Often, your defining details will be in the form of a relative clause. Study these examples of defining details before you write your sentences.

NOT GOOD: An ear is a body part *that is on the head.*

This defining detail is too general. It does not clearly define *an ear* because *eyes, nose,* and *mouth* are also body parts on the head.

GOOD: An ear is a body part *that is used for hearing.*

This defining detail is better. It is more specific. The only answer is *ear.*

Activity 4-13   Self-editing

Edit your sentences for the grammar of written definitions. Correct any errors that you find. After you have edited for these features, check (✓) the box.

☐ the term being defined

☐ simple present tense verbs (with subject-verb agreement)

☐ the general category that the term belongs to

☐ defining details that separate the term from other terms

☐ appropriate generic articles with nouns

☐ capitalization and punctuation to end your sentences

Other Definition Structures

In addition to the formal definition format, writers sometimes use other structures for definitions. These structures, such as dashes or parentheses, can define important terms and add detail.

GLR   See page 242 of the GLR for more information about definition structures.

READING 2   STAGES OF SLEEP (TEXTBOOK)

Read the following excerpt about sleep and dream research.

STAGES OF SLEEP

In 1952, Dr. Nathaniel Kleitman, an important sleep researcher at the University of Chicago, was curious about the way eyes moved during sleep. He assigned Eugene Aserinsky, a young graduate student, to study this. Aserinsky noticed that during sleep the eyes sometimes **darted**, or moved rapidly, just as if the person were awake.

At Kleitman's sleep lab, they used **an EEG machine** (a machine that records brain activ-   5
ity). The researchers began to see a connection between eye movements and sleep stages. In fact, the eyes only darted when people dreamed. According to Dr. William Dement, a famous

expert on sleep at Stanford University in California, this was *the* **breakthrough**—the discovery that changed sleep research.

Researchers realized that there was a difference between dreaming and nondreaming 10 sleep. Dement invented terms for these different stages: Rapid Eye Movement (REM) and Non-Rapid Eye Movement (NREM). **REM sleep** is the type of sleep that occurs only when people dream. During REM, the dreamer's eyeballs move quickly. **NREM sleep** means a period of quiet sleep when the eyes move slowly and the body is relaxed.

Source: Adapted from Rae Lindsay, *Sleep and Dreams* (Franklin Watts, Inc., New York, 1978, 17 and 20).

Activity 4-14   Checking Your Comprehension and Understanding of Cohesion

Use the previous reading to complete the following questions and tasks.

1. Who were Dr. Nathaniel Kleitman and Eugene Aserinsky?

_____

_____

2. What was Eugene Aserinsky studying?

_____

_____

3. During sleep, when do our eyes move rapidly?

_____

_____

4. What was the breakthrough in sleep research?

_____

_____

5. What is the difference between REM sleep and NREM sleep?

_____

_____

6. Find and underline examples of cohesion devices that show the relationship of ideas and sentences (logical organizers, repetition of key words/phrases, pronouns, different forms of the same word). Discuss those cohesion devices with your teacher and classmates.

Activity 4-15   Small Group Activity

Reading 2, page 112, contains several **boldfaced** words. Definitions for these words are also in the reading. With a small group of classmates, discuss how the writer provides definitions of these words. In other words, discuss the different definition formats in this excerpt. After your discussion, complete the following tasks:

1. circle the terms being defined

2. underline the definitions

3. highlight the definition structures (dashes, parentheses, commas, and so on)

> GLR   See page 242 in the GLR for more information about definition structures.

Activity 4-16   Identifying Definition Structures

In addition to textbooks on sleep and dreams, definition structures can be found in other books. Read the following excerpts from books about other subjects. Find the definition structures, and for each definition,

1. circle the word being defined

2. underline the definition

3. highlight the definition structure (dashes, parentheses, commas, and so on)

Source 1: A U.S. history text

Many immigrants came seeking freedom to practice their religion. They were fleeing religious persecution, or cruel treatment, in their native lands.

Philip L. Groisser and Sol Levine, U.S.A.: The Unfolding Story of America
(Amsco School Publications, Inc., 1995, 302).

Source 2: An anthropology text

In modern North America, divorce is fairly easy and common. And polygamy, marriage to more than one person, is against the law. As divorce grows more common, North Americans practice serial monogamy (people have more than one husband or wife but never legally at the same time).

Adapted from Conrad Phillip Kottak, Anthropology: The Exploration of Human Diversity
(McGraw-Hill, Inc., 1994, 358). Reproduced with permission of the McGraw-Hill Companies.

Source 3: A hospitality management text

Dependability is a trait that is valued highly by restaurant owners. It is a sign of maturity. Basically, it means that the employees will be responsible for their own actions.

> Anthony J. Strainese, *Dining Room & Banquet Management* (Delmar Publishers, Albany, NY: 1990, 164–165). Reproduced by permission.

Source 4: A cookbook

If metal is allowed to touch the walls of the microwave oven, arcing—a spark of electricity—may occur. Although arcing won't hurt you, it can damage the oven.

> *Micro Menus Cookbook* (Whirlpool Properties, Inc., copyright Meredith Corporation).

Source 5: A history text

In 1859, Edwin Drake drilled America's first oil well in Pennsylvania. At first, oil was made into kerosene, a fuel burned in lamps. Later, industries used refined oil to lubricate (grease) machines. Not until the 20th century would oil become an important source of power in industries.

> Philip L. Groisser and Sol Levine, *U.S.A.: The Unfolding Story of America* (Amsco School Publications, Inc., 1995, 281).

Activity 4-17   Writing Definition Structures

Some writers use only one or two of the same definition structures in their writing. However, using different definition structures can add variety to your writing. Review the excerpts in the previous activity. Copy four original sentences that contain definitions. Then, practice various definition structures by rewriting those sentences. Use a different definition structure for each one.

EXAMPLE

Original: They were fleeing religious persecution, **or cruel treatment,** in their native lands.

Rewrite: They were fleeing religious persecution **(cruel treatment)** in their native lands.

Activity 4-18   Finding Definition Structures in Academic Textbooks

Look through some of your own textbooks or some your teacher brings to class. Find two or three sentences using definition structures. Share those sentences with your classmates, and identify the definition structures.

Defining on Tests or Exams

In your academic classes, your teachers will ask about your knowledge of the classroom material. You may need to write a paper, give an oral presentation, or take an exam. In all of these situations, you will need to define important terms or concepts from your studies.

A common exam question is a short answer question that asks you to *explain* a concept or *define* a concept and give an *example*. Short answer questions may also ask you to *compare* two ideas or concepts. Short answer questions do not require a lot of detail. The answers are usually one to four complete sentences in length.

READING 3   SLEEP AND DREAMS TEST (SHORT ANSWER TEST)

Read the following test questions. They require short answer responses with definitions.

Name _____

SLEEP AND DREAMS TEST

Directions: Write an appropriate short answer response for each question.

1. Define a dream, and explain how often people usually dream each night.

2. What is an electroencephalograph machine? Why is it important?

3. What does REM sleep mean, and when does it occur?

4. Explain the difference between REM sleep and NREM sleep.

Activity 4-19   Analyzing Short Answer Questions and Responses

1. For each question in the previous test,

   a. underline the question word(s) (*define, explain, what, why,* and so on)

   b. circle the word(s) to be defined.

   EXAMPLE

   Define a (dream,) and *explain* how often people usually dream each night.

2. Study the following short answers. These answers are good because (1) they contain complete sentences, (2) they do not give a lot of detail, and (3) they are short. In addition, (4) the writer used the language of defining.

   EXAMPLES

   Define a dream, and explain how often people usually dream each night.
   A dream is a mental experience that seems very real. People usually dream one to two hours for every eight hours of sleep.

   or

   People usually have dreams—mental experiences that seem real—for about one to two hours every night.

Activity 4-20   Writing Short Answer Responses

Return to Reading 3, page 116, and answer each question with an appropriate short answer. Your answers should be one to four sentences in length, and you should use a variety of definition structures (formal definitions, dashes, commas, and so on).

Activity 4-21   Self-editing

1. Read your short answers again. Is the information in your short answers correct? Are your answers short but complete? Make any changes needed to improve the meaning of your writing.

2. Edit your short answers for the grammar of written definitions. Correct any errors that you find. After you have edited for these features, check (✓) the box.

   ☐ complete sentences

   ☐ the formal definition format or other definition structures

   ☐ simple present tense verbs (with subject-verb agreement)

☐ the general category that the term belongs to (for formal definition formats)

☐ defining details (for formal definition formats)

☐ appropriate generic articles with nouns

☐ appropriate cohesion devices

☐ capitalization and punctuation to end your sentences

Extended Definitions

READING 4   NIGHTMARES (ENCYCLOPEDIA AND STUDENT ESSAY)

Sometimes definitions are longer than a single sentence. Some definitions may even be more than one paragraph. These longer definitions are called extended definitions. Extended definitions may contain examples, comparisons, or other additional details.

1. Read this extended definition about nightmares. This definition is from the encyclopedia, *The New Book of Knowledge.*

NIGHTMARES

Nightmares are experienced by most people. They are long, frightening dreams that seem very lifelike. For example, the dreamer may dream of wild animals, dangerous people, or running from danger. Sometimes normal, everyday objects become frightening parts of our nightmares. For instance, in your dream, when you sit in a favorite chair, it may try to eat you.

Nightmares are usually more frequent when a person is anxious. They may also occur   5 during traumatic events such as war. Nightmares are more common during childhood. At least half of all children experience nightmares. However, as children grow older, their nightmares usually decrease.

Source: Adapted from "Dreaming," *The New Book of Knowledge*, Vol. 4D (Grolier, Inc., 1991, 318).
Reproduced by permission.

2. Read this extended definition about nightmares by a student.

> **NIGHTMARES**
>
> A nightmare is a dream that is scary and often very real. A nightmare includes scary people or dangerous situations. I often have nightmares about monsters or falling from a building. These dreams scare me, and I frequently wake up at night. In my opinion, a horror movie or a spicy meal might cause nightmares. If I watch a scary movie, I usually have a bad dream at night. Therefore, I try not to watch scary movies or eat late at night anymore.   5
>
> Juan Pinzon
Colombia

The Parts of Extended Definitions

You can define words like *ear* or *police officer* in one or two sentences, but in some situations, extended (longer) definitions are required. For instance, it would be very difficult to give an effective short definition of words like *success* or *love*. When you write an extended definition, you can make your definition clear and interesting to read by including some or all of the following:

a formal definition format or other definition structures
examples
comparisons
personal experience
opinions

Activity 4-22   Identifying the Parts of Extended Definitions

With your teacher and classmates, identify and label the parts of an extended definition in the excerpts in Reading 4.

Activity 4-23   Collecting Ideas About Sleep Problems

Collect ideas about sleep problems by reading the following three paragraphs from brochures about sleep issues. Use complete sentences to answer the questions that follow each paragraph.

SNORING

When people snore, they breathe during sleep with harsh, sometimes loud sounds. An estimated 10% to 30% of adults snore. Snoring is usually not serious. However, loud snoring may mean that something is seriously wrong. For example, snoring indicates that the airway is not fully open. The noise of snoring comes from forcing air through the throat. For about five in 100 people—usually overweight, middle-aged men—very loud snoring is the first sign of a possible life-threatening problem: sleep apnea. Sleep apnea is a disorder where the sleeper briefly stops breathing. People with sleep apnea don't breathe properly during sleep, so they don't get enough oxygen and have poor-quality sleep. This may cause health problems.

Source: Adapted from *Sleep Apnea and Snoring*, American Sleep Disorders Association, 1992, 1–2. Reproduced by permission.

1. How many adults snore?

   _____

2. Who usually snores?

   _____

3. What is one possible cause of snoring?

   _____

INSOMNIA

Trouble falling asleep or staying asleep is called insomnia. One in three American adults has insomnia. Insomnia usually affects people for a night or two, but sometimes it affects them for weeks, months, or even years. One type of insomnia is transient insomnia. Transient insomnia refers to a person's inability to sleep well for several nights. This is usually caused by excitement or stress. For instance, if an adult has an important meeting or a disagreement with a spouse, he or she may sleep poorly. Most people sleep worse when they are away from home. Relief from the stressful situation will usually return sleep to normal.

Source: Adapted from *Insomnia*, American Sleep Disorders Association, 1992, 1–2. Reproduced by permission.

1. What is insomnia?

   _____

2. What percent of Americans suffer from insomnia?

   _____

3. List possible causes of transient insomnia.

   _____

4. What is one remedy for insomnia?

_____

SLEEPWALKING

A sleepwalker is a person who walks around while asleep. Sleepwalking is often seen in older children. Many sleepwalkers simply get up out of bed and walk around the room. Other sleepwalkers may go to another part of the house or even outside to the yard or garage. Sleepwalkers may return to bed, or they may awaken in the morning in a different part of the house. Sleepwalkers might talk in their sleep, too. Usually, no treatment is necessary. In children, the amount of sleepwalking often decreases with age.

Source: Adapted from *Parasomnias: Things That Go Bump in the Night*, American Sleep Disorders Association, 1992, 2–3. Reproduced by permission.

1. Who commonly sleepwalks?

_____

2. List things that a person might do when sleepwalking.

_____

_____

Activity 4-24   Identifying the Grammar in Extended Definitions

The three paragraphs about sleep problems use the grammar of informational writing, persuasive writing, and written definitions. Study and review this grammar by completing the following tasks in each paragraph.

1. Underline present tense verbs.

2. Circle logical organizers (*and, for instance*).

3. Place parentheses around structures that control the strength of generalizations:

opinion structures (*in my opinion, I believe*)

adverbs of frequency (*usually, often*)

modal auxiliaries *(may, might)*

expressions of quantity (*some, most*)

4. Underline conditional sentences.

5. Highlight formal definition formats or other definition structures.

LEARNER'S NOTEBOOK

Exploring Ideas

To explore your ideas about sleep problems, complete or answer the following in your learner's notebook. Begin a paragraph for each new idea.

1. Write the definitions of *nightmare, snoring, insomnia,* and *sleepwalking.*
2. Which of these sleep problems have you or someone you know experienced?
3. What opinions or feelings do you have about these terms?
4. Which of the previous extended definitions gives the clearest definition(s)? Why?

Activity 4-25   Small Group Discussion

With a small group of classmates, continue to collect ideas about sleep problems by discussing your responses from your learner's notebook. Add some of your classmates' ideas to your own learner's notebook.

PUTTING IT ALL TOGETHER

FINAL WRITING ASSIGNMENT: SLEEP PROBLEMS

You have collected ideas about *nightmares, snoring, insomnia,* and *sleepwalking* by reading, by exploring your ideas in your learner's notebook, and by discussing ideas with your classmates. Now, write your own extended definition about one of those sleep problems.

1. Begin by writing a formal definition of your chosen term.

2. Then, write four to six sentences about that term. Use examples, comparisons, personal experience, and/or opinions.

3. Use logical organizers and other cohesion devices (repetition of key words/phrases, pronouns, different forms of the same word) to connect your ideas and sentences.

Editing Your Writing

1. Read your extended definition again. Do you clearly explain or describe your chosen sleep problem? Should you provide more details (examples, comparisons, personal experience, and/or opinions) to help your audience understand this sleep problem? Do you move from general ideas to specific details? Make any changes needed to improve the meaning of your writing.

2. Edit for the grammar of informational writing, persuasive writing, and written definitions. Correct any errors that you find. After you have edited for these features, check (✓) the box.

❑ complete sentences

❑ correct verb tense (with subject-verb agreement)

❑ appropriate logical organizers and correct punctuation

❑ structures for accurate generalizations

    opinion structures

    adverbs of frequency

    modal auxiliaries

    expressions of quantity

❑ conditional sentences

❑ a complete formal definition

❑ possibly other definition structures (dashes, parentheses, and so on)

❑ cohesion devices (logical organizers, repetition of key words/phrases, pronouns, different forms of the same word)

Providing Peer Support

Exchange papers with a partner, and read each other's ideas.

1. On your partner's paper, label the parts of an extended definition:

    a complete formal definition
    possibly other definition structures (dashes, parentheses, and so on)
    examples
    comparisons
    personal experiences
    opinions

2. Tell your partner what you like best about the writing. In the margin of the paper, write a statement such as:

    I had an experience just like this.   I learned from your experiences.

    Your personal experiences are exciting.   I like the vocabulary you used.

    I like the way you combined your sentences.

3. Give one suggestion to improve your partner's writing. In the margin of the paper, write a statement such as:

    I don't understand this example.

    You should add more defining details to your writing.

    I would add an opinion structure to this sentence to make it more accurate.

4. Ask one question about information you need or would like to know about the term. In the margin of the paper, write a question such as:

    Have you experienced this problem?

    How might someone solve this problem?

    Do you think this problem is serious?

Revising Your Writing

1. With a partner, discuss her or his ideas and suggestions for your writing.

2. Make several changes to improve your writing.

Finalizing Your Writing

1. Make the corrections that you decided on during the self-editing and peer-support processes. You may want to refer to the check list on page 123 again.

2. Rewrite your extended definition to submit to your teacher.

L
O
O
K
I
N
G

A
H
E
A
D

In your academic courses, you will often need to provide definitions of important terms and concepts. This will show your understanding of the materials. In order to write effective answers and assignments, you must first understand the questions and the assignments.

Return to page 99, and review the *Sample Authentic College/University Defining Assignments*. For each assignment:

1. underline the question word(s) (*define, explain, what, why,* and so on)

2. circle the word(s) that needs to be defined

Chapter 5

*D*eveloping

Blue Jeans and Levi Strauss

GOALS

WRITING
◆ practice using description, examples, and personal experience to develop your writing

GRAMMAR
◆ practice the grammar of past time narrative writing

CONTENT
◆ learn about the history of blue jeans and Levi Strauss, the creator of blue jeans

ACADEMIC FIELD

History

Sample Authentic College/University Developing Assignments

In your academic classes, you will use the skills you learn in this chapter to complete assignments and exam questions like these:

Sociology

In what ways does crime affect the public? Give examples from the broadcast news or newspaper.

Economics

What rights do you have as a worker, investor, consumer, and taxpayer? Provide an example of each one.

Anthropology

Describe the special courtship and marriage customs in your family. What do your family members value in a potential spouse? Be specific.

Consumer Behavior

People play many different roles in their lives, and their consumption behaviors may differ depending on the role they are playing at the time. Do you agree or disagree with this statement? Give examples from your personal life to support your opinion.

CNN video support is available for this chapter.

Turner Le@rning
A Time Warner Company

GETTING READY

Introduction to Developing

In academic classes, you are often expected to develop your writing. *Developing* means adding specific details to explain your general ideas. To develop your writing, you first need to generate ideas through collecting (reading, listing, outlining, writing in your learner's notebook, and so on). Then, you support those ideas with description, examples, personal experience, and/or comparisons. Developing can make your writing more interesting and enjoyable to read.

LEARNER'S NOTEBOOK

Warm-up Writing

How many students in your classroom are wearing blue jeans? Is your teacher wearing blue jeans? In your learner's notebook, write whether you think the popularity of jeans is increasing, decreasing, or staying the same. Develop your opinion with comparisons, specific examples, and/or personal experiences.

Grammar Preview

Past time narrative is often used in writing where the author tells a story about the past. It can also be used to give past time examples and experiences to support ideas in your writing. This chapter focuses on the following aspects of *past time narrative writing: chronological organizers, past tense verbs, proper nouns,* and *personal pronouns.*

You will also study *grammar common to all types of academic writing,* including the use of *non-restrictive relative clauses* and *appositives* to give information about people you mention in your writing.

> **GLR** See pages 210–220 and 221–225 in the GLR for more information on the grammar common to all types of academic writing and the grammar of past time narrative.

FOCUSING

The History of Jeans

Activity 5-1   Pre-reading Vocabulary

The following words are *italicized* in the next reading. Find the italicized words, and read the sentences. Then, match each definition to the appropriate word. One answer is provided.

1. ____ miner	a. cloth
2. ____ textile mill	b. king or queen and family
3. _a_ fabric	c. power to make something attractive or interesting
4. ____ equator	d. length of three feet or 36 inches (0.91 meter)
5. ____ yard	e. person who removes minerals from under the earth's surface
6. ____ royalty	f. person who makes or fixes an item on a machine, especially parts of the object
7. ____ to appeal	
8. ____ machinist	g. imaginary line around the earth halfway between the North and South Poles
	h. factory where cloth is made

READING 1   BLUE JEANS: YESTERDAY AND TODAY (ECONOMICS TEXTBOOK)

Past time narrative writing usually has two parts: (1) the background information that leads up to a story and (2) the actual story about the past. Read the following excerpt, which contains background information about the history of blue jeans.

BLUE JEANS: YESTERDAY AND TODAY

[1]The world's most popular pants today are blue jeans. [2]Once, jeans were the pants of working people—*miners*, *machinists*, and construction workers. [3]Today, people wear jeans at home, at movies, at parties, and even at formal occasions. [4]Lawyers, doctors, housewives, and students all wear them. [5]Hollywood stars appear in them on opening nights of movies. [6]You may even find *royalty* wearing them.

[7]About 20 years ago, United States' *textile mills* produced 400 million square *yards* of denim, the *fabric* from which jeans are made. [8]That was enough denim to circle the earth's

equator nine times with a strip one yard wide! [9]However, that was still not enough denim to meet the demands of our jeans-hungry world. [10]In fact, the shortage of denim production in 1973 was about 100 million square yards.

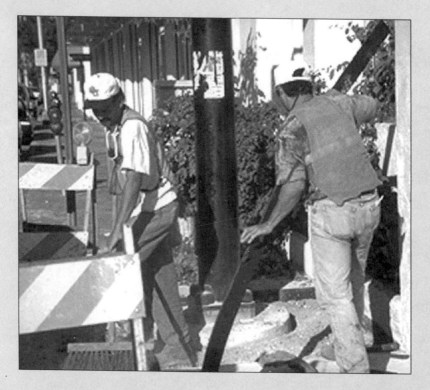

[11]In the 1940s and early 1950s, blue jeans were children's play clothes. [12]Teenagers had a difficult time getting the approval of parents and school administrators to wear them at school. [13]Young people in the early 1960s, the civil rights marchers, and teenagers at rock concerts all made blue jeans their special dress. [14]One author said that jeans express freedom. [15]Maybe this is their *appeal* even today.

[16]Many young people did not like the idea of wearing the same things as their parents, but they also did not want to give up their favorite clothes. [17]So they developed their own style. [18]For example, nowadays, many young people wear jeans with holes. [19]In fact, for some people, the older the jeans, the more desirable they are.

[20]The company that created blue jeans more than 100 years ago is the Levi Strauss Company. [21]Today, this San Francisco–based company is the largest in the jeans industry. [22]The company sells about 24 percent of all jeans that are marketed.

Source: Adapted from Elmer U. Clawson, *Our Economy: How it Works,* 3rd Ed. (Addison-Wesley Longman Publishing Company, 1988, 52–57). Reproduced by permission.

The Grammar of Past Time Narrative: Chronological Organizers

Chronological organizers help the reader understand when events happened. In other words, they build cohesion in the writing. Chronological organizers like *today* or *now* tell the reader the event is in the present. Chronological organizers like *yesterday, last month,* or *in 1980* tell the reader the event happened in the past. Chronological organizers are very common in past time narrative writing.

> **GLR** See page 223 in the GLR for more information on chronological organizers.

Activity 5-2 Identifying Chronological Organizers

1. Return to Reading 1 on page 129. Identify and highlight the chronological organizers in sentences 1, 2, 3, 7, 10, 11, 13, 15, 18, 20, and 21.

2. Make a list of each chronological organizer and the main verb in each sentence. An example is provided.

Sentence No.	Chronological Organizers	Verbs
1	today	are
2		
3		
7		
10		
11		
13		
15		
18		
20		
21		

3. Some of the chronological organizers in Reading 1 on page 129 refer the reader to the present and others refer the reader to the past. Write each chronological organizer

from the reading in the appropriate column below. An example is provided for each column.

CHRONOLOGICAL ORGANIZERS

Present	Past
today	once

The Grammar of Past Time Narrative: Past Tense Verbs

The basic story in a narrative is told using simple past tense. Other verbs, such as the past progressive and the past perfect, are used to give additional information. The following chart explains the purposes and gives examples of these verb tenses.

PAST TENSE VERBS

Verb Purposes	Examples
Simple Past to tell a story	regular: Sometimes, a tired old horse *pulled* a cart. irregular: Levi's story *began* in a small village in Bavaria.
Past Progressive to provide background information to the story	They joined many other immigrants who *were struggling* to fulfill their dreams in America.
Past Perfect to provide background information to the story	The German Jews *had lived* in the Bavarian village of Buttenheim for at least several generations.

Understanding the task

GLR See page 221 of the GLR for more information on past tense verbs.

For a list of irregular verbs, see Appendix D.

Activity 5-3 Identifying Simple Past Tense Verbs

1. Return to Reading 1. Use the chronological organizers to help you see when the writer moves from present tense verbs to past tense verbs.

2. Circle the simple past tense verbs. Then, decide if each verb is regular or irregular, and write the verb in the following chart.

3. Finally, write the base form of each verb. For words you do not know, use your dictionary or Appendix D. Examples are provided.

SIMPLE PAST TENSE VERBS: REGULAR AND IRREGULAR

Regular Verbs	Base Form	Irregular Verbs	Base Form
produced	produce	were	be

LEARNER'S NOTEBOOK

Clothing Styles

Blue jeans have been a favorite clothing item for many years, but it wasn't until the 1960s that students were permitted to wear blue jeans to most public schools in the United States. Describe what you wore to school as a child or young teenager. How has your clothing style changed over the years? Include comparisons, examples, and personal experiences in your learner's notebook.

Developing Your Writing

When you write, you should *tell* the reader your main idea. This is your general statement. You should then *show* your reader what you mean by providing specific details about your general statement. You can do this by providing description, personal experience, examples, and/or comparisons. This is called *developing* your writing.

In this paragraph from Reading 1, the writer moved from a general statement (telling) to specific details (showing) by providing examples.

general statement   specific details

The world's most popular pants today are blue jeans. Once, jeans were the pants of working people—miners, machinists, and construction workers. Today, people wear jeans at home, at movies, at parties, and even at formal occasions. Lawyers, doctors, housewives, and students all wear them. Hollywood stars appear in them on opening nights of movies. You may even find royalty wearing them.

In this chapter, we discuss developing your writing through description, personal experience, and examples. (For a review of comparisons, see Chapter 3.) You can combine several of these development strategies when you write.

Developing Your Writing

Description   Personal Experience   Examples   Comparisons

Immigrating to the U.S.

Activity 5-4   Pre-reading Vocabulary

The following words are *italicized* in the next reading. Find the italicized words, and read the sentences. Then, match each definition to the appropriate word. One answer is provided.

1. _____ belongings   a. rising and falling sounds in song or speech

2. _____ remarkable   b. dull in color, uninteresting, depressing

3. _____ generation   c. rounded stone once used to pave streets

4. _____ synagogue   d. image of a person, animal, or thing from stone or metal

5. _____ drab   e. outstanding, noticeable, unusual

6. _____ odds and ends   f. place of religious worship for Jewish people

7. _____ cart   g. many small items without much value

8. _____ struggle   h. personal property like clothes, books, etc.

9. _____ cobblestone   i. small, light vehicle used to carry goods or people

10. _____ statue   j. difficult effort or fight

11. _a_ lilt   k. different age levels in a family, such as grandparents, parents, and children

READING 2   PASSPORT TO A NEW LIFE (BOOK)

As you read earlier in this chapter, past time narrative writing usually has two parts: (1) the background information that leads up to a story and (2) the actual story about the past. Reading 1 provided the background information about blue jeans. The following excerpt tells the actual story of blue jeans. Like many stories, it also includes background information and description to help you understand the story. Read this excerpt about Levi Strauss, the creator of blue jeans.

PASSPORT TO A NEW LIFE

[1]When you think of "blue jeans," the name Levi probably comes to mind. [2]Actually, Levi was the name of a *remarkable* man—Levi Strauss.

[3]Levi's story began in a small village in Bavaria, a land in the southern part of Germany. [4]Levi was born on February 26, 1829. [5]He was the youngest of six children. [6]Levi's family was part of a small community of German Jews who had lived in the Bavarian village of Buttenheim for many *generations*. [7]His father, Hirsch Strauss, made a living selling dry goods—bolts of cloth, clothing, and notions like needles, pins, thread, and scissors.

[8]Bavaria was a beautiful land. [9]Its high mountains were snow-covered in winter and green in summer. [10]Pretty villages with rows of wooden houses stood along the river banks. [11]A traditional church, a *statue*, and fountains stood in the central square of each town. [12]A *synagogue* was often located behind the central square. [13]Jews had lived on this land since Roman times.

[14]As Levi grew older, the Buttenheim Jewish community became smaller. [15]In addition, anti-Semitism (hatred of Jews because of their religion or race) increased. [16]Many people saw that there was no future in Buttenheim—perhaps none in all of Bavaria—for a young Jew to make a living. [17]The Strausses sold whatever they could, including their house, and packed their *belongings*. [18]They were ready to sail to America.

[19]When Levi, a young man of eighteen, first saw New York in 1847, the city was full of activity. [20]Levi heard unfamiliar words of many different languages. [21]English, Portuguese, and Spanish mixed with Swedish, German, and French. [22]Dark-haired Italians with blue work pants hurried next to light-skinned Scandinavian sailors. [23]Irish women in long, *drab* dresses spoke English with a special *lilt*. [24]They pushed against fashionably dressed "uptown ladies" who had come to meet passengers from a ship.

[25]Levi also saw neat rows of narrow houses that were built of wood or brick along *cobblestoned* streets. [26]Stores sold merchandise of every description. [27]Merchandise could also be found on carts that were piled high with *odds and ends*. [28]Sometimes, a tired old horse pulled a *cart*. [29]More often men, too poor to own a shop or even a horse, pushed their carts. [30]Men and women fought or worked while children were playing on the streets.

[31]The Strauss family became a part of this busy life. [32]They joined many other immigrants who were *struggling* to fulfill their dreams in America.

Source: From Sondra Henry and Emily Taitz, *Levi Strauss: Everyone Wears His Name* (DillonPress, imprint of Silver Burdett Press, Simon & Schuster Elementary, 1990, 7–15). Reproduced by permission.

Activity 5-5   Checking Your Comprehension

Complete the following tasks about the previous reading. Use complete sentences.

1. Describe Levi's homeland.

_____

_____

_____

2. Give three reasons why Levi and his family left Bavaria.

_____

_____

_____

3. Describe what Levi heard when he arrived in New York City.

_____

_____

_____

4. Describe what Levi saw in New York City.

_____

_____

_____

LEARNER'S NOTEBOOK

Hometown and Childhood

In your learner's notebook, describe your hometown (the place where you grew up) and your childhood for someone who did not know you then. Answer some or all of the following questions. Use a paragraph for each new idea.

1. What did your hometown look like when you were a child?
2. What do you remember about summer evenings with your family or with friends?
3. What activities and games do you remember doing or playing as a child?
4. What were your friends or classmates from your hometown like?

Activity 5-6   Identifying the Grammar of Past Time Narrative Writing

Study and review the grammar of past time narrative writing by completing the following tasks in Reading 2 on page 135.

1. Highlight the chronological organizers.

2. Underline the simple past verbs (regular and irregular). Write the base form above each verb.

3. The writer used the past progressive verb _were playing_ in sentence 30. Find and draw a box around another past progressive verb in the story.

4. The writer used the past perfect verb _had lived_ in sentence 6. Find and place brackets [ ] around another past perfect verb in the story.

Non-Restrictive Relative Clauses and Appositives: Giving Information About People and Places

Non-restrictive relative clauses give additional information about nouns. They have relative clause structure. Non-restrictive relative clauses are separated from the noun and the rest of the sentence by commas.	John Adams, *who was an honored leader of the Revolution,* was elected Vice President in 1789.
Appositives are non-restrictive relative clauses without the relative pronoun and the verb *to be.* Appositives also give additional information about nouns, and they are separated from the noun and the rest of sentence with commas.	Electors also voted for George Washington, *the first President of the United States.*

GLR   See pages 219–220 in the GLR for more information on non-restrictive relative clauses and appositives.

Activity 5-7   Recognizing Non-Restrictive Relative Clauses and Appositives in Past Time Narrative Sentences

Place brackets [ ] around the non-restrictive relative clauses and appositives in the following sentences. Then, draw an arrow from each non-restrictive relative clause or appositive to the noun it is describing.

EXAMPLE

Levi's story began in a small village in Bavaria, [a land in the southern part of Germany.]

1. His father, Hirsch Strauss, made a living selling dry goods.

2. When Levi, a young man of eighteen, first saw New York in 1847, the city was full of activity.

3. More often men, too poor to own a shop or even a horse, pushed their carts.

4. When Levi arrived in the United States, his brothers, Jonas and Louis, were already settled in New York City.

5. In 1858–1859, prospectors found a small amount of gold near Pikes Peak, an area in Colorado Territory.

6. In 1862, the federal government developed the Homestead Act, which provided free land for those who moved west.

7. Andrew Jackson, who was now the President of the United States, moved thousands of Indians to new lands.

Developing Your Writing: Description

When you write a description, you include details about what something looks like, smells like, feels like, and so on. In other words, the five senses (seeing, hearing, smelling, tasting, and touching) can help you describe something and help your readers form pictures in their minds.

Writers often develop their writing by using description. The authors of Reading 2 describe Bavaria and New York City by using many adjectives and prepositional phrases that help the reader form a mental picture of these places.

> **GLR** See pages 215 and 262 in the GLR for more information on prepositional phrases and adjectives.

For an adjective chart, see Appendix C. For a list of common prepositions, see Appendix B.

Activity 5-8   Identifying Adjectives in Descriptions

When you develop your writing, adjectives can add important detail to your descriptions. Underline the adjectives in the following sentences. Then, for each adjective, draw an arrow to the noun it is describing. An example is provided.

EXAMPLE

Levi was the name of a remarkable man.

1. Levi's story began in a small village in Bavaria.

2. Levi's family was part of a small community of German Jews.

3. Bavaria was a beautiful land.

4. Its mountains were snow-covered in winter.

5. Pretty villages with rows of wooden houses stood along the river banks.

6. A traditional church stood in the central square.

7. In New York, Levi heard unfamiliar words of many different languages.

8. Irish women in long, drab dresses spoke English with a special lilt.

9. Levi also saw neat rows of narrow houses.

10. Sometimes, a tired old horse pulled a cart.

Activity 5-9   Recognizing Prepositional Phrases in Descriptions

Prepositional phrases can also add important detail to your descriptions. However, some ESL students have trouble recognizing prepositional phrases. In the following sentences, place parentheses ( ) around each prepositional phrase. An example is provided.

EXAMPLE

Levi's story began (in a small village) (in Bavaria).

1. Levi was born on February 26, 1829.

2. He was the youngest of six children.

3. Levi's family was part of a small community of German Jews.

4. Bavaria's high mountains were snow-covered in winter and green in summer.

5. Pretty villages with rows of wooden houses stood along the river banks.

6. Fountains stood in the central square of each town.

7. A synagogue was often located behind the central square.

8. Levi first saw New York in 1847.

9. Levi heard unfamiliar words of many different languages.

10. Dark-haired Italians with blue work pants hurried next to light-skinned Scandinavian sailors.

Activity 5-10   Using Description to Write About a Memorable Place

Write about a memorable or interesting place you visited in the past.

1. Begin by making a list of words and phrases for the things you saw, heard, smelled, and/or tasted. Include adjectives and prepositional phrases to describe those things.

    EXAMPLES

    sweet lemonade   people on the beach

    bright, hot sun   music from a band

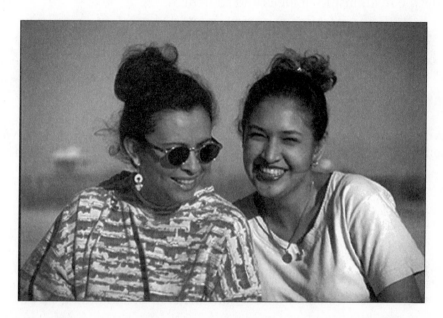

2. Write a general statement about this memorable or interesting place. Your general statement should tell where this place is and when you visited it.

3. Then, develop your ideas into a paragraph by writing four to five sentences that describe what you saw, heard, smelled, and/or tasted. Use some words and phrases from your list in your description. Begin a new paragraph for each main idea.

Activity 5-11   Self-editing

1. Read your paragraph(s) again. Do you clearly describe your memorable place? Should you provide more details to make your description more interesting? Do you move from general ideas to specific details? Make any changes needed to improve the meaning of your writing.

2. Edit for the grammar of past time narrative writing. Correct any errors that you find. After you have edited for these features, check (✓) the box.

☐ complete sentences

☐ past tense verbs

☐ non-restrictive clauses and appositives

☐ adjectives and prepositional phrases to develop your ideas

☐ chronological organizers and other cohesion devices (logical organizers, repetition of key words/phrases, pronouns, different forms of the same word) that show the relationship of ideas and sentences

The Levi Legend

Activity 5-12   Pre-reading Vocabulary

The following words are *italicized* in the next reading. Find the italicized words, and read the sentences. Then, match each definition to the appropriate word. One answer is provided.

1.	____ settle	a.	fabric, clothing, bed linens, etc.
2.	_a_ dry goods	b.	story from the distant past
3.	____ brave	c.	thick, rough cloth used for ships' sails, tents, etc.
4.	____ sturdy	d.	move in, make a home
5.	____ swell	e.	statement or comment about something
6.	____ remark	f.	person who makes, sews, or repairs clothing
7.	____ canvas	g.	strong, well-built, durable
8.	____ legend	h.	unafraid of danger
9.	____ leftover	i.	expand in size
10.	____ tailor	j.	what remains, such as some food after a meal

READING 3   SHOULD HAVE BROUGHT PANTS (BOOK)

Read the following excerpt that tells the story about Levi Strauss' first years in the United States. The authors provide background information, description, and examples to develop their writing.

SHOULD HAVE BROUGHT PANTS

¹When Levi arrived in the United States, his brothers, Jonas and Louis, had already *settled* in New York City. ²They earned a living in the *dry goods* business. ³Levi worked for his brothers when he first came to New York. ⁴He learned many important things from his brothers. ⁵For example, Levi selected goods with his brothers' help, listened to their advice, and learned the skills of buying and selling.

⁶In January 1848, less than a year after Levi Strauss had arrived to the United States, gold was discovered in California. ⁷Anyone who was *brave*, adventurous, or hard-working enough could go and find it. ⁸All kinds of people went to California to find gold. ⁹By 1850, San Francisco's population had *swelled* from several hundred to 25,000. ¹⁰Buildings, such as hotels, shops, and warehouses, were built all over the city. ¹¹People could easily find jobs. ¹²By 1853, the city had 70,000 people. ¹³Levi was one of those people. ¹⁴He went to California with dry goods to sell: needles, thread, scissors, and other sewing supplies, as well as rolls of *canvas*. ¹⁵His brothers in New York City had supplied all the goods.

¹⁶The Levi *legend* really began in San Francisco. ¹⁷According to one story, Levi quickly sold everything he had brought except the canvas. ¹⁸People still tell stories about that *leftover* roll of canvas. ¹⁹When he tried to sell the cloth, Levi was told that he should have brought pants. ²⁰Pants didn't last long in the mines, and they were always in great demand. ²¹After he had heard this *remark*, Levi brought his canvas to a *tailor* and had his first pair of work pants made. ²²Later, the demand for Levi's *sturdy* pants was so great that he could not get enough cloth. ²³And, as they say, the rest is history.

Source: From Sondra Henry and Emily Taitz, *Levi Strauss: Everyone Wears His Name* (DillonPress, imprint of Silver Burdett Press, Simon & Schuster Elementary, © 1990, 17–30). Used by permission.

Activity 5-13   Checking Your Comprehension

Complete the following tasks about the previous reading. Use complete sentences.

1. List things that Levi learned from his brothers when he first arrived in the United States.

    _____

    _____

2. Give reasons why people were going to California.

    _____

    _____

3. List some things Levi tried to sell in California.

    _____

    _____

Activity 5-14   Identifying the Grammar of Past Time Narrative Writing

Study and review the grammar of past time narrative writing by completing the following tasks in Reading 3 on page 142.

1. Highlight chronological organizers.

2. Underline simple past verbs (regular and irregular). Write the base form above each verb.

3. The writer used the past perfect verb *had settled* in sentence 1. Find and draw a box around other past perfect verbs in the story. (There are no examples of past progressive verbs in this excerpt.)

4. Place parentheses ( ) around several adjectives and prepositional phrases that develop ideas in this excerpt.

The Grammar of Past Time Narrative: Proper Nouns and Personal Pronouns

Proper nouns and personal pronouns are often used in past time narrative writing. *Proper nouns* are nouns like Jim Nguyen, New York City, or IBM. Proper nouns are always capitalized. In past time narrative writing, proper nouns are usually names of people or places. *Personal pronouns* (*I, you, them*) are used in place of subject nouns or object nouns.

> GLR   See pages 224 and 225 in the GLR for more information on proper nouns and personal pronouns.

Activity 5-15   Recognizing Proper Nouns and Personal Pronouns in Past Time Narrative Writing

In Reading 3 on page 142, circle each proper noun, and draw an arrow to any personal pronouns that refer to those proper nouns.

EXAMPLE   (Levi) worked for his brothers when he first came to (New York.)

145

LEARNER'S NOTEBOOK

A Person to Admire

Levi Strauss and his hard work and creativity is admired by many people. Write about a person that you admire.

1. To begin, make a list of reasons why you admire this person.
2. Then, write a general statement about this person, which includes who this person is.
3. Develop your ideas into a paragraph. Provide description and examples about the person you admire.

Developing Your Writing: Personal Experience

Your supporting details don't always need to come from a book, a graph, the WWW, or another person. You can use your own experiences to develop ideas in your writing. In other words, to explain or prove your general statement, you can write about things that happened to you.

Activity 5-16   Recognizing the Use of Personal Experience in Past Time Narrative Writing

In this chapter, you read about Levi Strauss' trip to the United States. The following paragraphs describe experiences about students' trips to different places. For each, underline the general statement and circle the personal experiences that explain or prove the general statement.

Student Writing Model 1

Brazil is a beautiful country to visit. Last summer, I went to Sao Sebastias with my family. Everywhere we went, there were beautiful beaches. The Brazilian coast is very pretty, and the sea water is very clear. I saw many of my friends and relatives, and we had a wonderful time.

Francisco Maldonaldo
Portugal

Student Writing Model 2

My trip last year to the United States from Spain was exciting. Before my trip, I got my passport and packed my suitcases. Then, I went to Manuses Airport in Valencia, and I flew to London. I visited London for one day. I went to see Big Ben, and then I went to Heathrow Airport. From there, I flew to Washington, where my friend Cass was waiting. We drove in her car through Virginia and Ohio, but afterwards we returned to Virginia to stay at my friend's house. Then, I flew home on August 19th.

Luis Rodenas
Spain

Activity 5-17   Recognizing the Grammar of Past Time Narrative Writing

For each of the previous paragraphs, complete the following steps:

1. Highlight chronological organizers.

2. Underline past tense verbs.

3. Circle proper nouns and personal pronouns.

4. Place parentheses ( ) around several adjectives and prepositional phrases that develop ideas.

Developing Your Writing: Examples

Examples can make your writing more interesting and enjoyable to read. Examples can also help your readers understand difficult concepts. You can use examples from personal experience or from someone else's experience, so they are often the easiest way to provide detail to your writing. Make sure, though, that your examples are related to your main idea.

Activity 5-18   Identifying Examples

In addition to description and personal experiences, writers often develop their writing with examples. Writers use example structures (logical organizers, parentheses, dashes, and so on) with their examples. The authors of Reading 3 on page 143 use several example structures to develop their ideas. With a partner, find the examples in Reading 3, and identify the example structures that are used.

See Chapter 1, page 21, and Chapter 6, page 165, for further explanations, examples, and activities on example structures. For a list of different example structures, see Appendix E.

Activity 5-19   Using Example Structures

Writers often use only one or two of the same example structures, but using different example structures (like parentheses and dashes) can add variety to your writing. Read the following sentences and circle the example structures. Then, practice various example structures by rewriting these sentences.

EXAMPLE

Jeans were the pants of working people—miners, machinists, and construction workers.
Jeans were the pants of working people (miners, machinists, and construction workers).

1. Levi's father made a living selling dry goods—bolts of cloth, clothing, and notions.

   _____

   _____

   _____

2. In New York City, Levi heard unfamiliar words of many different languages. For example, he heard English, Portuguese, and Spanish.

   _____

   _____

   _____

3. Levi went to California with merchandise to sell: needles, thread, scissors, and other sewing supplies.

   _____

   _____

   _____

4. Levi may have also brought larger items. For instance, he probably brought kettles, books, shoes, and bed linens.

    _____

    _____

    _____

5. In San Francisco, just about anything could be purchased (food, clothing, tools, buildings, and even mining claims).

    _____

    _____

    _____

6. Some miners came with equipment to blow up the rock. For instance, they brought hammers, drills, and gunpowder.

    _____

    _____

    _____

LEARNER'S NOTEBOOK

Things I Have Learned

Levi Strauss learned many things about the dry goods business from his brothers. Write about a person who has taught you many things. Who is this person? What did you learn?

1. Think about a person who has taught you many things. Make a list of the things that you learned from this person.
2. Write a general statement about this person.
3. Then, develop your ideas into a paragraph by writing four or five sentences that describe this person and your personal experiences. Include specific examples.

PUTTING IT ALL TOGETHER

FINAL WRITING ASSIGNMENT: PERSONAL SUCCESS

Some people believe that Levi Strauss' success was luck. He was in the right place at the right time. Others believe his intelligence and hard work attributed to his success. Think of something you have been successful at (e.g., learning another language, meeting new people, playing a sport or musical instrument). Explain to your teacher how you became successful.

Collecting Ideas

1. Begin by making a list of all the things you enjoy and/or are good at.

2. Then, spend a few minutes thinking about the ideas on your list. Do you enjoy these things because you are good at them? Why are you good at the things on your list?

3. Select one thing from your list to develop into a paragraph.

Organizing and Developing Your Ideas

1. Write a general statement about your success.

2. Then, develop your ideas by writing four or five sentences about your success. Use descriptive adjectives and prepositional phrases, and use specific details like description, personal experience, and examples to develop your ideas.

Editing Your Writing

1. Read your paper again. Do you clearly discuss something you have been successful at? Do you need to provide more detail to make your writing more interesting? Do you move from general ideas to specific details? Make any changes needed to improve the meaning of your writing.

2. Edit for the grammar of past time narrative writing. Correct any errors that you find. After you have edited for these features, check (✓) the box.

   ❑ complete sentences

   ❑ past tense verbs

   ❑ chronological organizers

☐ non-restrictive relative clauses and appositives

☐ proper nouns and personal pronouns

☐ development of ideas through description, personal experience, and examples

Providing Peer Support

Exchange papers with a partner, and read each other's ideas.

1. On your partner's paper, <u>underline</u> the general statement.

2. Place an X next to the development detail you like the best.

3. Explain why you like that development detail. In the margin of the paper, write a statement such as:

> I laughed when I read this personal experience.
>
> This example is very interesting.
>
> I learned from your examples.
>
> Great detail!
>
> I had an experience just like this.

4. Give one suggestion to make the writing better. In the margin of the paper, write a question such as:

> I don't understand. Could you use an example to help me?
>
> What did this look like? Can you describe it more?
>
> How did this experience make you feel?
>
> Could you please give more details?
>
> What things did you see and hear during this experience?

Revising Your Writing

1. With your partner, discuss her or his ideas and suggestions for your writing.

2. Make several changes to improve your writing.

Finalizing Your Writing

1. Make the corrections that you decided on during the self-editing and peer-support processes. You may want to refer to the check list that begins on the previous page again as you do this.

2. Rewrite your paper to submit to your teacher.

When you are deciding which academic classes to take, you should ask students who have completed the classes to share their experiences. Ask them to describe the class, share personal experiences they had while taking the class, and give examples of assignments and class discussions. This will help you make wise decisions about your class selection.

With a partner, discuss a class you completed. Describe the class, share personal experiences, and give examples of assignments and discussions.

Chapter 6

*C*lassifying

People and Places

GOALS

WRITING
◆ study and practice classifying

GRAMMAR
◆ practice the grammar of informational writing and past informational writing

CONTENT
◆ learn about the field of geography, focusing on the relationship between people and places

ACADEMIC FIELD

Geography

Sample Authentic College/University Classifying Assignments

In your academic classes, you will use the skills you learn in this chapter to complete assignments and exam questions like these:

Agriculture

Explain three important events or inventions that make milk today the best ever.

Psychology

Summarize the evidence that suggests people need to dream.

Sociology

Discuss some ways in which clothing can be used symbolically.

Economics

Describe three actions that could reduce poverty.

GETTING READY

Introduction to Classifying

Classifying is a way to organize your ideas. When you classify, you divide or separate your ideas into groups. This helps you explain how those ideas are related. It also helps others understand the organization of the ideas that follow.

A paragraph or paper that is classified can be divided into two parts:

1. a classification sentence
2. the development of your ideas

Warm-up Activity

Geographers are people who study the relationship between people and places. Geographers often travel throughout the world to study people and their environments. With a partner, discuss four or five places that you want to visit. Explain why those places interest you. Then, select three of your most interesting places, and complete the sentence that follows.

Three places that I want to visit are _____

_____, and _____

In your sentence about interesting places, you classified your ideas into three groups. This sentence is a *classification sentence.* To *develop your ideas,* you can explain why each of those three places interest you. When you classify, sometimes you only need one paragraph to develop your ideas. At other times, you may want to form a new paragraph for each of your ideas.

The following paragraph shows how one writer developed her ideas.

classification sentence

Three places that I want to visit are Paris, Venice, and Hong Kong. *The first*
development of ideas
place I want to visit is Paris. Paris has many interesting art museums, and visitors can see some of the greatest art in the world. Also, the city has a feeling of romance. *A second interesting place is Venice,* a city that is full of unique architecture. In Venice, you can study the uncommon combination of water and buildings. *Finally, Hong Kong has the excitement of business and pleasure.* The food is delicious, and the nightlife is fascinating.

Grammar Preview

In this chapter, you will practice the *grammar of informational writing* because this grammar is often used during classification. This chapter focuses on the following aspects of informational writing: *present tense verbs, complex noun phrases, passive sentences,* and *logical organizers.*

You will also practice past tense verbs used in *past informational writing.* When you write statements of fact or habit about the past, you use past informational writing.

> **GLR** See pages 221–222 and pages 226–237 in the GLR for more information on the grammar of past informational writing (past tense verbs) and the grammar of informational writing.

FOCUSING

People and Places

READING 1   WHAT IS GEOGRAPHY? (GEOGRAPHY TEXTBOOK)

Read this excerpt to learn more about the field of geography.

WHAT IS GEOGRAPHY?

The term *geography* comes from two Greek words—"geo" for *earth* and "graphia" for *write about.* Geographers study physical and cultural features on or near the surface of the earth. **Physical features** are those that occur naturally, such as mountains, rivers, and oceans. **Cultural features** are those created by people, such as boundaries, towns, and roads. Geographers also look at living things—plants, animals, and people. They want to know how 5 people shape and are shaped by their **environment**—all the things that surround us.

Geography, then, is the study of the earth in a way that shows the relationship between humans and their environment. That makes geography a story of people, places, and relationships.

Source: Edwin L. Jackson, Mary E. Stakes, Lawrence R. Hepburn, and Mary A. Hepburn, *The Georgia Studies Book* (Carl Vinson Institute of Government, University of Georgia, 1992, 28–29). Reproduced by permission.

Activity 6-1   Analyzing an Excerpt That Uses Classification

Use the previous reading to complete these tasks and questions.

1. Several terms are defined in this excerpt. For each of the boldfaced terms,

    a. highlight the definition structure (formal definitions, parentheses, and so on)

    b. underline the definition

    For a review of definition structures, see Chapter 4 and page 242 of the GLR GLR .

2. What two broad features do geographers study?

    Geographers study

    a. _____

    b. _____

3. According to the excerpt, what are some examples of each feature?

    a. _____

    b. _____

Organizing Your Ideas

In Chapter 2, you learned about making lists to collect ideas. When you make lists, you can group similar ideas together and put them into general categories. Grouping ideas is one way to classify. You can use a *chart* or an *outline* to classify or organize your ideas. Those ideas are organized from general to specific. Study the following examples of these two organizational formats, and compare the charts and outlines to the excerpts on pages 154 and 155.

CLASSIFYING CHARTS

PLACES I WANT TO VISIT (*general*)

Paris — art museums romance

Venice — architecture water

Hong Kong (*specific*) — business food entertainment (*more specific*)

FEATURES STUDIED BY GEOGRAPHERS

physical features — mountains rivers oceans

cultural features — boundaries towns roads

CLASSIFYING OUTLINES

PLACES I WANT TO VISIT *(general)*

I. Paris *(specific)*

    A. art museums *(more specific)*

    B. romance

II. Venice

    A. architecture

    B. water

III. Hong Kong

    A. business

    B. food

    C. entertainment

FEATURES STUDIED BY GEOGRAPHERS

I. physical features

    A. mountains

    B. rivers

    C. oceans

II. cultural features

    A. boundaries

    B. towns

    C. roads

Activity 6-2   Using Charts and Outlines to Organize Ideas

The following subjects relate to the field of geography. With a partner, discuss and collect ideas related to these subjects. Organize your ideas using charts and outlines. Remember, move from general ideas to specific details. For each item, some answers are provided. There may be more than one correct answer.

1.   COMMUNICATION SYSTEMS FOR THE 21ST CENTURY

telephone _____   _____   _____

2.   HOW GEOGRAPHERS CLASSIFY BODIES OF WATER

lakes

Pacific   Nile

3. TODAY'S POLLUTION PROBLEMS

    I. _____ air _____

    II. _____

    III. _____

4. FOOD FOR HEALTHY LIVING

    I. _____ vegetables _____

        A. _____

        B. _____

    II. _____

        A. _____ chicken _____

        B. _____

    III. _____

        A. _____

Classification Sentences

After you have collected and organized your ideas, you can write a *classification sentence*. A classification sentence explains (1) *what you will classify* and (2) *how you will organize and develop your ideas.* Study the following examples of classification sentences.

EXAMPLES

¹   ²
X can be divided into <u>three groups</u>.

        ²   ¹
There are <u>several categories</u> of <u>X</u>.

      ¹   ²
You can group <u>X</u> in <u>a variety of ways</u>.

Writers often (3) *list their ideas* with their classification sentences.

EXAMPLES

¹
X can be divided into <u>three groups</u>. <u>These groups are a, b, and c</u>.
(1)   (2)   (3)

There are <u>*several categories*</u> of X: <u>a, b, and c</u>.
(2)   (1)   (3)

You can group X in <u>a variety of ways</u>, <u>including a, b, and c</u>.
(1)   (2)   (3)

| **Activity 6-3   Identifying the Parts of a Classification Sentence** |

In the following sentences, label the parts of a classification sentence with 1, 2, and 3.

EXAMPLE   There are <u>several categories</u> of <u>communication systems for the 21st century,</u>
(2)   (1)

<u>including the telephone, the fax machine, and the Internet</u>.
(3)

1. There are several ways that geographers can divide bodies of water: oceans, lakes, and rivers.

2. Today's pollution problems can be grouped according to their effects on the public. This paper describes the effects of three kinds of pollution: air, noise, and water.

3. Geographers may study the food that is eaten in different environments. They divide food into several main groups, including vegetables, meat, and dairy products.

Subdivisions of Geography

READING 2   THE SUBDIVISIONS OF GEOGRAPHY (GEOGRAPHY TEXTBOOK)

Read the following excerpt. The authors use classification to organize their ideas.

THE SUBDIVISIONS OF GEOGRAPHY

There are two broad subdivisions of geography. These subdivisions are physical geography and human geography. Physical geographers study natural features and the climatic, geologic, and other processes that shape our world. Human geographers focus on people and their patterns of settlement and activity.

To describe and explain our world, geographers study findings in many related fields by   5
looking at the interconnection of people, places, and things. This interest in the relationship of people, places, and things is the great attraction of geography.

Source: Adapted from *Exploring Your World: The Adventures of Geography*
(National Geographic Society, 1989, 243). Reproduced by permission.

Activity 6-4   Analyzing an Excerpt That Uses Classification

Use the previous reading to complete these tasks.

1. Highlight the classification sentence in this excerpt. Then, label the three parts of a classification sentence with 1, 2, and 3.

2. On another piece of paper, draw both a chart and an outline to illustrate the organization of ideas in this excerpt.

The Grammar of Informational Writing: Complex Noun Phrases and Prepositional Phrases

Informational writing includes complex noun phrases and prepositional phrases. A complex noun phrase is a long, complicated noun phrase. A prepositional phrase is a phrase that begins with a preposition and ends with a noun or noun phrase. One common complex noun phrase is the *noun phrase + of prepositional phrase* structure.

EXAMPLE

When humans live in groups, they develop and share *similar ways of behavior.*

The complex noun phrase *similar ways of behavior* is the object of this sentence.

GLR   See pages 215 and 227 in the GLR for more information about prepositional phrases and complex noun phrases.

For a list of common prepositions, see Appendix B.

| **Activity 6-5** | **Recognizing the Complex Noun Phrase + *of* Prepositional Phrase Structure** |

1. The following sentences from this chapter contain the *noun phrase + of prepositional phrase* structure. Find this structure in each sentence, and place brackets [ ] around it.

   EXAMPLE

   Physical items (food, clothing, houses, and tools) are [a part of culture].

   a. In Venice, you can study the uncommon combination of water and buildings.

   b. Geography is the study of the earth in a way that shows the relationship between humans and their environments.

   c. Geographers study physical and cultural features on or near the surface of the earth.

   d. There are several ways that geographers can divide bodies of water: oceans, lakes, and rivers.

2. Return to Reading 2 on page 159, and find examples of the *noun phrase + of prepositional phrase* structure. Place brackets [ ] around each of these structures.

Punctuation in Classification Sentences

When you list three or more ideas, use *commas* to separate them. Study these classification sentences for the use of commas.

EXAMPLES

Three places that I want to visit are Paris, Venice, and Hong Kong.

Geographers study physical and cultural features on or near the earth's surface.

That makes geography a story of people, places, and relationships.

Colons (:) are often used to introduce a list or series of ideas. A colon directs a reader's attention to that list. Do not use a colon immediately after the verbs *be* or *include*. Study these classification sentences for the use of colons.

EXAMPLES

There are two main factors for voluntary migration: push factors and pull factors.

There are two broad subdivisions of geography. These subdivisions are physical [1]
geography [2] and human geography.

We can separate most of Europe into three major language groups: Romance, [1]
Germanic, [2] and Slavic [3] languages.

Activity 6-6   Using Commas and Colons

In the following sentences, place commas and colons where appropriate.

1. The earth's land area is divided into seven continents North America South America Europe Asia Africa Australia and Antarctica.

2. Africa's Sahara Desert doesn't have many trees people or bodies of water.

3. Throughout most of history, the huge Sahara has divided Africa into two parts the north and the south.

4. The rivers of Africa include the Nile Congo Niger and Zambezi.

5. A visit to Africa would not be complete without mentioning some of its animals elephants giraffes zebras lions and leopards.

6. The climate in Africa's jungles is hot humid and rainy.

Activity 6-7   Writing Classification Sentences

Write a classification sentence for each of the following topics. Use a variety of classification structures and correct punctuation.

1. reasons for small group discussion (see Chapter 1, page 10, for a review)

2. three kinds of learning styles (see Chapter 1, page 13, for a review)

3. three ways to collect ideas for writing (see Chapter 2, page 34, for a review)

4. three sleep problems (see Chapter 4, page 118, for a review)

Developing Your Ideas

When you classify, you divide or separate your ideas into general groups or categories. Then, you develop those ideas by giving specific details. You can give details by providing definitions, description, personal experience, examples, comparisons, and/or reasons.

READING 3   THE LANGUAGES OF EUROPE (GEOGRAPHY TEXTBOOK)

Read the paragraph on the next page, and notice the development of its ideas.

THE LANGUAGES OF EUROPE

We can separate most of Europe into three major language groups: Romance, Germanic, and Slavic languages. The first group is clustered around the Mediterranean Sea in the south. These people speak Romance languages. This means that their languages are based on Latin, the language of ancient Rome. French, Spanish, Italian, Romanian, and Portuguese are Romance languages. The second group is located across the northwestern 5 part of the continent. These people speak Germanic languages. This includes German, of course, as well as English, Dutch, Swedish, Norwegian, Danish, and Icelandic. The third group is in eastern and northeastern Europe. They speak Slavic languages like Russian, Polish, Bulgarian, Czech, Serbo-Croatian, and Slovenian.

Source: Adapted from Paul Rosenthal, *Where on Earth: A Geografunny Guide to the Globe*
(Alfred A. Knopf, Inc., Random House, 1992, 89). Reproduced by permission.

Activity 6-8   Analyzing an Excerpt That Uses Classification

Use the previous reading to complete these tasks.

1. Highlight the classification sentence in this paragraph. Then, label the three parts of a classification sentence with 1, 2, and 3.

2. On another piece of paper, rewrite the classification sentence, using another classification sentence format (see page 158).

3. On another piece of paper, draw a chart or an outline to illustrate the organization of ideas in this paragraph.

4. The author developed his ideas in two ways: by giving definitions and by giving examples.

    a. What definition(s) are in this paragraph?

    b. What example(s) are in this paragraph?

(To review the development of ideas with extended definitions, see Chapter 4, page 118.)

The Grammar of Informational Writing: Passive Sentences

Reading 3 uses the grammar of informational writing, which includes simple present tense verbs. Informational writing also often includes passive verbs (a form of the verb *to be* + past participle). For example, in the following sentence, *want* and *shape* are simple present tense verbs. The verb *are shaped* is passive.

Geographers *want* to know how people *shape* and are *shaped* by their environments.

> **GLR**   See page 232 in the GLR for more information about passive sentences.

Activity 6-9   Identifying Grammar Structures

Study and review grammar structures by completing the following tasks in Reading 3.

1. Underline simple present tense verbs and circle passive verbs.

2. Place brackets [ ] around the three *noun phrase* + *of prepositional phrase* structures.

Developing Ideas with Logical Organizers: Example Structures

As you have studied, you can develop your ideas by providing examples to support your general opinions or statements. In Chapters 1 and 5, you practiced using examples in your writing, using the logical organizers *for example* and *for instance*, and using other example structures. You can also use *such as* and *like* to provide examples. To understand the use of these logical organizers, study the sentences in this chart.

LOGICAL ORGANIZERS: EXAMPLE STRUCTURES

for example	general statements specific detail→ There are many different meanings for the term "city." *For example,* a settlement in Japan must have at least 30,000 to be considered a city.
for instance	general statement specific detail→ Most of these jobs require specialized skills. *For instance,* business people, construction workers, and police officers all have special skills for their jobs.
such as	general statement specific detail→ Cultural features are those created by people, *such as* boundaries, towns, and roads.
like	general statement specific detail→ They speak Slavic languages *like* Russian, Polish, Bulgarian, Czech, Serbo-Croatian, and Slovenian.

> **GLR**   See pages 230–231 in the GLR for more information about logical organizers.

For a list of example structures, see Appendix E.

Activity 6-10   Understanding Example Structures

1. Study the following about the use of these logical organizers.

   a. A complete sentence includes a subject and a verb. A complete sentence often follows the logical organizers *for example* and *for instance*.

   b. A noun phrase is group of words (without both a subject and a verb) that together act as a subject or an object. A noun phrase follows the logical organizers *such as* and *like*.

2. With your classmates and teacher, identify the punctuation used with each logical organizer in the previous chart.

> **GLR**   See page 267 and page 270 in the GLR for more information about noun phrases and sentences.

Activity 6-11   Using Example Structures

Read the following sentences about places around the world. Rewrite each group of sentences using *such as* or *like*.

> **EXAMPLE**
>
> The state of New York is home to a variety of wild animals. *For example,* you can find deer, rabbits, squirrels, and raccoons in New York.
>
> The state of New York is home to a variety of wild animals, *such as* deer, rabbits, squirrels, and raccoons.
>
> **or**
>
> A variety of wild animals, *such as* deer, rabbits, squirrels, and raccoons, lives in the state of New York.

1. There are snow-covered mountains on the South Island in New Zealand. People do various activities on and near those mountains. For example, skiing, fishing, deer hunting, skating, and riding are popular sports.

   (*such as*) _____

   _____

   _____

2. Many of Brazil's crops (coffee, soybeans, sugarcane, cocoa, and rice) are exported to other countries.

   (*like*) _____

   _____

   _____

3. The hot season for Rangoon, the capital of Burma, is not much worse than some American cities. For example, St. Louis, Cincinnati, and Louisville may get as hot as the city of Rangoon.

   (*such as*) _____

   _____

   _____

4. In Nigeria's tropical forests, there are animals of all kinds. For instance, elephants, gorillas, and leopards are commonly found in Nigeria.

   (*like*) _____

   _____

   _____

Activity 6-12   Developing Ideas with Reasons

An additional way to develop ideas is to provide reasons for your general opinions or statements. In the Warm-up Activity, page 154, you wrote about three places you want to visit. With a partner, discuss the reasons for your choice of places. Then, on another paper, develop your ideas by completing the following paragraph.

   Three places that I want to visit are _____,
   _____, and _____. First,
   I want to visit _____ because _____.
   Second, _____ is interesting
   because _____. Finally, I want to visit
   _____ because
   _____.

Using Logical Organizers for Cohesion

As you know, when you write, you want your reader to be able to easily move from one idea to the next idea. This makes your writing coherent. Logical organizers show

how ideas are related and help the reader understand the organization of your writing. The following logical organizers are often used in classification writing.

LOGICAL ORGANIZERS IN CLASSIFICATION WRITING	
For example, ... (For instance, ...)	First, ... (Second/Third, ...)
Another *noun phrase + verb* ...	Next, ... (Then, ...)
In addition, ...	Finally, ... (Lastly, ...)
Also, ...	

Commas are usually used after these logical organizers, except for *another*. Discuss the use of *another* with your teacher and classmates. Reading 4 provides an example of the use of *another*.

GLR   See page 230 in the GLR for more information about logical organizers.

READING 4   A CITY (GEOGRAPHY TEXTBOOK)

Read the following paragraph about cities, which researchers in human geography often study. This paragraph uses logical organizers to show the relationship of ideas.

A CITY

Generally, a city is a large settlement whose residents perform activities not related to agriculture (farming). However, throughout the world, there are many different meanings for the term "city." For example, a settlement in Japan must have a population of at least 30,000 to be a city. In the United States, another definition of a city is used: Places with populations of 2,500 or more are defined as urban, which means "characteristic of a city." In   5 addition, if an area in Sweden has a population of 200, it is considered a city. In general, the term "city" is used by geographers to describe any urban center where people live and work close together.

Source: Adapted from *Exploring Your World: The Adventures of Geography*
(National Geographic Society, 1989, 92). Reproduced by permission.

Activity 6-13   Identifying Classification and Grammar Structures

Use the previous reading to complete the following tasks.

1. Highlight the classification sentence.
2. Place a box around the logical organizers that connect ideas to that classification sentence. Identify the punctuation used with these logical organizers, and discuss this with your teacher and classmates.
3. Underline simple present tense verbs, and circle passive verbs.
4. Place brackets [ ] around the *noun phrase* + ***of** prepositional phrase* structures.

Activity 6-14   Using Appropriate Logical Organizers for Classification

For each of the following paragraphs, (1) highlight the classification sentence, and (2) add appropriate logical organizers to connect ideas. Use a variety of logical organizers from the chart on page 168. There may be more than one appropriate answer.

CHARACTERISTICS OF CITIES

The definition of a city may be slightly different, but all cities share several characteristics. _____, cities are densely populated. A large number of people live in one area. _____, the residents of a city hold a wide variety of jobs. Most of these jobs require specialized skills. For instance, business people, construction workers, and police officers all have special skills for their jobs. _____, people who live in 5 a city depend upon one another for services and survival. However, one job that city residents don't do is farming. For example, in a city, we buy our food from the owner of a grocery store. We cannot grow our own food.

Source: Adapted from *Exploring Your World: The Adventures of Geography*
(National Geographic Society, 1989, 92–95). Reproduced by permission.

THE AMAZON

Three geographical features make the Amazon particularly interesting. _____, it is alive with a large variety of plants, animals, insects, and fish. _____, most of the plants and animals in the forest don't live in the forest. They live *above* it, in the canopy—the cover formed by the treetops. Millions of monkeys, bugs, and plants spend their whole lives in the canopy, a hundred feet off the ground.   5 _____, the Amazon has what botanists call "crummy soil." (Botanists are scientists who study plants.) Many of the giant trees live in only one inch of fertile earth.

Source: Adapted from Paul Rosenthal, *Where on Earth: A Geografunny Guide to the Globe* (Alfred A. Knopf, Inc., Random House, Inc., 1992, 42). Reproduced by permission.

LEARNER'S NOTEBOOK

My Community

Two of the previous excerpts in this chapter are about cities ("A City" and "Characteristics of Cities"). There are good and bad things about every city. For example, the transportation system or the beautiful parks might be good things. The pollution or the cost of living may be bad things. In your learner's notebook, make a list of the good and bad things in your community. Use a chart like the one that follows. Then, write one classification sentence that explains the positive things and one classification sentence that explains the negative things.

POSITIVE THINGS	NEGATIVE THINGS
transportation system	pollution
beautiful parks	the cost of living

Parallelism in Your Writing

When you classify, parallelism is important. *Parallelism* means that each item is *similar in form* and *similar in content*. Parallelism also refers to *the order of your ideas*. Parallelism needs to occur in your *classification sentence* if you list your ideas. It also needs to occur *in the development of your ideas*. See how the following classification sentence is followed by the development of ideas.

EXAMPLE

classification sentence
<u>Geographers study physical and cultural features on or near the surface of the earth</u>. Physical features are those that occur naturally, such as mountains, rivers, and oceans. Cultural features are those created by people, such as boundaries, towns, and roads.

Grammatical Parallelism: Parallel in Form

When the logical connector *and* combines words, the words must be the same part of speech. In the previous example, study the classification sentence. In this classification sentence, *physical* and *cultural* are connected with *and*. Both *physical* and *cultural* are adjectives that give more information about the features. These two words are parallel in form.

Logical Parallelism: Parallel in Content and in the Order of Ideas

Combinations of words and phrases need to be grammatical, but they also need to have parallel meaning. In the previous example, both development sentences give a definition and some examples of each feature. This information is parallel in content. Finally, the example is parallel because of the order of ideas. For example, in the classification sentence, the writer lists *physical features* first and *cultural features* second. So, the writer develops *physical features* first and *cultural features* second.

Activity 6-15   Using Parallelism in Your Writing

Read these sentences about places around the world. The sentences are either grammatically or logically not parallel. On another piece of paper, rewrite each group of sentences to make them parallel.

EXAMPLE

incorrect, not grammatically parallel
Except for the higher mountain areas, Lebanon is *hot, sunshine, and dry* in the summers.

correct
Except for the higher mountain areas, Lebanon is *hot, sunny, and dry* in the summers.

1. There are many natural features in Colorado, including Rocky Mountain National Park, Trail Ridge Road, and there is the Black Canyon.

2. During the annual Mardi Gras celebration in New Orleans, people are carefree, happiness, and relaxed.

3. Togo, in West Africa, is bordered on the west by Ghana, on the east by Benin, and Upper Volta is north of Togo.

4. In Cyprus, society is divided into two major ethnic communities: Greek and Turkish. The Turkish Cypriots speak Turkish, are Muslims, and identify themselves with Turkish tradition. The Greek Cypriots identify themselves with Greek tradition, speak Greek, and are Greek Orthodox.

Activity 6-16   Writing Classification Sentences with Parallelism and Correct Punctuation

Write a classification sentence for each of the following. Be sure to use parallelism and correct punctuation.

> EXAMPLE   three kinds of storms
>
> There are various kinds of storms, including *snow storms, rain storms,* and *wind storms.*

1. three interesting places to visit in your hometown

2. three important reasons to recycle

3. three characteristics of a beach

4. three or more environmental problems

Migration

LEARNER'S NOTEBOOK

Reasons for Migrating

In your learner's notebook, explain why you or your family migrated (moved) to your current community.

Activity 6-17   Pre-reading Vocabulary

The following words are *italicized* in the next reading. Find the italicized words, and read the sentences. Then, match each definition to the appropriate word. One answer is provided.

_____ **1.** shortage   a. area where people have decided to live

_____ **2.** rural   b. related to a city, city-like

_____ **3.** urban   c. cruel treatment of people, usually for differences in belief or race

_____ **4.** voluntary   d. not having enough

_____ **5.** persecution   e. the act of taking something away

_a_ **6.** settlement   f. done without being forced or paid

_____ **7.** removal   g. related to the countryside

_____ **8.** slave   h. person who is owned by someone else and who works for no money

READING 5   MIGRATION (GEOGRAPHY TEXTBOOK)

Read the following excerpt to learn more about why people migrate from one place to another.

MIGRATION

Migration is the movement of people from one place to another for the purpose of *settlement*. Migration can be internal (within a country) or external (from one country to another). With internal migration, people usually migrate from *rural* areas to *urban* areas. In the case of external migration, people emigrate from their country of origin and immigrate to a new country. For instance, you might know someone who emigrated from the U.S. 5 and immigrated to Australia.

Migrations can be *voluntary* or forced. Most people migrate by choice and do so to improve their lives. There are two main factors for voluntary migration: push factors and pull factors. "Push" factors are the factors that encourage people to emigrate, or leave their place of origin. Things such as food or housing *shortages*, lack of employment, and *perse-* 10 *cution* are push factors. "Pull" factors are those things that attract people to immigrate to a new place. Economic opportunity and religious or political freedom are common pull factors. Usually, both push and pull factors affect migration.

In contrast, forced migration is the *removal* of people from their place of origin by a government or other powerful group. For example, from the early 1500s to the late 1800s, 15 millions of Africans were forced to leave their homelands to work as *slaves* in the Americas.

Source: Adapted from *Exploring Your World: The Adventures of Geography*
(National Geographic Society, 1989, 337). Reproduced by permission.

Activity 6-18   Identifying Classification and Grammar Structures

Use the previous reading to complete the following tasks.

1. This excerpt classifies several ideas. Highlight the three classification sentences.

2. The authors developed their ideas in two ways: by giving definitions and by giving examples.

   a. Underline the definitions, and circle the terms that are being defined.

   b. Place a box around the example structures, and circle the specific examples.

3. With your teacher and classmates, find examples of grammatical and logical parallelism in this excerpt.

4. Place brackets [ ] around the complex noun phrase + *of* prepositional phrase structures.

Activity 6-19   Understanding Reasons for Migrating

People choose to migrate to another place for many reasons. These reasons may be personal, political, educational, or financial. With a small group of classmates, discuss the meaning of these four reasons. Then, give one or two examples for each. One example is provided.

1. personal reasons _____ *a desire to experience a new culture* _____

   _____

2. political reasons _____

   _____

3. educational reasons _____

   _____

4. financial reasons _____

   _____

Activity 6-20   Student Reasons for Immigrating to the United States

Read the following paragraphs from students who immigrated to the United States from other countries. These students had different reasons for moving. For each paragraph, write the reason(s) on the line. There may be more than one appropriate answer.

EXAMPLE

I migrated to the United States from Hong Kong for several reasons. One of those reasons was my interest in knowledge. In Hong Kong, the educational system depends mainly on your memorizing skills. For example, if you memorize all the things from your books or lectures, you will pass your exams and get high scores. In contrast, I think that you learn more in the United States. You don't just memorize information. ___*educational*___

Angus Cheng
Hong Kong

1.   There are several reasons I moved to the United States. One reason was to be independent. For instance, if I lived with my family, they would take care of me and do everything for me all the time. I wanted to learn to take care of myself.

_____

Srivilai (Joy) Sirirojvisuth
Thailand

2.   I migrated to the United States for several reasons, including employment and educational opportunities. First, I can earn more money here than in Turkey. As a result, I can have more of the material things I want, such as a house, a nice car, and other luxuries. Second, I can get a good education here.

_____

Caner Eroglu
Turkey

3.   There are many reasons why I emigrated from India, but the main reason was for personal freedom. In India, women have to tolerate many things compared to men. For example, girls have to obey their parents' rules before their marriage, and they have to obey the rules of their husbands' parents after their marriage.

_____

Dipti Patel
India

4.   My family and I moved to the United States three years ago for several reasons. However, the most important reason was for my brother. To illustrate, my brother was in the war between Azerbaijan and Armenia. He was injured several times, and my family was worried about him. We decided to move to the United States to save him. _____

Mila Magomedova
Azerbaijan

5.   My family and I came here to look for a better future. Before the communists ruled
Vietnam, my father was in the army of the former government. After the communists came, my father was a political prisoner. He was not treated well, so we came
here for freedom. _____

Lien Nguyen
Vietnam

6.   My family immigrated here for one main reason: my father's health. My father
needs fresh air, but the air is very polluted in Seoul. It is difficult for many people to
live in Seoul, so people with health problems often try to move away from the city.

_____

Sook Lee
South Korea

7.   I came to the United States for several reasons, such as work and school. First, in
my country, it is difficult to find a job. I didn't see a good future for me. On the other
hand, in the United States, there are a lot of possibilities for everyone. I can earn
money for my future. Second, I can get a good education in this country. This is
important to me. _____

Evelina Balan
Madova, Russia

Activity 6-21   Analyzing Paragraphs

1. With a partner, complete the following tasks in the previous student paragraphs.

    a. Underline classification sentences.

    b. Label general statements (G) and specific details (S).

    c. Circle logical organizers that show the relationship of ideas and sentences.

    EXAMPLE

    <u>I migrated to the United States from Hong Kong for several reasons.</u> One of ⎤ G
    those reasons was my interest in knowledge. In Hong Kong, the educational ⎤
    system depends mainly on your memorizing skills. (For example), if you memo-
    rize all the things from your books or lectures, you will pass your exams and get   S
    high scores. (In contrast), I think that you learn more in the United States. You
    don't just memorize information. ⎦

2. As you have studied, you generally use the grammar of informational writing when you write statements of fact or habit. When those statements are about the past, you use past informational writing. The grammar features of past informational writing are very similar to informational writing, except for the verbs and time expressions. With your teacher and classmates, find and discuss examples of the grammar of informational writing and past informational writing in the previous paragraphs.

LEARNER'S NOTEBOOK

Immigration Stories

In your learner's notebook, write your opinions about the various immigration stories in Activity 6-20, page 174. Answer the following questions. Begin a new paragraph for each new idea.

1. Which personal story interested you the most? Why?
2. Which reason for migrating to the United States did you like the least? Why?
3. Which story would you like to know more about? What would you like to know?

PUTTING IT ALL TOGETHER

FINAL WRITING ASSIGNMENT: MIGRATING TO YOUR COMMUNITY

Write about why you or your family migrated to your current community. Use the grammar of informational writing and/or past informational writing.

Collecting Ideas

To begin, review your learner's notebook, "Reasons for Migrating" (page 172). Add ideas to your learner's notebook.

Organizing and Developing Your Ideas

1. Select several ideas from your learner's notebook to use in your final writing assignment. Make a chart or an outline to organize those ideas.

2. Write a classification sentence about your ideas. Your classification sentence should explain (a) what you will classify and (b) how you will organize and develop your ideas. You might also choose to (c) list your ideas.

3. Develop your ideas by providing description, definitions, comparisons, personal experience, examples, and/or reasons.

4. Use logical organizers (*first, second, next,* and so on) to help the reader move from one idea to the next.

5. Combine some of your ideas and sentences with other logical organizers (*and, so, however,* and so on) to develop cohesion and to show the relationship of those ideas.

Editing Your Writing

1. Read your paper again. Have you explained several reasons for migrating to your current community? Do you move from general ideas to specific details? Should you develop your ideas more to make your paper more interesting or clear? Make any changes needed to improve the meaning of your writing.

2. Edit for the grammar of informational and past informational writing. Correct any errors that you find. After you have edited for these features, check (✓) the box.

   ❑ a classification sentence

   ❑ development of ideas through description, comparisons, definitions, personal experience, examples, and/or reasons

   ❑ appropriate logical organizers to show the relationship of ideas and sentences

   ❑ parallelism

   ❑ complete sentences

   ❑ correct verb tense (present tense or past tense verbs)

   ❑ grammar of informational writing and past informational writing

Providing Peer Support

Exchange papers with a partner, and read each other's ideas.

1. On your partner's paper, <u>underline</u> the classification sentence. Then, label the parts of the classification sentence with 1, 2, and possibly 3.

2. Place a box around logical organizers (*first, second,* and so on) that help the reader move from one point to the next.

3. Circle logical organizers (*and, but, so*) that combine ideas and show the relationship of those ideas.

4. Place an X next to the developing detail you like best.

5. Explain why you like that detail. In the margin of the paper, write a statement such as:

> I smiled when I read this example.
>
> I had this same reason for migrating here!
>
> This reason for moving to the United States was very interesting to me.
>
> This example is very clear.

6. Give one suggestion to make the writing better. In the margin of the paper, write a question such as:

> Could you please give more details here?
>
> I don't understand. Can you use another example to help me?
>
> Why do you feel this way? Can you give a reason?
>
> How can you make your ideas parallel?

Revising Your Writing

1. With your partner, discuss her or his ideas and suggestions for your writing.

2. Make several changes to improve your writing.

Finalizing Your Writing

1. Make the corrections that you decided on during the self-editing and peer-support processes. You may want to refer to the check list on page 178 again.

2. Rewrite your paper to submit to your teacher.

• •

The main field that you study in college is called your *major*. Selecting your major takes time and careful thought.

You may have already decided your major. If not, think about possible majors that may interest you. Then, with a partner, discuss the reasons for selecting your major (or possible major). Write a classification sentence to explain your choice.

LOOKING AHEAD

EXAMPLE

I selected my major, Elementary Education, for several reasons. I want to be a teacher, I love children, and I think I will be a good role model.

Discovering

Consumer Behavior

GOALS

WRITING
◆ complete, design, and write about tables and surveys

GRAMMAR
◆ review the grammar of academic writing

CONTENT
◆ learn about the field of consumer behavior

ACADEMIC FIELDS
Consumer Behavior
Marketing

Sample Authentic College/University Discovering Assignments

In your academic classes, you will use the skills you learn in this chapter to complete assignments and exam questions like these:

Hospitality Management

Many people say that Equal Employment Opportunity laws have affected the hospitality industry more than many other industries. Discuss this with your classmates. Then, give some reasons why you agree or disagree with this statement.

Marketing

Blockbuster's 1,200 video rental stores dominate the video rental industry. In fact, Blockbuster is bigger than the next 15 video chains combined. With your classmates, discuss why this chain is so successful. Do any factors threaten its success in the future? Discuss this, and write about your opinions.

Sociology

With a group of classmates, find out from the local welfare agency the amount of the typical weekly food allowance for an unemployed family of four. Ask how much aid the agency provides and what is available through food stamp, surplus food, and free school lunch programs. Now imagine that you must manage the weekly food shopping on this budget. Go to the local supermarket, and make a list of purchases that uses the money wisely. Is it possible to buy enough food for a healthy diet? Write a brief report about your experience.

Consumer Behavior

Using the library and the Internet, research the life cycle of a recent fad. From your study, determine how marketing affected the fad.

 CNN video support is available for this chapter.

GETTING READY

Introduction to Discovering

Discovering means learning or finding out new information and ideas. In your academic classes, you discover information and ideas by reading, listening to lectures and oral presentations, using the Internet, and discussing issues with your teachers and classmates. You may also discover information by giving or taking surveys.

To understand and apply the information that you discover, you may need to compare, define, develop, and classify your ideas. In other words, you will use the skills that you have studied throughout this textbook.

Warm-up Activity

Review the writing assignments in *Sample Authentic College/University Discovering Assignments*. For each assignment, decide how students discover or learn new information. There may be more than one appropriate answer. One answer is provided.

1. Hospitality Management   use the Internet and the library, discuss ideas and
   information with your teacher and classmates

2. Marketing _____

3. Sociology _____

4. Consumer Behavior _____

Grammar Preview

In this chapter, you will use several features of academic writing that you have studied in earlier chapters. Since you will be asking questions as part of the discovery process for the writing activities in this chapter, you will use the *grammar of interactive communication* in writing. This includes *asking questions* and *using you, we, and I pronouns.*

In addition, you will practice *present and past informational writing.* When you write about things that are true now, you generally use *present tense verbs* and *subject-verb agreement.* When you write about things that were true in the past, you usually need to use *past tense verbs.*

> **GLR**   See pages 221–222, 226–237, and 255–261 in the GLR for more information about the grammar of past informational writing (past tense verbs), informational writing, and interactive communication

FOCUSING

Consumer Behavior

Activity 7-1   Pre-reading Vocabulary

The following words are *italicized* in the next reading. Find the italicized words, and read the sentences. Then, match each definition to the appropriate word. One answer is provided.

1. _____ consumer
2. _____ typical
3. _____ marketing
4. _____ product
5. __a__ service
6. _____ hobby
7. _____ commercial
8. _____ data

a. anything a business does to meet customers' needs

b. radio or television advertisement

c. activity done for pleasure

d. person who buys and uses goods and services

e. facts, information

f. showing the more common characteristics of a particular group

g. activities by which goods or services are advertised and sold

h. anything grown or made with materials and labor

READING 1   UNDERSTANDING CONSUMER BEHAVIOR

Read this brief introduction to consumer behavior.

UNDERSTANDING CONSUMER BEHAVIOR

Consumer behavior is a broad field. It investigates the *products* and *services* that we buy and use and how we select and purchase those products and services. Consumer behavior also studies why we buy and use products and services and how they affect our lives. To understand consumer behavior, people in *marketing* often collect *data* to study *consumers*. Marketers like to look at consumers' backgrounds to get information, such as age, educa- 5 tion, and income. They might want to know consumers' interests and *hobbies*. Many times, they want to know how people are influenced by *commercials*, product labels, and the opinions and behaviors of family and friends. Sometimes, they look at the *typical* consumer (the average person who buys and uses products and services). This information helps businesses decide how to market their product or service most effectively. 10

Activity 7-2   Checking Your Comprehension

Use the previous reading to complete the following tasks.

1. List several things that the field of consumer behavior studies.

    _____

    _____

    _____

    _____

2. Describe what marketers study about consumers.

    _____

    _____

    _____

    _____

3. Give reasons why marketers study consumers.

    _____

    _____

    _____

    _____

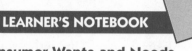

LEARNER'S NOTEBOOK

Consumer Wants and Needs

Products and services aren't successful if they don't meet consumers' wants or needs. In your learner's notebook, write a letter to the marketer of a product or a service that you feel clearly meets (or does not meet) your wants or needs. In your opinion, what makes this product or service successful (or unsuccessful)?

The Grammar of Interactive Communication in Writing: *You, We,* and *I* Pronouns

In conversations, we often ask questions, refer to the other people in the conversation as *you,* and talk about *we* and *I.* Writers sometimes use these features of conversational grammar in their academic writing. This style reaches out to the reader. The writer tries to interact with the reader. For example, in the following sentences from Reading 1, the writer uses *we* instead of *people* or *consumers.* Using *we* allows the writer to interact with the reader. *We* means that the writer and reader are alike, or that they share the same ideas.

Consumer behavior is a broad field. It investigates the products and services that *we* buy and use and how *we* select and purchase those products and services.

GLR   See pages 259–261 in the GLR for more information about the use of *you, we,* and *I* pronouns.

Activity 7-3   Identifying *You, We,* and *I* Pronouns in Interactive Writing

Read the following paragraph from a consumer behavior textbook. The author uses interactive communication in his writing. Circle the *you, we,* and *I* pronouns. An example is provided.

(We) live in a world full of sensations. Every day, we come into contact with colors, sounds, and smells. Some of these sensations occur naturally, such as the shades of an evening sky, the loud barking of a dog, or the smell of a rosebush. Other sensations come from people. The person sitting next to you in class might have bleached blonde hair, bright pink pants, and enough cologne to make your eyes water. Marketers add to these colors, 5 sounds, and smells. As a consumer, you see and hear product packages, radio and television commercials, and billboards. When you do make a decision on a purchase, you are responding to these influences.

Source: Adapted from Michael R. Solomon, *Consumer Behavior: Buying, Having, and Being,* 2nd Ed.
(Allyn and Bacon, Prentice-Hall, Inc., 1994, 48).

Activity 7-4   Analyzing the Meaning and Purpose of Interactive Writing

1. Read the following paragraph from a sociology textbook, and revise it to make it more interactive. Examples are provided.

we
What ~~people~~ think, do, and say are reflections of what ~~they~~ have learned from
                                                                                        we
parents, friends, and other members of society. Sociologists refer to this learning as socialization. All through life, people are constantly having to adapt to new situations. Think, for example, of the transition from childhood to adulthood and of the many things a young person must learn during this transition. Think of the challenges many young people face in the demands of college or the labor market.

Source: Adapted from Peter I. Rose, Penina M. Glazer, and Myron Peretz Glazer,
Sociology: Understanding Society (Prentice-Hall, Inc., 1990, 191).

2. Which do you prefer: the original excerpt or the revised excerpt with interactive writing? Why? Discuss your opinions with your teacher and classmates.

The Typical Consumer

READING 2   THE "TYPICAL" AMERICAN CONSUMER (NEWSPAPER ARTICLE)

Depending on its goals and resources, a company may focus on a certain type of American consumer, such as tennis players, people over age 50, or African Americans. It is also important for companies to understand the "typical" American consumer: the average person who makes purchases or uses services in the United States. We can identify the typical consumer from the available data, but no one can be the exact typical consumer.

1. Read the following table, which provides information about the typical American consumer. This information is based on data from the 1990 Census and marketing surveys.

2. Check (✓) each description that is similar to you. For example, if you are married and are a mother *or* a father, place a check next to "*She is married*" and "*She is a mother.*" (Because the typical American consumer is female, each statement refers to a woman.)

THE "TYPICAL" AMERICAN CONSUMER

The Basics	_____	The typical American is a white woman.
	_____	She is 32.7 years old.
	_____	She is married.
	_____	She is a mother.
	_____	Her family income was $35,225 in 1989.
Home	_____	The typical American family owns a home.
	_____	It is in the suburbs.
	_____	The total monthly ownership cost is $737.
	_____	The house has three bedrooms.
Work	_____	The typical American drives to work alone.
	_____	She works for a private manufacturing company.
	_____	She is a clerical worker.
Possessions	_____	The typical American house has two telephones.
	_____	There is no answering machine in the house.
	_____	The house has two or more television sets.
	_____	There is a VCR in the house.
	_____	The typical American does not own a gun.
	_____	She owed $2,317 on her credit cards at the end of 1991.

	_____	She generates about three pounds of garbage every day.
Characteristics	_____	The average female is 5 feet 3.7 inches tall and weighs 144 pounds. (The average American male is 5 feet 9.1 inches tall and weighs 172 pounds.)
	_____	They think this current weight is just about right.
	_____	The typical American is a Democrat.
	_____	She considers herself an environmentalist.
Health	_____	The typical American missed 5.1 days of work or school in the last year because of illness.
	_____	She was in contact with a doctor 5.5 days in the last year.
	_____	The typical American does not smoke.
Activities	_____	The typical American spent one or two hours driving yesterday.
	_____	She read a newspaper yesterday.
	_____	She watched 28 hours and 13 minutes of television last week, about one-quarter of her waking hours.

Source: Excerpts from Anne Cronin, "A Statistical Portrait of the 'Typical' American: This Is Your Life Generally Speaking," *New York Times* (July 26, 1992: ES5. Copyright 1992, The New York Times Company). Reproduced by permission.

LEARNER'S NOTEBOOK

The Typical Consumer

How do you compare to the typical American consumer? To begin, make a chart listing at least three similarities and three differences that interest you. Then, answer the following questions. Begin a paragraph for each new idea.

1. Why do you find these similarities and differences interesting?
2. What was most surprising to you about the typical U.S. consumer?
3. Do you think that you are a typical American consumer? Why or why not?

Activity 7-5   Understanding the Format and Grammar of a Table

Read the following list of suggestions for a table. With a partner, find several examples of each in "The 'Typical' American Consumer" table (page 187). Share your findings with your classmates. An example is provided.

In a table, you should

1. move from a general idea to specific details

               general idea   specific details
    Example   *Possessions*   The typical American house has two telephones.

2. have one specific idea for each statement

3. include generalizations about the present (with present tense verbs) or about the past (with past tense verbs)

Activity 7-6   Designing a Table About the Typical Student

With a small group of classmates, design a table that provides information about the typical student in your small group.

1. To begin, collect ideas by discussing your work experiences, study habits, characteristics, hobbies and interests, and so on with your group members. You can use the survey results from "The 'Typical' American Consumer" to help you collect ideas.

2. As a group, select three general categories (like work experiences) to include in your table.

3. Write two or three statements for each category (refer to Activity 7-5, the format and grammar of a table). Your statements should be true for most (or all) of the members in your group. Because this writing is about facts or habits, use grammar appropriate for present time or past time generalizations. Be sure to use appropriate time expressions (*every week, yesterday*) with your generalizations.

EXAMPLES

general category   statement with specific details
Work   The typical student in our group works part-time (5 to 25 hours each week).

general category   statement with specific details
Study Habits   The typical student studies two to three hours outside of class every day. He or she studied in the library last Saturday.

Activity 7-7   Self-editing

With your small group, complete the following tasks.

1. Read your sentences again. Are the statements true for most or all of the members in your group? Are your specific details clear and easy to understand? Make any changes needed to improve the meaning of your writing.

2. Edit for the grammar of generalizations and the format of a table. Correct any errors that you find. After you have edited for these features, check (✓) the box.

   ❑ general categories and specific statements

   ❑ one specific idea for each statement

   ❑ complete sentences

   ❑ correct verb tenses (with necessary time expressions)

   ❑ subject-verb agreement for present tense verbs or past tense forms of the verb *to be* (*was/were*)

Activity 7-8   Sharing and Discussing Your Table

Share your table with other students in your class. How are your tables similar and/or different? Which statements are most interesting to you? Which are most surprising? Discuss this with your teacher and classmates.

Surveys

People in marketing often use surveys to collect data about the consumers who buy and use their products or services. A survey asks people (called "respondents") to give their opinions. Surveys can be taken by mail, by telephone, or in person at your local grocery store or shopping mall, for example. Most surveys include a list of questions or statements for respondents to answer or complete.

READING 3   A SURVEY

Read and complete the following survey given by a video rental and music store.

VIDEO AND MUSIC PREFERENCES

To help us understand your movie and music preferences, please check (✓) the best response for you.

1. How many videos did you *rent* last month?
   _____ 0   _____ 1–2   _____ 3–4   _____ 5 or more

2. How many videos did you *purchase* last month?
   _____ 0   _____ 1–2   _____ 3–4   _____ 5 or more

3. How many movies did you see at the theater last month?
   _____ 0   _____ 1–2   _____ 3–4   _____ 5 or more

4. How many music CDs or tapes did you purchase last month?
   _____ 0   _____ 1–2   _____ 3–4   _____ 5 or more

5. What are your *music* preferences? (check all that apply)

   _____ adult contemporary   _____ country   _____ metal

   _____ alternative   _____ easy listening   _____ new age

   _____ blues   _____ instrumental   _____ rap

   _____ classical   _____ jazz   _____ rock

6. What are your *movie rental* preferences? (check all that apply)

   _____ comedy   _____ drama   _____ mystery

   _____ current releases   _____ foreign films   _____ science fiction

   _____ documentary   _____ horror

7. Do you own a CD player?   _____ Yes   _____ No

We appreciate your time and cooperation! Your responses will help us serve you better.

Activity 7-9   Comparing Results

With a small group of classmates, compare and contrast your survey results. Answer the following questions. Take notes on the lines to help you remember.

1. In what ways are you similar to your classmates? _____

   _____

   _____

2. In what ways are you different? _____

   _____

   _____

3. What surprises you about your classmates' results? Why? _____

_____

_____

4. What does not surprise you? Why? _____

_____

_____

Activity 7-10   Small Group Discussion

With a small group of classmates, discuss what the video and music store might do with the information it collects. List your ideas on another piece of paper, and share them with your teacher and other classmates.

Activity 7-11   Understanding the Format and Grammar of a Survey

Survey writers follow certain rules. Read the following list of survey rules, and, with a partner, find an example of each in the *Video and Movie Preferences* survey (page 191). Share your findings with your classmates. One example is provided.

In a survey, you should

1. include a statement to explain the purpose of the survey

To help us understand your movie and music preferences . . .

_____

2. provide brief directions for completing the survey

_____

3. use questions to seek information

_____

4. include one specific idea for each question

_____

5. include *you* and *we* pronouns to interact with the respondent

_____

6. include a statement to thank the respondent

_____

Survey Information

The questions or statements on a survey need to be clear and easy to read. Your audience (the people who complete your survey) should also understand the purpose of the survey. The purpose might be to collect consumer preferences, to learn about consumer complaints or satisfactions, and so on.

In addition, surveys need to provide useful information for the people who are seeking the data. When you design a survey, it is often best to develop and plan your questions with other people. This allows you to discuss ideas and share different opinions.

READING 4   PLANNING SURVEY QUESTIONS (DIALOG)

Read this dialog among three students. They are planning a survey to learn more about the eating habits of college students.

PLANNING SURVEY QUESTIONS

1. Peri: How many questions do we need?
2. Kerem: Ah, four to five, I think.
3. Peri: Any ideas?
4. Paul: How 'bout breakfast habits?
5. Kerem: Yeah, like, do people eat breakfast?
6. Peri: I think we should include a question on … on what they eat for breakfast, too.
7. Kerem: Yeah, good idea.
8. Peri: What do ya think about a question on where they eat lunch? And … umm … what, too.
9. Paul: Snack habits? Junk food?
10. Kerem: (laughter) Cooking meals or eating out? Ordering take-out food?
11. Peri: Yep, and, a food budget?
12. Paul: Okay, I think we have enough ideas, don't you? Let's start to write our questions.

Activity 7-12   Understanding the Characteristics of Spoken English

In Chapter 2, you studied the differences between spoken and written English. In spoken English, we often use fragments, informal vocabulary, and so on. In addition, we ask questions, refer to the other people in a conversation as *you*, and talk about *we* and *I*. Review and study the characteristics that make spoken English different from written English. If possible, find examples of these characteristics in the previous dialog, and write the line numbers below. Share your findings with your classmates.

_____ fragments   _____ repetition of words

_____ laughter   _____ conversational fillers (*umm, ah*)

_____ informal vocabulary (*yep* for *yes*)   _____ contractions (*can't* for *cannot*)

_____ turn taking   _____ eye contact

_____ questions   _____ *we, you,* and *I* pronouns

_____ immediate interaction with the other people

_____ short amounts of time to decide what to say

Activity 7-13   Turning Spoken Language into Written English

With a small group of classmates, write complete questions for a survey about eating habits of college students. Use the ideas from the dialog in Reading 4. In other words, change the spoken questions and ideas to written questions or statements. When you write your questions or statements, give your respondents a choice to make (like *yes/no*, *always/usually/never*, or *0–1 days/2–3 days*).

EXAMPLE

SPOKEN   "Yeah, like, do people eat breakfast?"

WRITTEN   Do you eat breakfast during the week?

            _____ always   _____ usually   _____ sometimes   _____ never

            or

            I eat breakfast during the week.

            _____ always   _____ usually   _____ sometimes   _____ never

GLR   See pages 256–258 in the GLR for more information about question formation.

1. SPOKEN   I think we should include a question on ... on what they eat for breakfast, too.

    WRITTEN _____

             _____

2. SPOKEN   What do ya think about a question on where they eat lunch? And ... umm
   ... what, too.

   WRITTEN _____

   _____

3. SPOKEN   Snack habits? Junk food?

   WRITTEN _____

   _____

4. SPOKEN   (laughter) Cooking meals or eating out? Ordering take-out food?

   WRITTEN _____

   _____

5. SPOKEN   Yep, and, a food budget?

   WRITTEN _____

   _____

Activity 7-14   Designing Your Own Survey

With a small group of classmates, design a survey about one of the following. You will
give your survey to respondents *not* in this class. If possible, design your survey on the
computer.

- preferred restaurants and/or meals
- favorite recreational and entertainment activities
- preferred stores, products, and/or brand names
- popular majors, classes, and/or professors
- (ask your teacher about other ideas you might have)

1. To help you design your own survey, review the *Video and Music Preferences* survey
   on page 191 and the format/grammar ideas for a survey (Activity 7-11) on page 192.

2. With your group members, decide what you will survey. Discuss possible questions
   or statements for your respondents and take notes about your ideas.

3. Write four or five questions/statements for your survey. There should be just one
   idea for each item, and your items should give people choices to make (*yes/no,
   always/usually/never*).

4. Include a statement to explain the purpose of your survey, brief directions for completing the survey, and a statement to thank the respondent.

5. When you finish, make a copy of the survey for each member of your group.

LEARNER'S NOTEBOOK

Designing a Survey

In your learner's notebook, describe your group's experiences when you developed your survey. Answer the following questions. Begin a paragraph for each new idea.

1. Was designing a survey difficult? Easy? Explain your opinions.
2. What did you learn? Be specific.
3. What did you enjoy/not enjoy about survey writing? Explain your opinions.

Activity 7-15   Providing Peer Support

Give and receive suggestions about your and other surveys by completing the following tasks.

1. Each group member from your small group in Activity 7-14 says a number: 1, 2, 3, or 4.

2. All students who are number 1 form one group. All students who are number 2 form another group, and so on.

3. In these new groups, share and read each group member's survey.

    If you don't understand a survey question or statement, ask the author about it.

    If you have a suggestion, give it to the author.

    If you like a survey question or statement, draw an X next to it.

Activity 7-16   Revising and Editing

Improve your survey by completing the following tasks.

1. Return to your first group.
    a. Share the comments and suggestions from your peer review group.
    b. Listen to the comments and suggestions from other group members, and together revise your survey to make it better.
    c. Edit each sentence for the following, and correct any errors you find. When you have edited for these features, check (✓) the box.

        ❑ a statement of purpose, directions, and a thank you
        ❑ correct question formation/complete sentences for your statements

❏ one specific idea for each item
❏ correct verb tenses (with necessary time expressions)
❏ subject-verb agreement
❏ appropriate use of *you* and *we* pronouns
❏ capitalization and punctuation

2. Each group should make 20 copies of your completed survey to give to respondents *not* in your class.

Activity 7-17   Giving a Survey

1. You will give your survey to five respondents not in your class, but before you ask respondents to complete your survey, practice role-playing with a partner. One person should be the person giving the survey. The other person should be the respondent. Possible questions and thank you's follow.

Excuse me. Could you complete this survey for my class? It should only take a few minutes.

Would you please fill out this short survey? It's for a class that I'm taking.

Pardon me. Do you have a couple minutes to complete a survey for me?

If the response is *no*,	If the response is *yes*,
Thank you anyway.	*Thank you.*
No problem.	*Thanks a lot.*
	Thanks. I appreciate it.

2. Each member of your group should give your survey to five respondents who are not in your class.

LEARNER'S NOTEBOOK

Experiences Giving a Survey

Write a paragraph to describe your experiences giving your survey. In your paragraph, compare and/or contrast two or three experiences you had with respondents and your survey. Use comparatives or logical organizers that show similarities and differences.

GLR See pages 212–215 and pages 230–231 in the GLR for more information about comparisons and logical organizers.

Collecting and Reporting Data

READING 5   VIDEO AND MUSIC PREFERENCES (TALLY SHEET)

After marketers give surveys, they tally the survey results. *To tally* means to count up or record responses. Read this informal tally sheet for the *Video and Music Preferences* survey on page 191.

**VIDEO AND MUSIC PREFERENCES
TALLY SHEET**

Date _____ February 5 _____

Total number of respondents __20__

Name of the person who gave the survey _____ Alper C. _____

1. How many videos did you *rent* last month?

   __卌 I__ 0   __卌 III__ 1–2   __IIII__ 3–4   __II__ 5 or more

2. How many videos did you *purchase* last month?

   __卌 II__ 0   __卌 卌 I__ 1–2   __I__ 3–4   __I__ 5 or more

3. How many movies did you see at the theater last month?

   __卌 II__ 0   __卌 卌__ 1–2   __I__ 3–4   __II__ 5 or more

4. How many music CDs or tapes did you purchase last month?

   __卌__ 0   __IIII__ 1–2   __卌 I__ 3–4   __卌__ 5 or more

5. What are your *music* preferences? (check all that apply)

   __II__ adult contemporary   __I__ country   _____ metal

   __III__ alternative   __I__ easy listening   __II__ new age

   _____ blues   __II__ instrumental   _____ rap

   __卌__ classical   __IIII__ jazz   __卌 I__ rock

6. What are your *movie rental* preferences? (check all that apply)

   __卌__ comedy   __卌__ drama   __III__ mystery

   __卌 卌__ current releases   __I__ foreign films   _____ science fiction

   _____ documentary   __II__ horror

7. Do you own a CD player? __15__ Yes   __5__ No

Activity 7-18   Understanding Tally Sheets

Use the previous tally sheet to answer the following questions. Write T (true) or F (false) on the line next to each statement.

_____ **1.** Most respondents rented three or four videos last month.

_____ **2.** Most respondents prefer going to the theater instead of renting videos.

_____ **3.** Fifteen respondents purchased music CDs or tapes last month.

_____ **4.** Only three respondents enjoy classical music.

_____ **5.** Current releases are the most popular movie rentals.

_____ **6.** Most respondents do not own a CD player.

Activity 7-19   Developing and Analyzing a Tally Sheet

Develop and analyze a tally sheet by completing the following tasks:

1. With your first group (from Activity 7-14), develop a tally sheet to collect your group's data (survey results).

2. Discuss your survey results with your group. Answer the following questions. Take notes on the lines to help you remember.

   a. What were the most common responses? _____

   _____

   _____

   b. What were the least common responses? _____

   _____

   _____

   c. What response(s) were answered almost equally? _____

   _____

   _____

   d. What is the most surprising result? Why? _____

   _____

   _____

e. What survey questions or statements did respondents have trouble with? Why?

_____

_____

3. Draw a chart or graph that illustrates the results of your survey. (For a review on chart and graph design, see Chapter 2, page 46.)

Activity 7-20   Planning a Presentation of Your Survey and Data

Each group will give a five-minute oral presentation to your class. The purpose of the presentation is to share your survey, your results, and the experiences you had when you gave your survey. Your group will have five minutes, including time for questions from the class.

1. With your group members, plan and take notes about your presentation. As you discuss this presentation with your group, be sure to plan to:

   a. introduce the main idea of your survey

   b. briefly explain the data that your group collected

   c. organize your material

   d. use your chart or graph

   e. have every group member participate

   f. leave time for possible questions from the class

2. With your group, decide how you will present your survey results to the class. Make a plan for your presentation. You can use these questions when you are planning.

   a. Who will introduce the presentation? _____

   b. Who will describe the funny or interesting experiences that your group members had? _____

   c. Who will present the survey and data from the survey? _____

   d. Who will prepare the chart or graph for the presentation? _____

   e. Who will answer questions from the class? _____

   f. _____

   g. _____

Activity 7-21   Suggestions for Giving an Effective Presentation

With your group members, discuss and practice the suggestions that follow for an effective presentation.

1. Do not write out your entire presentation. Instead, put ideas and important words on small note cards to use during your presentation. You will not read to your audience, but use the notes as a helpful reminder.

2. Practice your presentation with your group members several times. This will help you give the best presentation possible.

3. Look at your audience when you are talking. Smile, speak loudly and clearly, and put intonation in your voice.

4. Make sure your chart or graph is large enough for your audience to see.

5. Provide a handout of your chart or graph. Your chart should include a title and the names of the presenters.

6. Practice answering questions that you think your audience might ask.

Activity 7-22   Listening to Presentations

Listen to the presentations by your classmates, and take notes about their presentations on another piece of paper. Answer some of the following questions in your notes. Your teacher might choose to compile the notes as feedback for the presentations. In addition, you will use these notes to write an entry in your learner's notebook.

1. What was the main point of the presentation?

2. Did you understand the charts or graphs? Why or why not?

3. What did you learn from the presentation?

4. What was the best part of the presentation?

LEARNER'S NOTEBOOK

Group Presentations

Use your notes from the previous activity to write about one of the presentations. In your opinion, which group presentation was the best? Why do you think it was the best? Give specific examples and reasons to support your opinion.

PUTTING IT ALL TOGETHER

FINAL WRITING ASSIGNMENT: SURVEY AND DATA COLLECTION

Write two or more paragraphs about your survey and data collection. Because you and your group members have already given an oral presentation about your survey, much of your planning for this paper is complete. You will, however, need to change your ideas and spoken English from your presentation into written English for this paper. In addition, attach a copy of your group's survey, the tally sheet, and the chart/graph to your paper.

Organizing and Developing Your Ideas

1. Choose two of the following ideas to write about.

   a. *Describe* your survey and its purpose.

   b. *Classify* the responses to your survey and give the results.

   c. *Compare and/or contrast* your survey results with what you thought the results would be.

d. *Provide experiences* that you and your group members had when you designed your survey and gave it to respondents.

e. *Give reasons* why you did or did not enjoy the survey activity. Support your reasons with *specific examples.*

2. Begin each paragraph with a general statement that introduces the main idea of your paragraph.

3. Then, develop each paragraph by writing four or five sentences that use description, classification, comparisons, personal experience, reasons, and/or examples.

4. Use logical organizers to help the reader move from one idea to the next in each paragraph.

5. In addition to logical organizers, use other cohesion devices in your writing (repetition of key words/phrases, pronouns, different forms of the same word).

Editing Your Writing

1. Read your paper again. Do you develop your ideas in two different ways? Do you move from general ideas to specific details? Make any changes needed to improve the meaning of your writing.

2. Edit your paper for the following, and correct any errors that you find. When you have edited for these features, check (✓) the box.

   ☐ complete sentences

   ☐ correct verb tenses (with necessary time expressions)

   ☐ subject-verb agreement for present tense verbs or past tense forms of the verb *to be* (*was/were*)

   ☐ appropriate logical organizers and punctuation

   ☐ additional cohesion devices (repetition of key words/phrases, pronouns, different forms of the same word)

(For a review of the grammar of informational writing, past time narrative writing, and so on, see the appropriate chapters in this textbook.)

Providing Peer Support

Exchange papers with a partner, and read each other's report.

1. For your partner's paragraphs, <u>underline</u> each general statement.

2. Tell your partner what you like best about each paragraph. In the margin of each paragraph, write a statement such as:

    I had an experience just like this!

    This survey result is very interesting.

    I enjoyed reading about your survey and survey responses.

3. Give one suggestion to improve your partner's writing. In the margin of each paragraph, write a statement such as:

    I don't understand this information about your data collection.

    Try to write more about your personal experiences here.

    You should explain your survey results more.

4. Ask one question about information you need or would like to know. In the margin of each paragraph, write a question such as:

    Did you get the results you expected?

    I don't understand. Can you include an example here?

    How did this experience make you feel?

    Could you please provide more details about your experiences?

Revising Your Writing

1. With your partner, discuss her or his ideas and suggestions for your writing.

2. Make several changes to improve your writing.

Finalizing Your Writing

1. Make the corrections that you decided on during the self-editing and peer-support processes. You may want to refer to the check list on page 203 again.

2. Rewrite your paper to submit to your teacher.

In your academic classes, you will often complete surveys. You might complete surveys that

- give your instructor information about your educational background
- evaluate your instructors at the end of the class
- give your opinions about a textbook
- tell your department or college what you like or don't like about a program
- help a friend gather information for a research paper or a graduate thesis

DISCUSSION

With your teacher and classmates, discuss other ways that you might use surveys in college or university.

Grammar
and
Language
Reference

This Grammar and Language Reference (GLR) provides grammar explanations, examples, and activities. The grammar outlined in the GLR is often found in academic writing. The authentic examples are from textbooks and student writing.

CONTENTS

Section 1 Grammar Common to All Types of Academic Writing 210

   A Basic Sentence Structure 210
   B Comparison 212
   C Prepositional Phrases 215
   D Relative Clauses 217
   E Non-Restrictive Relative Clauses and
      Appositives 219

Section 2 Grammar of Past Time Narrative Writing 221

   A Overview 221
   B Past Tense Verbs 221
   C Chronological Organizers 223
   D Proper Nouns 224
   E Personal Pronouns 224

Section 3 Grammar of Informational Writing 226

   A Overview 226
   B Complex Noun Phrases 227
   C Generic Articles and Nouns 229
   D Logical Organizers 230
   E Passive Sentences 232
   F Present Tense Verbs 233
   G Subject-Verb Agreement 235

Section 4 Grammar of Written Definitions 238

   A Overview 238
   B Present Tense Verbs 239
   C Generic Articles and Nouns 239
   D Categorizing Nouns 240
   E Relative Clauses 241
   F Definition Structures 242

Section 5 Grammar of Persuasive Writing 246

   A Overview 246
   B Structures to Control the Strength of Generalizations: Opinion Structures 246
   C Structures to Control the Strength of Generalizations: Adverbs of Frequency 247
   D Structures to Control the Strength of Generalizations: Modal Auxiliaries 250
   E Structures to Control the Strength of Generalizations: Expressions of Quantity 252
   F Conditional Sentences 254

Section 6 Grammar of Interactive Communication in Writing 255

   A Overview 255
   B Using Questions 256
   C Using *You, We,* and *I* Pronouns 259

Section 7 Basic Grammar Terminology 262

   A Adjectives 262
   B Adverbs and Adverbials 263
   C Articles and Determiners 263
   D Auxiliary Verbs 264
   E Comma Splices 264
   F Complements 265
   G Conjunctions 265
   H Fragments 266
   I Nouns 267
   J Noun Phrases 267
   K Objects 268
   L Phrases and Clauses 269
   M Prepositions 269
   N Pronouns 270
   O Sentences 270
   P Sentence Adverbials 271
   Q Subjects of Sentences 272
   R Verbs in Sentences: Active or Passive 272
   S Verb Forms 273
   T Verb Tenses 273
   U Other Words Used to Talk about Verbs: Infinitives and Participles 274

Section 1: Grammar Common to All Types of Academic Writing

1A   Basic Sentence Structure

When you write sentences, it is important to understand the basic sentence structure of English. The basic sentence structure is made up of *subject + verb + (object/complement) + (adverbial)*. (For more information on basic grammar terminology, see page 262 in GLR Section 7.)

Sometimes, the basic sentence will have only a subject and verb or a compound subject and/or compound verb. In the examples, the subject is underlined once, and the verb is underlined twice. (See page 272 for information on compound subjects and compound verbs.)	Everyone dreams. They cook and clean.
Some verbs must have an object or complement. In this case, the basic sentence might have a subject, verb, and object or a subject, verb, and complement.	subject verb object These people speak Romance languages. subject verb complement The U.S. is a multi-cultural country.
Some sentences have only a subject, verb, and adverbial. The sentence might have more than one adverbial. Adverbials can often move to other positions in the basic sentence.	subject verb adverbials adverbials We dream (one to two hours) (each night). adverbial subject adverbial verb (Today,) teenagers (often) work.
Sometimes, all four parts of the sentence are used. In this type of sentence, the parts are *subject, verb, object/complement*, and *adverbial*.	subject verb direct object adverbial I finished (high school) (in my home country). adverbial subject verb complement (In Ukraine,) all colleges are (free).

Activity 1-1 Identifying the Parts of a Sentence (Subject, Verb, Object/Complement)

Read these sentences. They are from a grammar and writing course syllabus. For each sentence, underline the complete subject with one line. Underline the complete verb with a double line (two lines). Circle direct objects or complements.

EXAMPLE   <u>This syllabus</u> <u>provides</u> (a general plan).

1. This is a writing and grammar course.
2. We use a communicative approach.
3. Attendance is important.
4. We will not finish the entire textbook.
5. We will complete many writing assignments.
6. I do not accept late homework assignments.
7. You must pass the final examination.
8. The final examination is comprehensive.
9. Schedule changes may be necessary.

Activity 1-2 Identifying the Parts of a Sentence (Subject, Verb, Object/Complement, Adverbial)

Read this excerpt from a book about study skills. Some of the sentences are boldfaced. For each sentence in bold, underline the complete subject with one line. Underline the complete verb with a double line (two lines). Circle direct objects or complements. Place parentheses ( ) around adverbials. One answer is already given.

GET TO KNOW YOUR TEXTBOOK

(1) **Your textbook is an excellent study tool.** (2) **It is a bank of information.** Your textbook contains a table of contents. (3) **<u>The table of contents</u> <u>lists</u> (the chapters) (in the book).** In addition, (4) **many books have an index at the end of the book.** An index helps you find what you are looking for. Some books also have appendices. Appendices, which include additional useful information, may also be located at the end of textbooks.

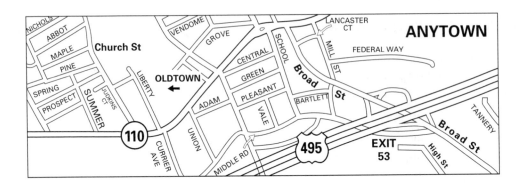

(5) **A road map and a textbook are similar.** (6) **A road map shows the main towns and cities in dark, large print.** In a textbook, the main topics and ideas are also boldfaced. Boldfaced means that the important ideas are blacker and heavier than the rest of the print. This boldfaced print shows that the words are important. The reader should pay attention to them. When you travel, (7) **a map guides you from one place to another place.** A textbook also leads you from topic to topic. It uses larger titles and headings to guide you. When you read, study those titles and headings. They will give you information about main ideas. Boldfaced and large print is not the only print that is used to focus your attention on key words and ideas. As you read sentence after sentence in a book, (8) **your eyes follow the words along the printed lines.** Suddenly, the text contains print that looks different. The print looks like script rather than printing. This style of print is called *italics*. Italics shows that (9) **the word or sentence is important.** The use of italics tells you to pay special attention to the words and their meaning.

Source: Adapted from Sigmund Kalina, *How to Sharpen Your Study Skills* (New York: Lothrop, Lee, and Shepard Company, A Division of William Morrow & Company, Inc., 43–46). © 1975 by Sigmund Kalina. Reproduced by permission.

1B Comparison

Comparison is one of the most common and most useful tools for students. It includes explaining how things are different and how they are similar. When you explain how things are different, you are contrasting. When you explain how things are similar, you are comparing. However, when professors ask you to compare two things, they often want you to look at both the differences and the similarities.

LOGICAL ORGANIZERS: WORDS OF DIFFERENCE

Four common logical organizers that show difference are *but, however, on the other hand,* and *in contrast.* These words show that two ideas or things are not alike (not similar). Study the use of these words in the following examples. (For more information about logical organizers, see page 230, GLR Section 3.)

but	My father needs fresh air, **but** the air is very polluted in Seoul.
however	I didn't see a good future for me in Russia; **however,** in the U.S., there are a lot of possibilities for everyone.
	I didn't see a good future for me in Russia. **However,** in the U.S., there are a lot of possibilities for everyone.
on the other hand	In my hometown, young students wear black pants and white T-shirts to school; **on the other hand,** older girls wear long white dresses and white pants.
	In my hometown, young students wear black pants and white T-shirts to school. **On the other hand,** older girls wear long white dresses and white pants.
in contrast	The towns in my country are developing quickly; **in contrast,** there is less progress in the villages.
	The towns in my country are developing quickly. **In contrast,** there is less progress in the villages.

LOGICAL ORGANIZERS: WORDS OF SIMILARITY

Sometimes, when you compare two ideas or things, you want to focus on their likenesses or similarities. Three common logical organizers that show similarity are *both, also,* and *too.* Study the use of these words in the following examples. (For more information about logical organizers, see page 230, GLR Section 3.)

both	**Both** coffee and emeralds are important products in Colombia.
	Coffee and emeralds are **both** important products in Colombia.
also	The people in my country are changing their lifestyles. They speak French at home. They **also** wear European clothes.
	The people in my country are changing their lifestyles. They speak French at home. They wear European clothes **also**.
	The people in my country are changing their lifestyles. They speak French at home. **Also,** they wear European clothes.
too	People from Morocco are helpful and honest. They are hospitable, **too**.

COMPARATIVES

Using comparatives is another way to show the difference between two ideas or things. In the following example, "home ownership" and "apartment renting" is being compared. *More expensive than* is the comparative.

EXAMPLE   Home ownership is **more expensive than** apartment renting.

Follow these rules when you are forming the comparatives of adjectives.

When you have one-syllable adjectives, use the adjective + *er.*	fast—*faster* slow—*slower* tall—*taller*
When you have two-syllable adjectives ending in a consonant + *y,* change the *y* to *i* and add *er.*	friendly—*friendlier* busy—*busier*
The word *more* comes before all other adjectives.	intelligent—*more intelligent* interesting—*more interesting*
The word *less* can also come before all other adjectives. *Less* means "not more."	difficult—*less difficult* beautiful—*less beautiful*

Activity 1-3 Understanding Syllables and Comparatives

1. Count the syllables in each of these adjectives, and write the number on the line.
2. Then, write a comparative form of that adjective.

EXAMPLES	poor	1	*poorer*
	relaxing	3	*more relaxing*

a. shy   _____   _____

b. happy   _____   _____

c. energetic _____ _____

d. short   _____   _____

e. assertive _____ _____

f. windy   _____   _____

g. cool   _____   _____

Continued

    h. productive   ____   _____

    i. cheap   ____   _____

    j. thirsty   ____   _____

Activity 1-4 Writing Sentences of Comparison

Write five sentences that describe the differences and similarities of a class you had in the past and this class. In your sentences, use a variety of logical organizers for difference, logical organizers for similarity, and comparatives.

1C   Prepositional Phrases

Prepositions are words like *of, in,* and *across.* Prepositions are used in three ways in English. Recognizing these different uses can help you learn to use prepositions more accurately.

Adverbial Phrases Prepositions are often used to make adverbial phrases. These adverbial phrases tell *where, when,* and *how.*	where **In modern North America,** divorce is fairly easy and common. how We can separate most of Europe **into three major language groups.**
Complex Noun Phrases Prepositions are very frequently found attached to a noun in a complex noun phrase.	**Young people in the early 1960s** made blue jeans their special dress. Nowadays, many young people wear **blue jeans with holes.**
Prepositional Verbs Prepositions are also closely connected to some verbs and need to be learned as part of the structure of those verbs. (See the website at http://www.gsu.edu/~wwwesl/egw/verbprep.htm for a list of these prepositional verbs.)	The term geography **comes from** two Greek words—*geo* for earth and *graphia* for write about. Human geographers **focus on** people and their patterns of settlement and activity.

(For a list of common prepositions, see Appendix B: Common Prepositions.)

Activity 1-5 Recognizing Three Ways That Prepositions Are Used in English

1. In the following sentences, underline the prepositions and place parentheses ( ) around the whole phrase.
2. Then, identify the type of preposition: (a) adverbial phrase, (b) complex noun phrase, or (c) prepositional verb.

EXAMPLES   To succeed (in the U.S. classroom), you must learn the expectations and styles
                                          a
                 (of your teachers).
                   b

                 The term geography comes (from two Greek words).
                                            c

a. In our society, most jobs require special knowledge or skills.

b. My classmates worked in groups, and we exchanged ideas and opinions.

c. Edward Tylor stated that culture includes knowledge, beliefs, art, law, customs, and any other habits of man.

d. The teacher and students approved of the revised test schedule.

e. You should complete your homework before class.

f. Stereotypes are exaggerated beliefs about people.

g. I don't think people in the United States play or like soccer.

h. My teacher does not approve of talking during tests.

i. In your learner's notebook, write your feelings, your thoughts, and your opinions.

j. The students listened to the teacher's explanation.

1D   Relative Clauses

Relative clauses are added to nouns to give more information and to make the nouns more exact. In this example, a relative clause is added to the noun *people*.	Researchers are people **who study a subject to learn new facts.**
In this next example, the writer has a sentence about the noun *trait*. She wants to add more information to this noun.	Dependability is a **trait.**
She starts with a sentence about that idea and changes the sentence to make it into a relative clause. She has to change the clause to get the best wording—using the pronoun *that* rather than repeating the same noun *trait*.	**This trait** is valued by restaurant owners. **that** is valued by restaurant owners
She adds the relative clause to the noun to make the complex noun phrase: a *trait that is valued by restaurant owners.*	Dependability is **a trait that is valued by restaurant owners.**
When you write sentences with relative clauses, you must understand relative pronouns. **Relative pronouns** replace the subject or object of the sentence. Relative pronouns are words like *who, whom, which, that,* and some others. The clauses created with these relative pronouns are called **relative clauses** or **adjective clauses.** (See Pronouns, page 270, and Phrases and Clauses, page 269.)	Levi's family was part of a small community of German Jews **who lived in Buttenheim.** One job **that city residents don't do** is farming.
The relative pronouns *who* and *whom* are for people. *Who* is a subject pronoun, and *whom* is an object pronoun. In spoken English, *that* is sometimes used for people. In these sentences, brackets [ ] are placed around the relative clauses.	A sleepwalker is a person [**who** walks around while asleep]. He was a teacher [**whom** everyone admired]. The teacher [**that** I had last term] rarely lectured in class.
The relative pronouns *that* and *which* are for animals and things. *That* and *which* can be both subject pronouns and object pronouns. *Which* can also be used for non-restrictive relative clauses. (See Non-Restrictive Relative Clauses, page 219.)	Electroencephalographs are machines [**that** record activity in the brain]. In the U.S., places with populations of 2,500 or more are defined as urban, [**which** means "characteristic of a city."]

Activity 1-6 Using Appropriate Relative Pronouns

Complete each formal definition of the following nouns with an appropriate relative pronoun. (For a review of the formal definition format, see Chapter 4, page 104, or the GLR, Section 4, page 238.) You may use each pronoun more than once, and there may be more than one appropriate answer.

- which
- that
- who
- whom

EXAMPLE   Legwork is work __which/that__ requires looking for and collecting information, such as by a reporter or detective.

1. A consumer is the ordinary person _____ buys and uses goods and services.

2. Luncheons are events _____ include lunch and usually speeches.

3. Colleagues are people with _____ one works.

4. A person's mother tongue is the first language _____ he/she speaks as a child.

5. A mayor is a person _____ is the head of a city's government.

Activity 1-7 Writing Definitions Using Relative Clauses

1. Select three nouns from your native language, and write them on a piece of paper. Then, in English, write a definition for each word, using the formal definition format and the grammar of written definitions. (For a review of this format and grammar, see Chapter 4, page 104, or page 238 in the GLR Section 4.) Do not tell your classmates the English meanings of your nouns.

EXAMPLES

pastel (Spanish)   (Cake)   is a dessert that people eat on their birthdays.

poza (Russian)   (A rose)   is a red flower that women often receive from their lovers.

2. Exchange papers with a classmate who does not speak your native language. Your classmate will try to guess the English words from your definitions. If your classmate cannot guess your words, rewrite your definitions to provide clearer details in your complex noun phrases: noun + relative clause.

1E   Non-Restrictive Relative Clauses and Appositives

Writers often need to give background information about people and places. This can be done with a non-restrictive relative clause or an appositive.

A **non-restrictive relative clause** has relative clause structure. It gives additional information about a noun. However, the noun is so completely identified that no additional information is needed to specify which noun. For example, a proper noun of a person (like Dr. Raymond Dart) tells you exactly who is meant. Non-restrictive relative clauses are separated from the noun and the rest of the sentence with commas.	In 1924, Dr. Raymond Dart, **who was a Dutch professor working in South Africa,** discovered the remains of the earliest known humanlike animals. The Cherokee Indians ended up in Indian Territory, **which was an area that later became part of the state of Oklahoma.**
An **appositive** is a non-restrictive relative clause that has been reduced by removing the relative pronoun and the verb *to be*. The examples show how appositives give information about people and places.	Dr. Nathaniel Kleitman, **an important sleep researcher,** worked at the University of Chicago. Prospectors found a small amount of gold near Pikes Peak, **an area in Colorado Territory.**
Writers often use non-restrictive relative clauses or appositives to give background information about a noun. This background information may include a person's professional title or other credentials. This may also include an explanation of a place or thing.	Educational advances were among the main accomplishments of the women's rights movement before 1850. For example, in 1836, Mary Lyon, **a Massachusetts teacher,** opened Mount Holyoke, **which was the nation's first permanent women's college.**

Activity 1-8 Recognizing Non-Restrictive Relative Clauses and Appositives

Place brackets [ ] around the non-restrictive relative clauses and the appositives in the following paragraphs. Then, draw an arrow from each non-restrictive relative clause or appositive to the noun it is describing. One answer is provided.

Paragraph 1

John F. Kennedy's father, [Joseph Kennedy,] was a businessman who made a huge fortune. Joseph Kennedy had nine children (John was the second oldest), and he gave each of them a million dollars when they became twenty-one. He also planned what his sons should do. Joseph Kennedy, Jr., the oldest boy, was to be the family politician. John—his family called him Jack—was to be a writer and teacher. He went to Harvard.

Source: Wyatt Blassingame, *The Look-It-Up Book of Presidents* (New York, Random House, 1996, 120).

Paragraph 2

The Sumerian people invented cuneiform, the first system of writing. In modern times, no one could read cuneiform until the secret of its meaning was unlocked, or decoded. This was done by Sir Henry Rawlinson, a 19th century British army officer and scholar. After two years of work, Rawlinson, who studied the cuneiform writings carved on a wall in Iran, was able to decode the first two paragraphs of the writings.

Source: Adapted from Henry Brun, *Global Studies: Civilizations of the Past and Present* (Amsco School Publications, Inc., 1995, 22).

Paragraph 3

In 1938, Prime Minister Neville Chamberlain of Great Britain and the leaders of France and Italy met in Munich with Adolf Hitler, the Nazi dictator, to discuss the problem of Czechoslovakia. Hitler had made many aggressive moves on the pretext of reclaiming German territory lost in World War I. Britain and other nations watched, but did nothing, until 1938. Then, Hitler moved to take the Sudetenland, which was a part of Czechoslovakia where Germans lived. At the Munich meeting, a deal was made. Hitler could have the Sudetenland in exchange for his promise to halt any further aggression. But Hitler had no intention of stopping with the Sudetenland.

Source: Adapted from Jodine Mayberry, *Leaders Who Changed the 20th Century* (Steck-Vaughn Company, 1994, 14).

Section 2: Grammar of Past Time Narrative Writing

2A   Overview

Past time narrative is used in writing where the writer tells a story of something that happened in the past. Past time narrative is used to write biographies, autobiographies, and case studies. It is also used to write history. In addition, it is often used to give past time examples to support ideas in a piece of writing.

Past time narrative writing requires you to use several grammatical features that are frequently found in this type of writing. These features include • <u>past tense verbs</u> (underlined twice) • chronological organizers (in parentheses) • <u>proper nouns</u> (underlined once) • *personal pronouns* (in italics) This excerpt shows how these grammatical features are used in academic writing.	(Early in 1879) <u>the Electoral College</u> <u>voted</u> for <u>the first U.S. President.</u> Every elector <u>voted</u> for <u>George Washington.</u> *They* <u>selected</u> another honored leader of <u>the Revolution, John Adams,</u> to be <u>the Vice President.</u> (Then), (on April 30) <u>Washington</u> <u>began</u> *his* first term.

2B   Past Tense Verbs

The **simple past** tense is the most frequently used verb in past time narrative. It is used to tell the basic story of the narrative. It is also used to give facts about the past and about things that began and ended in the past. For most verbs, you form the past tense by adding *ed* to the simple present tense. These verbs are called **regular verbs** (like *produced* in the example). For **irregular verbs** (like *became*), you form the past tense by changing the spelling (and pronunciation) of the basic verb. (For a list of common irregular verbs, see Appendix D: Irregular Verbs or the website at http://www.gsu.edu/~www.esl/egw/jones.htm.)	In 1973, the U.S. **produced** 400 million square yards of denim. Jeans **became** the symbol of defiance against authority. *Continued*

The **past progressive** is used to discuss a past event that happened over a period of time. It can also be used to write about two past time events that happened at the same time. You form the past progressive by using *was/were* and the *ing* form of the verb.	They joined many other immigrants who **were struggling** to fulfill their dreams in America. While men **were working** on the streets, children **were running and playing**.
The **past perfect** is used infrequently. The past perfect emphasizes that one past time event was completed before another past time event. You form the past perfect by combining *had* + the past participle of the verb. (For a list of past participles of irregular verbs, see Appendix D: Irregular Verbs or the website at http://www.gsu.edu/~www.esl/egw/jones.htm.)	They pushed against fashionably dressed "uptown ladies" who **had come** to meet passengers from a ship. Less than a year after Levi Strauss **had arrived** to the U.S., miners discovered gold in California.

Activity 2-1 Using Simple Past Tense

Read the following passage about Dr. Elizabeth Blackwell, the first female to earn a medical degree in the United States. Then, choose an appropriate verb from the list, place a check next to the verb, and write the correct past tense form of that verb on the line. There may be more than one appropriate answer, but use each word only once. One answer is provided.

- catch
- buy
- go
- accept
- lose
- study
- earn
- apply
- ruin
- be
- be
- return
- √ receive
- work

In 1849, when Elizabeth Blackwell ___*received*___ her M.D., or doctor of medicine degree,

20,000 people _____ there to watch her become the first woman to earn

a medical degree in the United States. However, she did not always get that kind of attention.

Blackwell _____ to 29 medical schools before Geneva College in New York

_____ her. And once there, many of the other students did not take her seriously.

Despite poor treatment from fellow students, Blackwell _____ an

excellent student. But after she _____ her medical degree, no American

hospital would hire her. So, Dr. Blackwell, who was British, _____

Continued

to England and _____ in a British hospital. Later, she

_____ midwifery in France. Unfortunately, though, she

_____ an illness from a baby and _____ the

sight of one eye. This _____ her hopes of becoming a surgeon.

    Eventually, she _____ to New York, where she _____ her

own hospital, the New York Infirmary for Women and Children, in 1857.

Source: Adapted from Sheila Keenan, *Scholastic Encyclopedia of Women in the United States* (New York: Scholastic Inc., 1996, 31).

2C   Chronological Organizers

An important feature of narratives is the use of chronological organization. This means that the story is told in the order in which it occurred. Chronological organizers are words that help the reader understand when events happened in a past narrative.

Chronological organizers can be words like *first, next, later,* and *then.*	**Later,** industries used refined oil to lubricate (grease) machines.
Chronological organizers can also be phrases such as: *at first* *before that* *100 years ago* *in 1862* *February 4, 1995*	**In 1973,** United States textile mills produced 400 million square yards of denim. **At first,** oil was made into kerosene, a fuel burned in lamps. On **February 26, 1829,** Levi was born.
In addition, chronological organizers can be clauses such as: *when he heard* *after she had finished*	**When Levi first saw** New York, the city was full of activity. **After Levi had heard** this remark, he brought his brown canvas to a tailor.

Activity 2-2 Recognizing Chronological Organizers

Return to the passage in Activity 2-1, and highlight all the chronological organizers. Label the chronological organizers as words, phrases, or clauses.

                        phrase

EXAMPLE   **In 1849,** when Elizabeth Blackwell _____received_____ her M.D., or doctor of medicine degree . . .

2D   Proper Nouns

Narratives involve the use of proper nouns to give the names of the people, places, events, and so forth that were involved in the story.

Proper nouns are usually the names of people and places.	**Noah Webster** was born in **West Hartford, Connecticut,** and lived in various places, including **Goshen, New York.**
When you are writing about people, the person's full name is usually given first. Later in the passage, this person is often referred to by a shorter form of her/his name. Usually, a person's family name is used.	**Noah Webster** published *An American Dictionary* in 1828. **Webster's** books strongly influenced the way Americans used the English language.
People are also referred to by using the appropriate personal pronoun.	**He** wanted to replace the standard British texts with American ones.

2E   Personal Pronouns

Because narratives can have many proper nouns to refer to particular people, places, events, and so forth, personal pronouns are another feature of this type of writing. The most difficult task for the writer is to be sure that the reader knows exactly what the pronoun is referring to.

Personal pronouns have a subject form, an object form, and one or more possessive forms.	Subject pronouns: *I, you, he, she, it, we, they* Object pronouns: *me, you, him, her, it, us, them* Possessive pronouns: *my/mine, your/yours, his, her/hers, its, our/ours*
After a noun is mentioned once, a pronoun can be used to refer back to the noun. Pronouns must match nouns in *number.* In other words, singular pronouns refer to singular nouns, and plural pronouns refer to plural nouns.	**Edgar Allan Poe** wrote some of the best stories of **his** time. **He** wrote both detective stories and horror stories. <div align="right">Continued</div>

Pronouns must also match the noun in *gender*. *He* and *she* refer back to masculine and feminine nouns.	**Sarah Josepha Hale** became the first female magazine editor in the country when **she** began to work for *Ladies' Magazine* in 1827.
Because academic writing often refers to concepts and processes, the pronoun *it* is frequently used.	**Understanding personal economics** can help you make better decisions. **It** can also help you live a more productive life.

Activity 2-3 Identifying Proper Nouns and Personal Pronouns

In the following paragraph, underline the proper nouns, and circle the personal pronouns. Then, draw a line to connect each personal pronoun to the noun it refers to. Examples are provided.

Philip Knight, the founder of Nike, Inc., grew up in a suburb of Portland, Oregon. In the 1950s, he was a mile runner on the University of Oregon track team. His coach was Bill Bowerman. At that time, only a few companies sold sneakers and athletic shoes in the United States. Athletes had few choices of styles or features when they bought shoes for their sports.

During his years at Oregon, Bowerman experimented with the running shoes he had. He took them apart and put them back together. He believed that taking an ounce or two off the weight of the shoes helped his athletes run faster.

A few years later, Knight was studying business at Stanford University. He remembered Bowerman's homemade shoes, and he wrote a paper on marketing running shoes for a class on small businesses. That paper contained the idea that would make Knight a billionaire.

Source: Adapted from Jodine Mayberry, *Business Leaders Who Built Financial Empires* (Steck-Vaughn Company, 1995, 34).

Section 3: Grammar of Informational Writing

3A   Overview

Informational writing is found throughout the textbooks in your academic courses. This type of writing is used to state facts, data, theories, and definitions (factual, scientific meaning). It is also used to discuss personal habits (personal, habitual meaning). In your academic work, you will often write about facts, data, theories, definitions, and personal habits. In other words, you will use informational writing.

All of the following grammar works together in informational writing:

- **Complex noun phrases** give detailed information about nouns. They are very important and common features of informational writing. (Examples are bold-faced.)
- **Generic nouns** are used to talk about groups rather than about individuals. (Examples are underlined once.)
- **Logical organizers** show the relationships among sentences. (Examples are in brackets.)
- **Passive sentences** are often used because this style focuses on processes and theories, not on people and actions. (Examples are italicized.)
- **Present tense verbs** are frequently used to make general truth statements. The most common verb form is the simple present tense. (Examples are underlined twice.)
- Because present tense is used, **subject-verb agreement** is a feature of informational writing.

   This excerpt shows the use of this grammar in informational writing.

The nine-digit Social Security number is divided into three parts. **The first three numbers** generally indicate the state of residence at the time <u>a person</u> applies for his or her first card. The middle two digits of a Social Security number <u>have</u> no special significance, [but] merely <u>break</u> the numbers into blocks of convenient size. The last four characters represent **a straight numerical progression of assigned numbers.**

   The Social Security Administration has issued about <u>380 million Social Security numbers,</u> [and] about *six million new numbers are assigned* each year.

Source: *Social Security: Your Number,* Social Security Administration, SSA Publication No. 05-10002, U.S. Government Printing Office, April 1996, 5.

Activity 3-1 Analyzing Informational Sentences

1. Read these informational sentences. For each sentence, underline the complete subject with one line and underline the complete verb with a double line (two lines).
2. With a partner, discuss the meaning of each of these informational sentences. Decide if each sentence has *factual, scientific meaning* or *personal, habitual meaning*, and write the meaning on the line. The first answer is provided.

Informational Sentences	Meaning
a. The sun heats to approximately 15,000,000 degrees C.	factual, scientific
b. Our class meets at 1:15 p.m. every weekday.	_____
c. Fire needs oxygen to burn.	_____
d. Children begin to talk around the age of 12 to 15 months.	_____
e. We try to write in our learner's notebooks each night.	_____

3B   Complex Noun Phrases

One of the basic features of academic writing is the use of complex noun phrases. Complex noun phrases give detailed and exact information about the main noun. They are formed in four different ways as shown below.

Adjective + Noun Phrase Adjectives are often attached to noun phrases. Adjectives add information to nouns to make them more exact and detailed. (See Adjectives, page 262, and Complements, page 265.)	In Colorado, you can find **many natural features.** Levi was **a remarkable man.**
Noun Phrase + Relative Clause Relative clauses are sometimes called adjective clauses because they are like adjectives. They add information to a noun to make it more exact and detailed. (See Relative Clauses, page 217)	Culture includes **the ways that people think and behave.** **People who wake up quickly** are more likely to recall their dreams.

Continued

Noun Phrase + Prepositional Phrase Prepositional phrases are frequently attached to a noun in a complex noun phrase. (See Prepositional Phrases, page 215, and Appendix B: Common Prepositions.)	Prospectors found **a small amount of gold** near Pikes Peak. **The norms in our society** say that pink is the color for baby girls.
Noun + Noun Phrase Two or more nouns may be combined to form a single noun phrase. While the noun *classroom* in *classroom environments* is being used like an adjective, it remains a noun in form. Usually, the noun that is used as an adjective will be singular in form—the noun *Olympics* changes in *Olympic swimmer.*	I like **the classroom environments** in the U.S. In the evenings, my daughter tells me about **her school day.**

Activity 3-2 Recognizing Complex Noun Phrases

1. In each of the following sentences, underline the complex noun phrases.
2. Then, identify the type of complex noun phrase: (a) adjective + noun phrase, (b) noun phrase + relative clause, (c) noun phrase + prepositional phrase, or (d) noun + noun phrase.

EXAMPLE   In <u>the college or university classroom,</u> you will participate in <u>many different learning activities.</u>

a.   Teachers use various methods in the U.S. classroom.

b.   His brothers in New York City had supplied the goods.

c.   Religion is found in every society on the globe.

d.   Families are formed to meet human needs.

e.   The level of knowledge in modern technological society is very high.

f.   An infant needs food, warmth, clothing, and physical contact.

g.   Parents have the greatest influence over the ways that we think of ourselves.

h.   Parents provide positive reinforcement with smiles, words of approval, a chocolate cookie, or a new toy.

i.   The anthropologist must make friends with a village resident who knows the people well.

j.   They share as much as possible about the life of the people.

3C   Generic Articles and Nouns

In informational writing, you often communicate about *groups* of people or classes of things, rather than about particular people or things. You do this when you are making generalizations or writing definitions. For example, in the formal definition below, the writer is not defining a particular government. Instead, the writer is defining government systems in general.

EXAMPLE   A government is a system of laws and customs that controls how people live with one another and with other groups.

When we communicate about groups of people or classes of things, we use generic articles and nouns. When you use a generic noun, you need to decide if the noun is singular, plural, or noncount. This will determine your article usage.

A or An + Singular Noun in Generalizations *A (an)* with a singular noun is used to refer to one person or thing. The meaning is about a person or thing in general, and not about a particular person or thing.	**A parent** sets expectations by letting **a child** know what he or she must do. **An empire** is **a group** of territories or people under one ruler.
The + Singular Noun in Generalizations *The* with a singular noun can also be used for generic meaning. But this generic type is usually used in technical or informative writing about plants, animals, inventions, and other technical topics.	**The EEG** is a machine that records activity in **the brain.** **The family** is currently the subject of much scholarly research.
Plural Nouns in Generalizations Plural nouns without articles can be used to refer to groups of people or classes of things. This meaning does not refer to particular people or things.	**Sleep laboratories** are **places** where **researchers** study sleep and **dreams.** **Attitudes, values,** and **rules** for behavior are learned, not inherited.
Noncount (Uncount) Nouns in Generalizations Noncount nouns are words like *information, mathematics, sugar,* and *water.* In addition, for generic meaning, noncount nouns do not have articles. Noncount nouns do not have a singular or a plural form. For subject-verb agreement, they use the same verb form as singular nouns.	**Water** is a colorless liquid made of **hydrogen** and **oxygen.** An infant needs **food, warmth, clothing,** and **physical contact.**

Activity 3-3 Using Appropriate Generic Articles

1. In these formal definitions from college textbooks, underline all nouns and noun phrases, and write S (singular), P (plural), or U (noncount/uncount) above each noun. Use a dictionary, such as the *Newbury House Dictionary of American English,* to determine noncount nouns. Most dictionaries use the symbol "U" for noncount (uncount) nouns.
2. Then, if necessary, insert the correct generic article.

EXAMPLE

<pre>
         S   P   S   P   S
   A Bill of rights is list of rights that are guaranteed by government. (history text)
</pre>

   a. On assembly line, workers stand alongside wide moving belt. (manufacturing text)

   b. Artifacts are physical items like food, clothing, houses, and tools. (anthropology text)

   c. Mortgage is document showing that loan has been made and will be repaid. (real estate text)

   d. Chimpanzees are large, dark-haired African apes with long arms. (anthropology text)

   e. To hunt sea animals, the Inuit people used kayaks. These are small, one- or two-person boats made of waterproof skins stretched over wooden frame. (global studies text)

   f. Function is any use of banquet facilities. Examples of functions are meetings, dinners, conferences, and cocktail parties. (banquet management text)

3D   Logical Organizers

Narrative writing includes chronological organization, but informational writing is organized in some "logical" manner. Recognizing the logic behind particular writing is a challenge for writers who come from different cultural and linguistic backgrounds. This chart provides a reminder of the vocabulary that you can use to show the logical relationships among the sentences in your writing.

Meaning	Coordinating Conjunctions	Subordinating Conjunctions	Transition Words
adding	and		also additionally furthermore in addition moreover

Continued

cause/result	so	if when	as a result consequently therefore thus
choice	or nor		instead on the other hand
comparison (similarities)			also similarly likewise
concession	yet	although even though	nevertheless nonetheless
condition		if unless	
contrast (opposites)	but	while	however nevertheless on the other hand in contrast
emphasis			as a matter of fact indeed in fact
example			for example for instance to illustrate to clarify in other words
reason/cause	for	because since as	
summary or conclusion			in conclusion finally overall in summary
time		before after when while	then

3E   Passive Sentences

Passive voice is a common feature of academic writing in scientific and technical fields, but passive sentences can be used in all other types of academic writing, too.

In English, sentences usually begin with the person or thing that does the action. This is called using the **active voice.** In this example, the writer focuses on *geographers* and the action that *geographers* do.	Geographers **study** physical and cultural features on or near the earth's surface.
But writers sometimes change the focus of a sentence to communicate about the action—not about the person or thing that did the action. This is called using the **passive voice.** This writing can happen when you write about: • things—rather than the people who use them • processes—rather than the people who do them • the history of a company, sport, or country—rather than the people who are involved	focus on the *process* of exportation, not *who* does the exporting Many of Brazil's crops **are exported** to other countries. focus on the *history* of an organization, not *the people* who were involved The organization, the Gray Panthers, **was formed** in 1970 to work for equal rights for old people.
The passive verb is a combination of *be* + the past participle of a verb. (For a list of past participles of irregular verbs, see Appendix D: Irregular Verbs or the website at http://www.gsu.edu/~www.esl/egw/jones.htm.)	In advertising, printed posters and brochures **are used** to communicate the features of a new product.

Activity 3-4 Recognizing Passive Sentences

Underline the passive verbs in the following paragraph. One answer is provided.

NATURE AND WASTE

What happens to wild birds and animals when they die? Where do all the leaves go once they have fallen in autumn? They <u>are dealt with</u> by nature's recycling system. All dead plants and animals decay and decompose. They are broken down by maggots, worms, bacteria, and fungi and so the chemicals and nutrients they contain return to the earth. They may go into the soil, the ocean, or perhaps a river, where they are used again by growing plants and animals. This is a natural process in which waste materials are reused. It is a never-ending cycle of death, decay, new life, and growth.

Source: Barbara James, *Waste and Recycling* (Steck-Vaughn Company, 1990, 6).

3F   Present Tense Verbs

For informational meaning, the simple present tense form of the verb is usually used. However, you may find other present tense verbs in informational writing, too. The following explains the use of present tense verbs in academic writing.

Simple present tense verbs are often used for informational meaning and generalizations. These generalizations can be made both about personal and non-personal information.	A kibbutz **is** a communal settlement, often a farm, where families **share** work and earnings. Children in a kibbutz **learn** from infancy that their peers **are** very important people in their lives.
Present progressive verbs are used with action verbs to show that something is ongoing at the present moment. This form is frequent in conversational English, but it can also be found in writing about things that are happening now.	Many families that **are living** in this neighborhood originally came from less wealthy homes.
Present perfect verbs are not as common in academic writing as the simple present tense. The present perfect is often used to introduce the topic and to show how the past is related to the present.	Studies **have shown** that television has a significant effect on children who watch it several hours a week. In particular, violence on television and its possible effects **have been** subjects of scientific study.

PRESENT TENSE VERBS: *S* ENDINGS

The spelling of the present tense verb *s* endings may differ slightly. Study the following chart for the various spellings of the *s* endings.

SPELLING OF *s* ENDINGS

Most verbs: Add final *s*.	write = *writes* learn = *learns*
Verbs ending in *ch, sh, s, x,* or *z:* Add final *es*.	discuss = *discusses* finish = *finishes*
Verbs *do* and *go:* Add final *es*.	do = *does* go = *goes*
Verbs ending in a consonant + *y:* Change the *y* to *i* and add *es*.	study = *studies* copy = *copies*
Verbs ending in a vowel + *y:* Add *s*.	obey = *obeys* pay = *pays*

Activity 3-5 Using *s* Endings

Write the present tense *s* ending for the following verbs.

EXAMPLE   share   _____shares_____

1. discover   _____
2. enjoy   _____
3. go   _____
4. worry   _____
5. focus   _____
6. do   _____
7. identify   _____
8. try   _____

9. watch   _____
10. use   _____
11. pass   _____
12. develop   _____
13. practice   _____
14. teach   _____
15. believe   _____
16. want   _____

Activity 3-6 Identifying Present Tense Verbs

Underline and label the present tense verbs in this excerpt. One answer is provided.

              simple present

Books <u>communicate</u> in many different ways. A novel provides entertainment on a long plane ride or on a cold, rainy night. Encyclopedias are great stores of useful facts and figures. You can refer to them instantly time and time again. In an encyclopedia, you can find the answers to work or school questions. Encyclopedias can even settle disagreements that arise when you are talking with family and friends.

    For those of us who cannot find time to read a newspaper or book, magazines are the answer for the printed word. Magazines are filled with color photographs and both serious news articles and entertaining features. People usually keep magazines for interest or reference long after they have thrown away the newspaper. In fact, many magazines provide several days' reading.

Source: Adapted from Lionel Bender, *Understanding Communication and Control* (Silver Burdett Company, 1984, 34–36).

3G   Subject-Verb Agreement

One of the most important characteristics of the simple present tense is the relationship between a subject and a verb. This relationship is called subject-verb agreement. Various subject-verb agreement rules and example sentences follow.

Rule 1: Basic Agreement If the subject of a sentence is a singular count noun (*teacher* or *book*), a singular proper noun (*Mr. Wald* or *Canada*), a noncount noun (*information* or *homework*), or the pronoun *he, she,* or *it,* add *s* to the verb. For the other pronouns *(I, you, we, they),* use the simple form of the verb (no *s* ending).	<u>Sera</u> <u>likes</u> to work with one friend. <u>My friend's advice</u> <u>helps</u> me to be successful in my college classes.
Rule 2: Compound Subjects A compound subject joins two or more nouns, two or more pronouns, or a noun and a pronoun. A compound subject is plural. If the subject of a sentence is a compound subject, use the simple form of the verb (no *s* ending).	<u>Tamer and Berrin</u> <u>like</u> to study in several ways. <u>He and I</u> <u>repeat</u> new ideas aloud.
Rule 3: Subjects with Prepositional Phrases Prepositional phrases can come between the subject and verb, but they do not affect subject-verb agreement. The verb agrees with the main subject noun.	<u>The thinking parts</u> of our brain <u>are</u> more active during dreams. <u>The size</u> of the waves <u>depends</u> on the strength of the wind.
Rule 4: There/Here When the sentence begins with *there* or *here,* the verb agrees with the noun that follows the verb.	There <u>are</u> <u>many aspects</u> of geography. There <u>is</u> <u>one main factor</u> for voluntary migration. Here <u>are</u> <u>the answers</u> to the activity.
Rule 5: Gerunds and Infinitives Verbs can be used as nouns either by being changed to *gerunds* (by adding *ing*) or to *infinitives* (by adding *to*). If the subject of a sentence is a gerund or infinitive, the present tense form of the verb adds *s.*	<u>To copy a classmate's answers</u> <u>is</u> not okay. <u>Snoring</u> <u>indicates</u> that the airway is not fully open. <u>Sleepwalking</u> often <u>causes</u> a problem for older children. <div align="right">*Continued*</div>

Rule 6: False Plurals Some nouns look like plurals, but they are singular. The names of many academic disciplines *(economics)* and diseases *(measles)* are in this group. Other false plurals include the words *news* and *athletics*.	<u>Economics</u> <u>studies</u> how a society uses resources. <u>Measles</u> <u>is</u> a childhood disease. <u>News</u> <u>is</u> important to concerned citizens.

Activity 3-7 Using Present Tense Verbs and Subject-Verb Agreement

Study these informational statements, and write the correct form of each verb on the line. Be sure your *s* ending is correct.

EXAMPLE   (include) Most surveys __include__ some type of questionnaire.

1. (be) In the U.S., there _____ many possibilities for everyone.

2. (mean) Developing _____ adding specific detail to your writing.

3. (help) Information about consumers _____ marketers understand the market.

4. (be) Products and services _____ not successful if they don't meet the wants and needs of consumers.

5. (wish) He _____ to learn computer programming skills and American business strategies.

6. (show) Information _____ what consumers desire or even demand.

7. (be) There _____ a close relationship between people and the places where they live.

8. (use) Students _____ different study techniques to help them learn.

9. (be) The company's wide selection of videos _____ emphasized in its advertisements.

10. (ask) An effective student _____ questions when he or she doesn't understand.

11. (be) Wants and needs _____ satisfied only if marketers understand consumers.

12. (freeze) Water _____ at 32 degrees F.

13. (listen) I _____ to soft music when I write my assignments.

14. (be) To graduate from college _____ a dream of mine.

Activity 3-8 Using Present Tense Verbs and Subject-Verb Agreement

Read the following informational excerpt about note-taking. Then, choose an appropriate verb from the list, place a check next to the verb, and write the correct present tense form of that verb on the line. There may be more than one appropriate answer, but use each word only once. One answer is provided.

√ be   • use   • be   • be   • start   • begin

THE TECHNIQUES OF NOTE-TAKING

Your homework actually _____ in the classroom. It _____ with your

note-taking. As you study your notes, there may be parts that confuse you. Perhaps, you can-

not understand the notes you took in class. What can you do? Learn to take better notes, and

you will begin to take the work out of homework.

The trick in taking good notes _____is_____ to be alert. Whenever your teacher is lec-

turing or explaining things, listen, concentrate, think, and then write. In this way, there

_____ a better chance of understanding what you are writing.

The first thing to do is practice how to listen. This may seem strange, but most people

never learn how to listen. Listening _____ a skill; it can be improved by practice

and training. Researchers testing thousands of people have found that most people

_____ only about twenty-five percent of their total ability to listen. It is as though

you were to listen to your favorite music group on stereo with only one speaker turned up

half way. Most people do not listen as much as they can.

Source: Sigmund Kalina, *How to Sharpen Your Study Skills*, (New York, Lothrop, Lee and Shepard Company, A Division of William Morrow & Company, Inc., 1975, 32–33). © 1975 by Sigmund Kalina. Reproduced by permission.

Activity 3-9 Practice Subject-Verb Agreement

On another piece of paper, write one or two example sentences for each of the subject-verb agreement rules on pages 235–236. Edit to make sure you have used the grammar of writing sentences and the correct verb form. Share your examples with a classmate.

Section 4: Grammar of Writing Definitions

4A   Overview

Academic writing includes many definitions for words that you need to understand and use in your own writing.

Textbooks will often mark these important words in special print. Sometimes, the words will be in **bold type** or in *italic type.* Words that you need to know many also be listed in special review sections at the end of each chapter. Generally, your instructors will expect you to learn these new words and be able to use them in your own writing.	**Polyandry,** the practice of having two or more husbands, and **polygyny,** the practice of having two or more wives, are family structures in some societies. The arrangement of individuals and families into graded layers is known as *social stratification.*

FORMAL DEFINITION FORMAT

Sometimes, formal definitions of important words are provided in your academic textbooks. A formal definition of a noun has four parts:

1. the term to be defined
2. the verb (often the verb *to be: is/are*)
3. the category that the term belongs to
4. the details that separate the term from other terms in the same category

Study these examples of formal definitions from a sociology textbook.

TERM	is/are	CATEGORY	DEFINING DETAILS
Sociology	is	the study	of society.
A social fact	is	any social activity or situation	that can be measured or observed.
Socialization	is	the process	by which all of us learn to become members of society.

Activity 4-1 Identifying the Parts of a Formal Definition

Label the parts of these formal definitions.

EXAMPLE   term   is   category   defining details
          A go-between is (a person) [who arranges marriages.]

1. Polyandry is the practice of a woman having more than one husband.

2. The kula ring is a complex system of exchange that is used among the Trobriand Islanders in the South Pacific.

3. A kibbutz is a type of small agricultural commune in present-day Israel.

4. Subsistence societies are societies which produce no surplus beyond a tiny amount.

5. The pyramids of Egypt were elaborate tombs for the dead god-kings.

6. Castes are inherited social classes that are found in some cultures, such as India.

7. Conspicuous consumption is the wasteful display of wealth.

4B   Present Tense Verbs

See Section 3, Grammar of Informational Writing, page 233.

4C   Generic Articles and Nouns

See Section 3, Grammar of Informational Writing, page 229.

4D   Categorizing Nouns

When you write a formal definition of a noun, you need to put the noun into a general category. Categorizing also occurs when you collect ideas by listing.

Activity 4-2 Writing General Categories

Write a general category to describe each of the following groups of ideas.

Example   _____seasons_____
             winter
             spring
             summer
             fall

1. _____   2. _____
   teacher   happy
   doctor   sad
   accountant   frustrated
   taxi driver   angry

3. _____   4. _____
   soccer   Vietnam
   volleyball   Ethiopia
   tennis   Brazil
   swimming   Canada

5. _____   6. _____
   water   mathematics
   orange juice   chemistry
   cola   history
   coffee   anthropology

Activity 4-3 Grouping and Categorizing Similar Ideas

On another piece of paper, separate these ideas into three groups. The ideas in each group should relate to each other. Then, write a general category to describe each group.

- classroom   • taxi   • office
- train   • library   • fried chicken
- pizza   • hamburger   • bus
- computer lab   • potato chips   • car

Activity 4-4 Writing Sentences with General Categories

Match each word with the appropriate general category, and write the general category on the line. Then, on another piece of paper, write a complete sentence for each, using correct generic articles and the correct form of the verb *to be*. (For more information about generic articles, see page 229.)

EXAMPLE	general category	sentence
a hammer	_a tool_	A hammer is a tool.

specific term		**general category**
1. anger	_____	electrical appliance
2. earrings	_____	writing instruments
3. pencils	_____	animal
4. microwave	_____	language
5. coffee	_____	musical instrument
6. teachers	_____	emotion
7. horse	_____	people
8. piano	_____	drink
9. Arabic	_____	pieces of jewelry

4E   Relative Clauses

See Section 1: Grammar Common to All Types of Academic Writing, page 217.

4F   Definition Structures

Students are expected to learn and use many new words in their college and university class-es. But the formal definition structure is not always used to provide definitions in your texts. Other formats may be used. Learning and using new words will be easier if you understand the ways that definitions can be structured in your texts.

    Definitions of words are often presented in the following formats. For each of these examples, X = the term and Y = the definition.

X is Y. Y is X.	*Archaeologists* **are** scientists who study the life and cul-ture of ancient people. The ability to control **is** *power.*
X means Y.	*Ethology* **means** the study of the behavior of animals in their natural environment.
X refers to Y.	*Prestige* **refers to** the honor or respect that a person is given by others in the community.

LEARNING TO RECOGNIZE DEFINITIONS: INDIRECT PRESENTATION OF DEFINITIONS

Some writing makes definitions easy to recognize, but other materials present definitions more indirectly. The following chart shows some common indirect presentations of defini-tions. Some of these definitions need to be restated to make them into full definitions. A possible restatement is given for each definition. Other ways are also possible.

Format Style	Authentic Definition	Possible Restatement
The definition is given after the term and set off from the term with commas + *or.*	*Social mobility,* **or** move-ment into a different stra-tum, is difficult but not impossible in some closed societies.	**Test Question:** What is social mobility? **Answer:** Social mobility means movement into a different stra-tum. It is difficult but not impos-sible in some closed societies.
The definition is placed near the term and put in parentheses.	Sociologists are concerned with the many *social dif-ferences* people exhibit (the variations they learn in their societies).	**Test Question:** What do social differences refer to? **Answer:** Social differences are the variations that people learn in their societies. For example, the food that we eat and the way that we dress are social differences. Continued

The term is followed by examples that suggest a definition.	People in *the upper class,* **such as owners of large businesses, top executives, and those with large investments,** live in the most beautiful neighborhoods.	**Test Question:** How would you describe members of the upper class in the United States? **Answer:** Members of the upper class live in nice neighborhoods, have powerful professional jobs, and earn a lot of money.
The definition is set off from the term with commas.	*The feudal estate system,* a system in which social position is determined by birth, allows some upward movement of a society's members.	**Test Question:** What is meant by a feudal estate system? **Answer:** A system in which a person's social position is determined at birth is a feudal estate system. In this system, people have limited opportunities to move up in society.
The definition is given as a non-restrictive relative clause. (For more information about non-restrictive relative clauses, see page 219.)	One sociologist identified *charismatic authority,* **which is based on the special personal qualities of a leader,** as a major base of power in any political system.	**Test Question:** Define charismatic authority. **Answer:** Charismatic authority refers to power that is based on a leader's special personal qualities. For instance, if a leader is a good speaker and has a positive personality, she may have charismatic authority.
The definition is introduced by a passive phrase like is *defined as,* is *called,* or is *known as.*	Groups that hold a great deal of social power in a society **are called** *elites.*	**Test Question:** Who is considered to be an elite in a society? **Answer:** Elites are people who have a lot of social power in a society. The director of a large corporation might be an elite.
The definition is set off from the term by dashes.	You must work out a *hypothesis*—an educated guess—about how two or more things are related.	**Test Question:** Define the term hypothesis. **Answer:** A hypothesis refers to an educated guess.

Activity 4-5 Identifying Definition Structures

In each of the following paragraphs,

1. circle the term(s) being defined
2. underline the definition(s)
3. highlight the definition structure(s)

One answer is provided.

Paragraph 1

The age when children start to become sexually mature **is known as** puberty. Adolescence refers to the period from puberty to maturity. During this time, both boys and girls go through a number of physical and emotional changes. Puberty is triggered by hormones from the pituitary gland, which causes changes in the adrenal glands and in the gonads—the ovaries and testes.

Source: Adapted from "Preventive Medicine-Senses," *The Marshall Cavendish Encyclopedia of Health* (New York, Marshall Cavendish Corporation, 1995, 607).

Paragraph 2

Benjamin Franklin was an avid reader. He wanted to know everything about everything, and he thought that the best way to do that was to read books. Because Ben was so fond of books and reading, it was decided that he would learn to be a printer. He would be an apprentice, a kind of student-worker, for his older brother James.

Source: Adapted from Eve B. Feldman, *Benjamin Franklin: Scientist and Inventor* (Franklin Watts, 1990, 14–15).

Paragraph 3

People are often unique in how they learn. Some students are effective learners when they listen to the teacher talk about the materials (auditory learners). Many engineering and science students like to learn with their hands (tactile learners). For example, they learn by building models, doing experiments, and taking notes.

Source: Joy M. Reid, Editor, *Learning Styles in the ESL/EFL Classroom* (Heinle & Heinle Publishers, 1995). Reproduced by permission.

Paragraph 4

Culture is many things. One anthropologist, Edward Tylor, stated that culture includes knowledge, beliefs, art, law, customs, and any other habits of man in a society. Artifacts (food, clothing, houses, and tools) are a part of culture. You can see, touch, and handle these things.

Source: Adapted from H. Leon, *Inquiry into Anthropology* (Globe Fearon [Simon & Schuster Education Group], 1987, 4–5). Reproduced by permission of Globe Fearon.

Activity 4-6 Writing Short Answers with Definitions

Use the definitions in Activity 4-5 to answer the following questions. Write your answers in complete sentences.

1. What is an apprentice?

   _____

   _____

2. Define puberty.

   _____

   _____

3. What is the purpose of the pituitary gland?

   _____

   _____

4. Describe the difference between an auditory learner and a tactile learner.

   _____

   _____

5. Define and give several examples of an artifact.

   _____

   _____

Section 5: Grammar of Persuasive Writing

5A   Overview

Writers in all situations are trying to be persuasive. We all want our readers to understand
our ideas and to believe that our writing is correct. When students write for their teachers,
they are trying to persuade the teacher that they know the material. One feature of most academic writing is the tone which writers use to persuade readers to believe their claims.
Another feature often found in academic persuasion is the use of conditional statements to
present cause-result statements. The following pages show how academic writers use both of
these features in persuasive writing.

5B   Structures to Control the Strength of Generalizations: Opinion Structures

OPINION STRUCTURES

In my opinion,	**In Freud's opinion,** dreams allow us to fulfill our unac- ceptable wishes.
I believe (that)	**People in some cultures believe that** dreams come from our soul and the travels it takes.
I think (that)	**Carl Jung,** one dream researcher, **thinks** dreams make up for things we don't have in real life.
I feel (that)	**Patricia Garfield,** author of the book *Creative Dreaming,* **feels that** we can train ourselves to dream about certain things.

Activity 5-1 Using Opinion Structures in Small Group Discussions

With a small group of classmates, collect ideas and opinions about the U.S. classroom. To
begin, return to your learner's notebook assignment in Chapter 1, page 6. Use various opinion structures to share your opinions, and move from general opinions to specific details. An
example is provided.

EXAMPLE   opinion structure   general opinion   specific details
              I believe that you can learn best when you work with other students, so pair
              or small group work is the best.

5C   Structures to Control the Strength of Generalizations: Adverbs of Frequency

always   usually   often/frequently   sometimes   seldom/rarely   never
100% ── 0%

Adverbs of frequency tell how often something happens. Adverbs of frequency range from *always* (100%) to *never* (0%).	Culture **always** influences the way we live.
Adverbs of frequency have positive and negative meanings. *Always, usually, often, frequently,* and *sometimes* have positive meanings. *Seldom, rarely,* and *never* have negative meanings.	People from the same culture **often** speak, dress, eat, think, and act in similar ways. People from different cultural groups **seldom** have identical customs.
Academic writers often use an adverb of frequency to limit the strength of a claim. You will seldom find words as strong as *always* or *never* in academic writing. If these words are used, the writer must have strong evidence to support the statement.	Culture is **never** just physical items. It also includes ideas and beliefs.
Adverbs of frequency have special placement, depending on the verb. Adverbs of frequency are located: • before the simple present or simple past tense verb • after the first auxiliary verb • after the main verb *to be* • before the imperative verb In addition, • the adverbs *usually, often, frequently,* and *sometimes* may also occur at the beginning of a sentence. The examples on the right illustrate each of these points in order.	People from the same culture **often** speak, dress, eat, think, and act in similar ways. The environment will **always** influence a person's culture. Culture is **never** just physical items. **Never** judge another culture as being right or wrong. **Sometimes,** people believe customs from another culture are wrong or bad.

Activity 5-2 Using Adverbs of Frequency to Make Accurate Generalizations

Writers often use adverbs of frequency when they make statements about habits and routines. Read the following statements about customs and habits in the classroom. Add an appropriate adverb of frequency to each sentence according to the expectations and customs of *this class*.

EXAMPLE   Students never whisper to each other during tests in this class.

1. Students stand up when answering a question in class.

2. Students in this class are allowed to share their opinions and ideas.

3. Students are late for this class.

4. Students in this class work in small groups.

5. In this class, students use the teacher's first name when they ask questions.

6. Students are permitted to submit their homework late.

7. In this class, students will take quizzes.

8. Students in this class knock on the classroom door if they arrive late.

9. Students eat and drink in this classroom.

10. Students stand up when their teacher enters the classroom.

Activity 5-3 Using Present Tense Verbs and Adverbs of Frequency

1. Read the following paragraphs about sleep disorders.
2. For each paragraph, choose an appropriate verb from the list, place a check next to that verb, and write the correct present tense form of that verb on the line.
3. When provided, include the adverb of frequency in the correct place.

There may be more than one appropriate answer, but use each word only once. One answer is provided.

Paragraph 1

              √ be   • occur   • include

Sleep disorders _____ in people of all ages, but they (frequently)

_____are frequently_____ more common in children. Sleep disorders

_____ sleepwalking and sleep terrors.

Paragraph 2

- become
- involve
- walk
- perform
- need
- be
- stop

Sleepwalking (usually) _____ simply sitting up in bed. But

children (often) _____ in their sleep, too. Some children even

_____ inappropriate behavior, such as urinating in a closet.

Sleepwalking _____ most frequent in children between the ages

of 4 and 8. Children (usually) _____ sleepwalking when they

_____ older. Until they do stop, however, sleepwalkers

_____ safeguards to prevent injury, such as window locks and gates

across stairways.

Paragraph 3

- become
- run
- stop
- be
- happen
- have
- scream
- be
- be
- grow

When a child _____ in the night, parents (often)

_____ to find their child sitting up in bed. The child (often)

_____ hot and sweaty but not awake. If the child is awakened,

she (frequently) _____ confused, and she

_____ likely to talk about "bad dreams." The child (usually)

_____ no memory of the event in the morning. Sleep terrors

_____ most common between the ages of 4 and 12. Like sleep-

walking, sleep terrors _____ in the first third of the night.

Fortunately, sleep terrors (usually) _____ as a child

_____ older.

Source: Adapted from *Sleep Problems in Children: A Parent's Guide* (American Sleep Disorders Association, 1996, 8–10). Reproduced by permission.

5D   Structures to Control the Strength of Generalizations: Modal Auxiliaries

Modal auxiliary verbs include *may, might, can, could, shall, should, must, will,* and *would.*	In this class, you **will interview** a classmate to find out her or his opinions about youth in another culture.
The modal auxiliary is followed by the simple form of a verb without *to.*	These changes **can make** women more independent.
Modals do not take a final *s.* The main verbs do not take a final *s.*	In Mexico, when a couple wishes to marry, the man **should ask** the woman's family for permission.
Each modal has more than one meaning, depending on the context of the sentence. In the first example, *must* means strong necessity; in the second, *must* means logical conclusion.	In my country, children **must obey** their parents. My neighbor has five children. She **must be** very busy.
The modal auxiliaries *might* and *may* are often used when the writer wants to persuade the reader. There is often little difference in meaning between *might* and *may.*	These customs **might seem** strange to others. These customs **may seem** strange to others.

Activity 5-4 Using Modal Auxiliaries to Make Accurate Generalizations

Read the following student paragraphs about other cultures. Then, make accurate generalizations about these cultures by writing *might* or *may* and the correct form of the verb on the line. One possible answer is provided.

Student Writing Model 1

Nowadays, the lives of women in Colombia are very different from 30 years ago. You will find that women (work) _____might work_____ outside the home. Most men respect the ideas and feelings of their wives. Also, men (assist) _____ with the house and the children. I think these changes (help) _____ women become more independent. In addition, the changes (make) _____ the family structure stronger than the past.

Cecilia Samaniego
Colombia

Student Writing Model 2

In my opinion, there are two kinds of high school students in Egypt. First, many students are often lazy and careless. Some students do not care about the last year in high school. They (feel) _____ that they can easily go to private colleges and universities after graduation. Second, some students study hard and do all their homework. This kind of student (want) _____ to be successful in her or his life. I believe these students will be someone in the future.

Tamer Adel Soliman
Egypt

Activity 5-5 Writing Accurate Generalizations with *Might* and *May*

On another piece of paper, write a complete sentence using the words and phrases below. Use *might* or *may* in your sentences to make the generalizations more accurate.

EXAMPLE   people in the United States — on the weekend
             People in the United States *might relax* with friends on the weekend.

1. people on vacation
2. students — before an exam
3. bride — on her wedding day
4. students — Friday evening
5. business person — before an important meeting

5E   Structures to Control the Strength of Generalizations: Expressions of Quantity

Academic writers often add various **expressions of quantity** (like *a number of*, *many*, and *several*) to sentences to make accurate statements of generalization.	Nowadays, **a number of Iranian women** are active. In fact, **most women** work outside the home.
Academic writers seldom use expressions of quantity like *all* or *no* because they make strong generalizations. If these words are used, the writer must have very strong evidence to support the statements. Otherwise, the reader will not be persuaded to agree with the writer.	inaccurate generalization, not based on facts **All Americans** like to wear casual clothes. accurate generalization, based on facts **All humans** have culture.
Expressions of quantity usually come before a noun. Some expressions of quantity are used only with plural nouns. Some expressions of quantity are used only with noncount nouns. Still others are used with both plural and noncount nouns.	**Some students** do not care about the last year in high school. In my home country, my teacher did not assign **a lot of homework**.

EXPRESSIONS OF QUANTITY IN ACCURATE STATEMENTS OF GENERALIZATION

Expressions of Quantity	Used with Plural Nouns	Used with Noncount Nouns
a number of many several	a number of cultures many cultures several cultures	
a lot of most some	a lot of cultures most cultures some cultures	a lot of information most information some information

Activity 5-6 Using Expressions of Quantity in Accurate Statements of Generalization

Fill in each blank with an appropriate expression of quantity to make a true statement. Use a variety of structures. Notice that some sentences also include opinion structures to further control the tone of the generalization. There may be more than one correct answer.

EXAMPLE   _____Most_____ Americans own a TV.

1. _____ students at this college study in the library.

2. _____ families in the U.S. have two cars.

3. I think that _____ drinking water in the U.S. is clean.

4. _____ students at this college are 18 to 23 years old.

5. In my opinion, _____ languages are easier to learn than English.

6. I feel that _____ homework provides effective practice and study for students.

7. _____ students ride bicycles to class.

8. I believe _____ advice from your parents is useful.

Activity 5-7 Writing Accurate Generalizations with Expressions of Quantity

On another piece of paper, write six sentences about the people in your neighborhood, school, and/or family. Use the following expressions of quantity to make accurate statements of generalization: *a number of, many, several, a lot of, most,* and *some.* You might also want to include opinion structures in your sentences.

EXAMPLES   **Several** classmates smoke cigarettes during the class breaks.
             In my opinion, most students at this university use backpacks to carry their books.

5F   Conditional Sentences

Academic writing often uses conditionals to set up cause-result statements. These can be used when the writer is trying to persuade a reader that a particular chain of causes and results will occur.

Conditional sentences are formed using an "*if*-clause" and a main clause. The "*if*-clause" gives the *cause*. The main clause gives the *result*.	**If a community's main source of income is lost,** it may shrink and even become a ghost town.
The main clause can have different modals (like *will* or *may*) depending on the strength of the information. In these examples, *may* means that the writer's evidence shows a possibility in the result. *Will* means that the writer's evidence strongly predicts the result.	If people become too unhappy, they **may leave** in search of another community. You **will learn** best when you combine learning styles.

Activity 5-8 Recognizing the Grammar of Persuasive Writing

1. Read the following passage about the Internet.
2. Place brackets [ ] around the conditional sentences. Then, label the *if*-clause (cause) and the main clause (result) in each conditional sentence.
3. Circle any modals in the main clauses. One answer is provided.

GAINING ACCESS TO THE INTERNET

if-clause (cause)

[If you want access to the Internet—the worldwide network of computer networks, which

includes thousands of databases, discussion groups, and files on every topic imaginable—you will

main clause (result)

need to set up an account with an Internet provider.] You can get a free account if you're a

student at certain colleges and universities, or you can sign up with a commercial online ser-

vice that will charge you a fee. Here are some places to try before you sign up with a com-

mercial service:

• A local college or university.

• A public library.

• Your place of employment.

Continued

If you're not able to obtain an Internet connection through one of these institutions, you might try:

- Talking to people at your local computer store.

- Browsing through a computer newspaper, often free at computer stores.

- Having a friend with access to the World Wide Web check out Yahoo's Index of Internet Service Providers at http://www.yahoo.com.

If all you want is access to the Internet, you can probably obtain it more economically using one of the methods above. If, however, you're interested in the many other resources available through commercial services, the Internet access you receive from them may be a valuable plus.

Source: *Getting Online: A Friendly Guide for Teachers, Students, and Parents* (U.S. Department of Education, ERIC 96-5029(R)).

Section 6: Grammar of Interactive Communication in Writing

6A   Overview

In conversations, we often ask questions, refer to the other people in the conversation as *you*, and talk about *we* and *I*. There are many other features that make conversations different from writing—using fragments, taking turns, being able to have eye contact and interact with the other people immediately, having short amounts of time to form ideas, using informal vocabulary, and more.

Writers sometimes use features of conversational grammar in academic writing. This style reaches out to the reader and tries to interact with the reader. Frequently, you will find academic writers using questions and also the pronouns *you, we,* and *I*.	Imagine that you are stranded on a desert island with a million dollars. How much is it worth? You can't eat it. You have nothing to spend it on. Basically, your money has no value. But once you are rescued, your money immediately becomes very valuable. Why? Because it can buy a lot. Source: Karen Bornemann Spies, *Our Money* (The Millbrook Press, 1992, 5).

6B   Using Questions

In college or university, you will ask and answer many questions every day. Usually, one person asks a question and another person answers it as part of a discussion or conversation. Questions are used for many purposes—to collect information, to make suggestions, and others.

YES/NO QUESTIONS

The following are yes/no questions that U.S. students frequently ask their teachers.

Can we use dictionaries during the test?   Is our quiz on Friday?

Do you accept late homework?   Is class attendance required?

To form a **yes/no question,** you change the basic sentence. To do that, change the word order, and change the final period to a question mark. The first auxiliary word or the form of the verb *to be* moves in front of the subject.	**We can use** our dictionaries during the test. **Can we use** our dictionaries during the test? Class attendance **is** required. **Is** class attendance required?
If there is no auxiliary verb or form of the verb *to be,* you must add *do* or *does.* For example, in these sentences, there are no words to move in front of the subject. To form a question, you must add a form of the word *do.*	Your teachers **accept** late homework. **Do** your teachers **accept** late homework? She **accepts** late homework. **Does** she **accept** late homework?
Subject-verb agreement must be followed for singular subjects with present tense verbs. In this example, use the singular form of *do (does)* and use the simple form of the verb (without the final *s*).	Your teacher **permits** you to eat in class. **Does** your teacher **permit** you to eat in class?
In American English, *have* is like other verbs in the formation of questions.	The U.S. classroom usually **has** desks and chairs for students. **Does** the U.S. classroom usually **have** desks and chairs for students?

Activity 6-1 Practice with Yes/No Questions

Change these sentences about cultural beliefs into yes/no questions.
1. Draw a circle around the word that moves to the beginning of the sentence to form a question.
2. Then, draw an arrow to show where the word should be placed, and change the period to a question mark.
3. Finally, write the complete question in the space provided.

EXAMPLE   Parents (should) choose their child's husband or wife?
             Should parents choose their child's husband or wife?

a. A newly married couple should live with the groom's family.

_____

b. Women must raise the children in a family.

_____

c. The man might be the "head" of the house.

_____

d. Some husbands may help clean the house and prepare the meals.

_____

e. A woman should marry before age 25.

_____

f. Students must stand up when their teacher enters the classroom.

_____

Activity 6-2 Writing Yes/No Questions Using *Do* and *Does*

The following sentences require the use of *do* or *does* to form a question. On another piece of paper, rewrite these sentences, making them yes/no questions. Capitalize the first word of each question, and put a question mark at the end of your question.

EXAMPLE   Your father cooks some of the family's meals.
             Does your father cook some of the family's meals?

1. You use your mother's last name.
2. Your mother works outside the home.
3. Your grandparents live with your family.
4. Your culture allows men to marry more than one wife.
5. Your father makes all the major decisions in the family.
6. Most women in your culture attend college.

INFORMATION QUESTIONS

Information questions use the words *who, what, where, when, why, how,* and a few others. These questions are used when you know part of the information, but not all of it. For example, you might know that something will happen but not know who will do it.	**What** do teenagers do for fun in France? **When** do young people graduate from high school in Brazil?
Each of the question words replaces a particular part of the sentence. For humans, *who* refers to the subject or the object of a sentence.	**Who** knows anything about the Turkish culture?
Whom is used only to refer to an object. It is required immediately after a preposition.	**From whom** did you learn this information?
What refers to either the subject or the object for everything not human.	**What** do you know about Turkey?
When refers to adverbials of time.	**When** did Turkey declare its independence?
Where refers to adverbials of place.	**Where** is Turkey located?
Why refers to adverbials of reason.	**Why** is Turkey an interesting place to visit?
How refers to adverbials of manner.	**How** has Turkey changed in the last 20 years?
How much and *how many* are used to refer to quantities. *How much* must always be used to refer to noncount nouns. *How many* refers to plural count nouns.	**How much information** do you know about another culture? **How many countries** have you visited?

Activity 6-3 Writing Information Questions

On another piece of paper, write information questions about habits and routines. Use question words, and use adverbs of frequency where appropriate. Capitalize the first word of each question, and put a question mark at the end of your question.

EXAMPLES when/get up   When do you usually get up?
          where/live   Where do you live?

1. what/full name
2. when/study for your classes
3. when/go to bed
4. what/do on the weekends
5. when/prefer to take classes
6. why/attend this college
7. where/complete your homework
8. what/interests and hobbies
9. where/eat lunch
10. why/in this class
11. (write your own question)
12. (write your own question)

6C   Using *You, We,* and *I* Pronouns

USING *YOU* AND *I* IN ACADEMIC WRITING

You and *I* are used in academic writing to give some of the flavor of conversation to written words. Using these pronouns correctly in academic writing can be a challenge. To better understand their use, writers need to study carefully all the examples they can find. Some examples are given.

When writers give advice, they often speak directly to the reader as *you*.	Put **yourself** in **your** instructor's head. What kind of questions would **you** ask? Make practice test questions.
Writers sometimes combine question asking with the use of *you*.	Do **you** know who or what is pictured on our paper money? Can **you** describe what is stamped on each U.S. coin? This chapter answers these questions.
In this excerpt, the writer first provides information about labor-saving devices. The writer then asks the reader a question, using *you*. The writer is trying to connect the material to the lives of the readers and what *you*, the readers, experience.	Many of the world's resources are used to enable the consumer society to have labor-saving devices. How many kitchen gadgets do **you** use in **your** home? Continued

Sometimes, the writer wants to express her or his opinion in an essay. Some teachers encourage you to write in this manner. Other teachers have different opinions about the use of *I* in an academic essay. Find out the opinions of your teachers and the customs in your academic major.	I think that a pass/fail grading system would be more fair. Still, I believe most students would work hard to learn the subject. At least, I don't think the grading system would affect it.

USING *WE* IN ACADEMIC WRITING

Writers use the pronoun *we* to suggest a bond, or connection, with their audience. *We* means that the writer and the reader share the same knowledge, ideas, experiences, or beliefs.

The writer uses *we* in this excerpt to suggest a close relationship between the writer and the reader—both the writer and the reader share the same society.	**We** live in a society that consumes, or uses, many resources. It is often called "the consumer society."
In this excerpt, the writer could use *you*, but *we* suggests a stronger connection with the reader. Both the writer and the reader can find examples of recycling in their shared world.	**We** can see examples of reuse and recycling all around us. The clothing, toys, and books passed on to friends, relatives, or thrift shops are being reused.

Activity 6-4 Identifying the Grammar of Interactive Communication in Writing

In the following paragraphs, underline questions and circle the pronouns *you, we,* and *I.* Then, with your teacher and classmates, discuss the effect that this grammar has on you and other readers. Examples are provided.

Paragraph 1

What can you do to prepare for college tests? To help you study for tests, you should create review tools, such as flashcards, chapter outlines, and summaries. This helps you organize and remember information. It also helps you condense material to a manageable size. Use 3 x 5-inch cards to review important information. Write ideas, formulas, concepts, and facts on cards to carry with you. Study on the bus, in the library, or whenever you have a few extra minutes.

Source: Adapted from *How to Study for and Take College Tests* (ACCESS ERIC, Office of Educational Research and Improvement, U.S. Department of Education, NLE 97-2527).

Paragraph 2

You need a job. Somewhere, an employer has the job you want. How do you get that job? By marketing your job talents. By showing employers you have the skills they need. Do you have job talents? YES! Homemakers, disabled individuals, veterans, students just out of school, people already working—all have skills and experience for many good jobs.

Source: *Tips for Finding the Right Job* (U.S. Department of Labor, Employment and Training Administration, 1996, 1).

Paragraph 3

Many of us got our Social Security number about the time we got our first job. It was a symbol of our right to work and our responsibility to pay taxes. And, like getting a driver's license, it was symbolic of becoming an adult. Today, many parents apply for a number for their newborns even before they leave the hospital!

Source: *Social Security: Your Number* (Social Security Administration, SSA Publication No. 05-10002, April 1996, 2).

Section 7: Basic Grammar Terminology

The following information will help you to talk about the grammar in your academic writing. The most important terms are given in helpful charts. The charts do not teach you how to use the grammar, but they provide examples of this grammar.

7A   Adjectives

Adjectives are words like *happy, important, colorful,* and many others. Adjectives usually are used in front of the main noun.	**good** friends **effective** students **small group** work
Adjectives can be used in the complement of a sentence. *Unique* and *strange* are complements in the examples. (See Complements on page 265.)	People are **unique** in how they learn. These customs may seem **strange** to others.
Most adjectives have comparative and superlative forms. Depending on the syllables in the adjective, comparatives are made with *er* or *more: happier* or *more important,* and superlatives are made with *est* or *most: happiest* or *most important.*	As divorce grows **more common,** North Americans practice serial monogamy. My new place is a lot **bigger** than my old apartment. He was the **youngest** of six children.
Another name for a **relative clause** is an **adjective clause.** This name is sometimes used because the clause combines with a noun and is like an adjective in its work. (See Phrases and Clauses on page 269 and Relative Clauses on page 217.)	Culture includes all the ways **that humans live in the environment.**

7B Adverbs and Adverbials

Adverbs are the kinds of words that give information about time, place, manner, and purpose. They answer questions such as *when, where, why, how,* and a few other similar questions. (See Sentence Adverbials on page 271.)	how A young graduate student noticed that the eyes moved **slowly** during sleep.
Groups of words that have this grammar are called **adverbials.** There are adverbial phrases and adverbial clauses. (See Phrases and Clauses on page 269.)	where **At the sleep lab,** they used an EEG machine. when Sleep researchers became important **in the 1940s and 50s.**

7C Articles and Determiners

Articles are often used in noun phrases. Articles are the words *a, an,* and *the.*	**a** college education **an** important sleep research **the** thinking part of **the** brain
Sometimes, articles are described as **determiners.** Determiners also include *this/that, these/those, each, no, another, some,* and several other words.	Jews had lived on **this** land since Roman times. **Another** way to prepare for tests is to create review tools, such as flashcards.
The **possessive personal pronouns** can be called determiners. (See Pronouns on page 270.)	During **his** years at Oregon, Bowerman experimented with the running shoes he had.

7D   Auxiliary Verbs

English verbs are often simple single words, but they can also be a combination of two or more words. For example, present and past progressive verb tenses combine a form of *be* with the *ing* form of the verb. In this situation, *be* is called the **auxiliary verb.** Another name for auxiliary verb is **helping verb.**	auxiliary verb + main verb (present progressive) **is completing** auxiliary verb + main verb (past progressive) **was completing** auxiliary verb + main verb (present perfect) **has completed** auxiliary verb + main verb (passive verb) **is completed**
Questions and negatives can also require *do*, *does*, or *did* as an auxiliary verb. (See Question Formation, page 256.)	*do* as auxiliary verb and *date as* main verb In Vietnamese high schools, **do** young people **date?** *did* as auxiliary verb and *want* as main verb My dad **didn't want** me to date until I was 15.
Modal auxiliary verb or **modal** is the name for words like *will, would, can, could, may, might, must, shall,* and *should*. They combine with main verbs for verb phrases.	Sleepwalkers **might talk** in their sleep. Relief from the stressful situation **will** usually **return** sleep to normal.

7E   Comma Splices

A **comma splice** is when two complete sentences are joined with only a comma. This example shows a comma splice.	There are two broad subdivisions of geography, these subdivisions are physical geography and human geography.
To correct a comma splice, you can separate the sentence to form two individual sentences. (See Sentences, page 270.)	There are two broad subdivisions of geography. These subdivisions are physical geography and human geography.

Continued

You can add a semicolon.	There are two broad subdivisions of geography; these subdivisions are physical geography and human geography.
You can add a coordinating conjunction. (See Logical Organizers, page 230, and Conjunctions, page 265.)	There are two broad subdivisions of geography, and these subdivisions are physical geography and human geography.

7F Complements

Complements are often nouns, noun phrases, or adjectives. The complement describes or renames the subject. **A linking verb** connects (or links) the complement to the subject. Common linking verbs include *be, become, feel, seem, taste,* and many others. In these examples, subjects are underlined once, verbs are underlined twice, and complements are circled. (For more information, see Appendix A: Linking Verbs or the website at http://www.gsu.edu/~wwwesl/egw/vanassch.htm.)	Culture is (many things.) These customs may seem (strange) to others. Students can become (more effective learners) if they understand how they learn best.

7G Conjunctions

One kind of conjunction is the **coordinating conjunction.** Coordinating conjunctions *for, and, nor, but, or, yet,* and *so* are used to combine words and phrases. They are also used to combine two or more sentences. (For more information, see http://www.gsu.edu/~wwwesl/egw/bryson.htm.)	*or* used to connect nouns Sometimes insomnia affects people for weeks, months, **or** even years. *and* used to connect adjectives A nightmare is a dream that is scary **and** often very realistic. *and* used to connect sentences These dreams scare me, **and** I often wake up at night.

7H Fragments

A **fragment** is a part of a sentence. In other words, a fragment is an **incomplete sentence.** When we talk, we often speak in fragments. But in written English, incomplete sentences are very seldom used. These examples are fragments.	Slaves who had been freed. Because they mistreated their slaves.
The use of an adverbial clause as a sentence is a common error in writing. An adverbial clause begins with a **subordinating word** like *because, when, after, while,* and some other words. (See Phrases and Clauses, page 269.)	**When Levi first saw New York in 1847.** The city was full of activity. Levi brought his canvas to a tailor. **After he had heard this remark.**
The examples in boldface are fragments. The simplest solution is to join the fragment to its related independent clause and to correct the punctuation. These examples are complete sentences.	When Levi first saw New York in 1847, the city was full of activity. Levi brought his canvas to a tailor after he had heard this remark.
Sometimes, it is possible to create two independent sentences by removing the subordinating word and making other changes to create a complete sentence of the fragment. These examples are complete sentences.	Levi first saw New York in 1847. At that time, the city was full of activity. Levi heard this remark, so he brought his canvas to a tailor.

7I   Nouns

A **noun** is a word like *student, computer, car, child, success,* or *mathematics.* Nouns are used in sentences as subjects, objects, complements, and a few other functions.	The typical American **family** owns a **home.** Most **respondents** rented three to four **videos** last **month.**
Count nouns have singular or plural forms. **Regular count nouns** form their plurals by adding *s* for the spelling. **Irregular count nouns** have some other way to form the plural. In these examples, the first two nouns are regular. The next two are irregular.	**Count Nouns Have Two Forms** **singular count** **plural count** student students computer computers child children woman women
Noncount (or **uncount**) nouns are not singular and not plural. They cannot be used with *a* or *an; -s* is not added to make a plural. (For more information, see the website at http://www.gsu.edu/~wwwesl/egw/sansom.htm.)	**Noncount Nouns Have Only One Form** water mathematics information food music vocabulary health money

7J   Noun Phrases

Noun phrase is the name for the combination of a noun with other words. The combination functions in a sentence just like the simple nouns do—as a subject, object, or complement.	noun phrase as subject **The world's most popular pants** are blue jeans. noun phrase as direct object They did not want to give up **their favorite clothes.**
A noun phrase can include several different kinds of structures. An article or determiner, one or more adjectives, and other words can combine with the main noun to form a noun phrase.	**Many young people** did not like the idea of wearing the same things as their parents. **A suitable environment** is quite important for my writing. <div align="right">Continued</div>

| A **complex noun phrase** is a noun phrase that is long and complicated with words attached before and/or after the main noun. (In these examples, the main nouns are underlined, and the complex noun phrases are boldfaced.) | Pretty <u>villages</u> with rows of wooden houses stood along the river banks.

This will help you learn from <u>teachers</u> who use different methods in the classroom. |

7K   Objects

The word **object** is used for two different types of grammar structures. Verbs can have objects. Prepositions can also have objects.

A **transitive verb** must have a direct object. Sometimes, this **direct object** is called the object of the verb. Direct objects provide information about *who?* or *what?* (The transitive verbs are double underlined, and the direct objects are circled in these examples.)	<u>Athletes, dancers, and musicians</u> <u>improve</u> (their abilities) by practicing physical movements. <u>Language students</u> <u>increase</u> (their language skills) when they present role-plays and dialogs with their entire bodies.
Some transitive verbs can have another object called the **indirect object.** The indirect object "receives" the direct object. Indirect objects provide information about *for whom? to whom? for what?* or *to what?* You cannot have an indirect object unless you also have a direct object. (In the first example, the direct object is circled and the indirect object is in brackets.) Label the direct object and indirect object in the second example.	<u>Levi's brothers</u> <u>taught</u> [him] (many important things.) Many parents give their children a car.
Prepositions can have objects, too. The combination of a preposition with its object is called a **preposition phrase** or **prepositional phrase.**	A dream is one kind **of mental experience.** They were fleeing religious persecution, or cruel treatment, **in their native lands.**

7L   Phrases and Clauses

A **phrase** is a group of words that works together as a single unit. Phrases include noun phrases, verb phrases, and prepositional phrases. The examples on the right illustrate these three.	**A horror movie** might cause nightmares. Loud snoring **may mean** that something is seriously wrong. Sleepwalkers may awaken **in a different part of the house.**
A **clause** is different from a phrase because a clause has a subject and a verb. The most important clause types are adverbial clauses, noun clauses, and relative clauses. These three are illustrated in the examples on the right.	Most people sleep worse **when they are away from home.** Most people think **that their customs are natural, right, and good.** The company **that created blue jeans more than 100 years ago** is the Levi Strauss Company.

7M   Prepositions

Prepositions are words like *on, in, by,* and many others. Another term that is used is **preposition phrase** or **prepositional phrase.** This term refers to the combination of a preposition with its object. Prepositional phrases are often used as adverbials to tell *when, where, why,* and so forth. (For a list of prepositions, see Appendix B: Common Prepositions.)	prepositional phrase as an adverbial to tell *where* Houses often have yards **between the house and the neighbor's house.** two prepositional phrases as adverbials to tell *why* If owners need to move out **because of work** or **for personal reasons,** they cannot easily do so.
Prepositional phrases are also often attached to nouns in complex noun phrases. (In these examples, the complex noun phrases are underlined, and the prepositional phrases are boldfaced.)	The relationship **of people, places, and things** is the great attraction of geography. About 20 years ago, United States textile mills produced 400 million square yards **of denim.**

Continued

In addition, prepositions are closely connected to some verbs and need to be learned as part of the structure of those verbs. (See the webesite at http://www.gsu.edu/~wwwesl/egw/prepverb.htm for a list of these prepositional verbs.)	You should **look at** different models, sizes, and styles. Human geographers **focus on** people and their patterns of settlement and activity.

7N   Pronouns

Pronouns are words like *I/me, you, we/us, he/him, she/her,* and *it.* These are also called **personal pronouns** because they refer to "persons."	**I** studied in a small classroom with only four to eight people in **my** class.
Other words are also called pronouns. These include the following types: 1. **demonstrative pronouns** (*this/that* and *these/those*) (These are sometimes called **determiners**—see page 263.) 2. **relative pronouns** (*who, whom, that, which,* and some others). (See page 217.) 3. **interrogative pronouns** (*who, whom, whose, why, how,* and some others). (See page 258.)	1. **This** activity lets you share your ideas and opinions. 2. Culture includes all the ways **that** humans live in the environment and with each other. 3. **What** is your favorite way to learn new things?

7O   Sentences

A **sentence** is a complete unit that contains a subject and a verb. In writing, a sentence begins with a capital letter and ends with a period, question mark, or exclamation mark.	All humans have culture. What is culture?
Sometimes, a verb requires a direct object. **Direct objects** are nouns, pronouns, and other words that complete the meaning of the verb. This kind of verb is called a **transitive verb.** (In these examples, subjects are underlined once, transitive verbs are underlined twice, and direct objects are circled.)	These women have a difficult life. Often students might not complete their homework. Continued

Sometimes, the verb requires a complement. **Complements** are often nouns, noun phrases, or adjectives. The complement describes or renames the subject. A **linking verb** connects (or links) the complement to the subject. (See Complements on page 265 and Appendix A: Linking Verbs.) In these examples, subjects are underlined once, linking verbs are underlined twice, and complements are circled.	<u>Stereotypes</u> <u><u>are</u></u> (exaggerated beliefs about people.) In my opinion, <u>many young Americans</u> <u><u>are</u></u> (disrespectful.)
Sentences can also have **adverbs.** These adverbs answer questions like *when, where,* and *how.* (See Adverbs and Adverbials on page 263)	I believe most young Americans like to dress **informally.**
This example sentence does not have either a direct object or a complement. The verb is called an **intransitive verb.** An intransitive verb never has an object or a complement. It can be followed by an adverb (*naturally* in the example).	<u>A need for a product</u> <u><u>can arise</u></u> naturally.

7P   Sentence Adverbials

Some sentences include information about *when, where, why, how,* or other adverb information. The adverbial can be a single word, a phrase, or a clause.

A **single word adverb** can be used.	Physical features are those that occur **naturally,** such as mountains, rivers, and oceans.
A **prepositional phrase** can be used as an adverbial.	A dream happens **in the mind.**
An **adverbial clause** can be used.	I make a space for writing **because my desk is always messy.**

7Q   Subjects of Sentences

Subjects can be nouns, noun phrases, or pronouns—or any structure that works like a noun. Subjects can be very simple and short or very long and complicated.	<u>I</u> do many things before I start to write. <u>My own habit</u> is to find a sofa, soft light, some paper, and some pencils.
A sentence can also have two or more subjects. This is called a **compound subject.**	<u>A road map and a textbook</u> are similar.
In the first example, the **main subject** is the noun *person.* The **complete subject** is the noun phrase *the average person.* Find the main subject and the complete subject in the second example.	<u>The average person</u> has about five dream periods. Hollywood stars appear in jeans on opening nights of movies.

7R   Verbs in Sentences: Active or Passive

Each English sentence must have a subject and a verb. The verb in a sentence is often called the **verb phrase.** A sentence can also have two or more verbs. This is called a **compound verb.**	I <u>dress</u> in simple clothes to help me relax. He <u>must see</u> the new information before he can understand the lectures. The students <u>can understand or practice</u> more easily when they work in pairs.
Verbs can be **active** or **passive.** In active sentences, the subject does the action. In passive sentences, the subject "receives" the action that someone else does. (See page 232 for more information on passive verbs.)	<u>Igor</u> <u>spends</u> $800 per month on rent. <u>Pollution</u> <u>can be grouped</u> in a variety of ways.

7S   Verb Forms

Verbs are words like *require* or *speak*. They are used in sentences in the verb phrase.	Most of these jobs <u>require</u> specialized skills. They <u>speak</u> Slavic languages like Russian, Polish, and Bulgarian.
Require and most other verbs are **regular verbs.** They form their simple past tense and past participle by adding *ed* to the basic word. *Speak* and many other verbs are **irregular verbs.** They form their past tense and past participle in ways different from the regular verb. (For more information, see Appendix D: Irregular Verbs or the website at http://www.gsu.edu/~wwwesl/egw/jones.htm.)	The teacher <u>required</u> them to type all essays. Before I came to the U.S., I <u>spoke</u> just a little English.

7T   Verb Tenses

simple present tense	The residents of a city <u>hold</u> a wide variety of jobs. Economics <u>studies</u> how a society uses resources, such as money, labor, and materials.

simple past tense
  regular
  irregular
	I <u>migrated</u> to the U.S. from Hong Kong for several reasons.
	My family and I <u>came</u> here to look for freedom and a better future.

present perfect tense	Society <u>has changed</u> over the years.
past perfect tense	The German Jews <u>had lived</u> in the Bavarian village of Buttenheim for at least several generations.
present progressive tense or present continuous tense	The people in my country <u>are changing</u> their lifestyles.
past progressive tense or past continuous tense	They joined many other immigrants who <u>were struggling</u> to fulfill their dreams in America.

7U   Other Words Used to Talk about Verbs: Infinitives and Participles

infinitive (*to* + **verb**) **Infinitives** are used in three major ways: as direct objects, as adverbials, and with nouns. The three ways are illustrated in the examples.	He wants **to write** about the culture of his native country. I came to the university **to study** engineering. Many people in the downtown area are hungry and don't have a place **to live**.
present participle or *ing* participle The present participle is used to form present and past progressive verb tenses. These verbs are illustrated in the examples.	The towns in my country **are developing** quickly. They **were fleeing** religious persecution, or cruel treatment, in their native lands.
past participle or *ed* participle or *en* participle The past participle is used to form present and past participle verb tenses. It is also used to make passive verbs. These verbs are illustrated in the examples.	Society **has changed** over the years. Under King Louis XVI, France **had become** an ally of the United States. At first, oil **was made** into kerosene, a fuel burned in lamps.

APPENDIX A: LINKING VERBS

Linking verbs connect (link) a subject to a complement. A complement is a word that renames or describes the subject. (For more information about linking verbs, visit the WWW at http://www.gsu.edu/~wwwesl/egw/vanassch.htm.)

Be Linking verbs include all of the forms of *be*. Notice that *be* is used as the verb (not as an auxiliary).	Your textbook **is** an excellent study tool. A textbook and a road map **are** similar. Bavaria **was** a beautiful land.
Senses Linking verbs also include verbs related to the senses such as *feel, look, smell, sound,* and *taste.*	She always **feels** nervous on the first day of class.
Other Verbs Linking verbs include other verbs such as *appear, become, grow, prove, remain,* and *seem.*	Children generally stop sleepwalking when they **become** older.

Here is an alphabetized list of some common linking verbs.

appear (to be)	prove
be (am, is, are, was, were)	remain
become	seem
feel	smell
grow	sound
look	taste

APPENDIX B: COMMON PREPOSITIONS

This is an alphabetized list of common prepositions. It is not a complete list. When you learn a new preposition, add it to this list. Review the list frequently. (For more information about prepositions, visit the WWW at http://www.gsu.edu/~wwwesl/egw/index1.htm.)

about	beneath	into	toward(s)
above	beside	like	under
across	besides	near	underneath
after	between	of	until
against	beyond	off	up
along	by	on	upon
among	down	out	with
around	during	over	within
at	for	since	without
before	from	through	
behind	in	throughout	
below	inside	to	

APPENDIX C: ADJECTIVES

Improving your knowledge and use of adjectives will help you provide detail and description to your writing. One way to improve your adjective vocabulary is to study adjectives in categories and groups, such as *weather* or *shapes*. When you learn a new adjective, add it to the appropriate category or develop a new category. Complete and review your adjectives chart frequently.

Personality	Places	Size	Weather	Shapes/Textures	Age
shy	relaxing	large	windy	round	old
aggressive	beautiful	tiny	rainy	smooth	young
outgoing		huge	foggy		

APPENDIX D: IRREGULAR VERBS

The following is an alphabetized list of common irregular verbs. You should know the meaning and spelling of these irregular verbs. (For more information about irregular verbs, visit the WWW at http://www.gsu.edu/~wwwesl/egw/jones.htm.)

Base Form	Simple Past	Past Participle	*ing* Form
be	was/were	been	being
become	became	become	becoming
begin	began	begun	beginning
bite	bit	bit	biting
bleed	bled	bled	bleeding
break	broke	broken	breaking
bring	brought	brought	bringing
build	built	built	building
buy	bought	bought	buying
catch	caught	caught	catching
choose	chose	chosen	choosing
come	came	come	coming
cost	cost	cost	costing
cut	cut	cut	cutting
dig	dug	dug	digging
do	did	done	doing
draw	drew	drawn	drawing
drink	drank	drank	drinking
drive	drove	driven	driving
eat	ate	eaten	eating
fall	fell	fallen	falling
feed	fed	fed	feeding
feel	felt	felt	feeling
fight	fought	fought	fighting
find	found	found	finding

Base Form	Simple Past	Past Participle	*ing* Form
forget	forgot	forgotten	forgetting
forgive	forgave	forgiven	forgiving
freeze	froze	frozen	freezing
get	got	gotten	getting
give	gave	given	giving
go	went	gone	going
grow	grew	grown	growing
hang	hung	hung	hanging
have	had	had	having
hear	heard	heard	hearing
hold	held	held	holding
keep	kept	kept	keeping
know	knew	known	knowing
leave	left	left	leaving
lent	lent	lent	lending
let	let	let	letting
lose	lost	lost	losing
make	made	made	making
mean	meant	meant	meaning
meet	met	met	meeting
pay	paid	paid	paying
prove	proved	proved/proven	proving
put	put	put	putting
quit	quit	quit	quitting
read	read	read	reading
ride	rode	ridden	riding
ring	rang	rung	ringing
rise	rose	risen	rising
run	ran	run	running
say	said	said	saying
see	saw	seen	seeing

Base Form	Simple Past	Past Participle	*ing* Form
sell	sold	sold	selling
send	sent	sent	sending
shake	shook	shaken	shaking
show	showed	shown	showing
shut	shut	shut	shutting
sing	sang	sung	singing
sit	sat	sat	sitting
sleep	slept	slept	sleeping
speak	spoke	spoken	speaking
spend	spent	spent	spending
stand	stood	stood	standing
steal	stole	stolen	stealing
take	took	taken	taking
teach	taught	taught	teaching
tell	told	told	telling
think	thought	thought	thinking
understand	understood	understood	understanding
wake	woke	woken	waking
wear	wore	worn	wearing
win	won	won	winning
write	wrote	written	writing

APPENDIX E: EXAMPLE STRUCTURES

In English, we often begin by writing or saying something general. We then provide specific details that support or prove our general statement. Using example structures is one way to add specific details and support to your writing.

Format Style	Authentic Examples
Examples are introduced with logical organizers like *for example* or *for instance*. Usually, a comma and a complete sentence follow these logical organizers. (For other logical organizers that introduce examples, see the GLR, page 230.)	A function is any use of banquet facilities. *For example,* functions include meetings, dinners, conferences, and cocktail parties. I am a visual learner. *For instance,* I improve my vocabulary by reading the new words several times.
Examples are introduced with *such as* or *like*. Usually, noun phrases (not complete sentences) follow these words.	People in the upper class, *such as* owners of large businesses, top executives, and those with large investments, live in the most beautiful neighborhoods. Castes are inherited social classes that are found in some cultures *like* India.
A list of more than two or three examples is introduced with a colon (:).	Levi went to California with merchandise to sell: needles, thread, scissors, and other sewing supplies.
Examples are set off by one or more dashes (—). (Note: On many word processors, you can create a longer dash by inserting two hyphens between two words. There are no spaces on either side of the dash.)	Sufferers of migraine headaches experience many different side-effects. These range from the common—dizziness, nausea, diarrhea—to the strange—memory loss and speech disorders.
Examples are placed in parentheses ( ).	Artifacts (food, clothing, houses, and tools) are a part of culture.

Credits

Chapter 1
Page 9: "The U.S. Classroom." Adapted from "Classroom Management Techniques," by Becky Bodnar and Sharon Cavusgil, Annual Georgia TESOL Conference, Atlanta, GA, March 9, 1996.
Page 14: "Discover Your Learning Styles." Excerpted from Joy M. Reid, Editor, *Learning Styles in the ESL/EFL Classroom* (Boston: Heinle & Heinle Publishers, 1995).

Chapter 2
Page 34: "What Is Culture?" Adapted from H. Leon Abrams, Jr., *Inquiry into Anthropology,* Globe Fearon, Simon & Schuster Education Group, 1987).
Pages 47 and 48: "The One Thing Teens Want Most from Life" and "The Single Worst Influence Facing Today's Teens"; pages 49 and 50, "The Mood of American Youth". All adapted from a survey sponsored by the Horatio Alger Association for Distinguished Americans, Inc., in partnership with the National Association of Secondary School Principals, and reported by Dianne Hales in "How Teenagers See Things," *Parade Magazine,* August 18, 1996, 4-5. Reprinted by permission from Parade, © 1996 , the Horatio Alger Association, and Dianne Hales.

Chapter 3
Page 60: Photo © Michael Newman. PhotoEdit, Long Beach, CA.
Page 62: "Understanding Economics." Adapted from Allen W. Smith, *Understanding Economics* (New York: Random House, Inc., 1986, preface and pp. xxiii-xxvi).
Page 86: "Buying a Car." Adapted from *Facts for Consumers: New Car Buying Guide,* Federal Trade Commission, March 1992.
Page 87: Adapted from *Consumer Reports,* December 1977, 34-35.
Page 88 (top): Photo ©David Young-Wolff.

PhotoEdit, Long Beach, CA; (bottom): Photo © Robin L. Sachs. PhotoEdit, Long Beach, CA.

Chapter 4
Page 102: "Dreaming." Adapted from "Dreaming," *The New Book of Knowledge,* Vol. 4D. (Grolier, Inc., 1991, 317-8). Reproduced by permission.
Page 112: "Stages of Sleep." Adapted from Rae Lindsay, *Sleep and Dreams* (New York: Franklin Watts, Inc., Grolier Publishing Company, 1978, 17, 20).
Page 114: (top) Philip L. Groisser and Sol Levine, *U.S.A.: The Unfolding Story of America.*(Amsco School Publications, Inc., 1995, 302); (bottom) Adapted from Conrad Phillip Kottak, *Anthropology: The Exploration of Human Diversity* (McGraw-Hill, Inc., 1994, 358). Reproduced with permission of the McGraw-Hill Companies.
Page 115: (top) Anthony J. Strainese, *Dining Room & Banquet Management* (Albany, New York: Delmar Publishers, 1990, 164-5). Reproduced by permission; (middle) *Micro Menus Cookbook,* Whirlpool Properties, Inc., copyright Meredith Corporation; (bottom) Philip L. Groisser and Sol Levine, *U.S.A.: The Unfolding Story of America* (Amsco School Publications, Inc., 1995, 281).
Page 118: "Nightmares." Adapted from "Dreaming," *The New Book of Knowledge,* Vol. 4D. (Grolier, Inc., 1991, 317-8. Reproduced by permission.
Page 120: (top) "Snoring." Adapted from *Sleep Apnea and Snoring,* American Sleep Disorders Association, 1-2. Reproduced by permission; (bottom) "Insomnia." Adapted from *Insomnia,* American Sleep Disorders Association, 1-2. Reproduced by permission.
Page 121: Adapted from *Parasomnias: Things That Go Bump in the Night,* American Sleep Disorders Association, 1992, 2-3. Reproduced by permission.

Chapter 5
Page 130: "Blue Jeans: Yesterday and Today." Adapted from Elmer U. Clawson, *Our Economy: How It Works*, 3rd ed. (Addison-Wesley Longman Publishing Company, 1988, 52-57). Reproduced by permission.
Page 136: "Passport to a New Life." From Sondra Henry and Emily Taitz, *Levi Strauss: Everyone Wears His Name* (Dillon Press, an imprint of Silver Burdett Press, Simon & Schuster Elementary, ©1990). Used by permission.

Chapter 6
Page 155: Edwin L. Jackson, Mary E. Stakes, Lawrence R. Hepburn, and Mary A. Hepburn, "What Is Geography?" *The Georgia Studies Book* (Carl Vinson Institute of Government, University of Georgia, 1992, 28-9). Reproduced by permission.
Page 160: Adapted from *Exploring Your World: The Adventures of Geography,* National Geographic Society, 1989, 92-5, 243. Reproduced by permission.
Page 164: Adapted from Paul Rosenthal, *Where on Earth: A Geografunny Guide to the Globe,* (Alfred A. Knopf, Inc., Random House, Inc., 1992, 42, 89). Reproduced by permission.

Chapter 7
Page 184: (top) Adapted from Michael R. Solomon, *Consumer Behavior: Buying, Having, and Being,* 2nd ed. (Allyn and Bacon, Prentice-Hall, Inc., 1994, 48); (bottom) Adapted from Peter I. Rose, Penina M. Glazer, and Myron Peretz Glazer, *Sociology: Understanding Society,* (Prentice-Hall, Inc., 1990, 191).
Page 187: "The 'Typical' American Consumer." Excerpts from Anne Cronin, "A Statistical Portrait of the 'Typical' American: This Is Your Life Generally Speaking", *New York Times,* July 26, 1992, ES5. Copyright 1992, The New York Times Company. Reproduced by permission.

Grammar and Language Reference
Page 212: Adapted from Sigmund Kalina, *How to Sharpen Your Study Skills* (New York, Lothrop, Lee and Shepard Company, A Division of William Morrow & Company, Inc., 1975, 43-46). © 1975 by Sigmund Kalina. Reproduced by permission.
Page 220: (top) Wyatt Blassingame, *The Look-It-Up Book of Presidents.* (New York, Random House, 1996, 120); (middle) Adapted from Henry Brun, *Global Studies: Civilizations of the Past and Present* (Amsco School Publications, Inc., 1995, 22); (bottom) Adapted from Jodine Mayberry, *Leaders Who Changed the 20th Century* (Steck-

Vaughn Company, 1994, 14.)
Page 222: Adapted from Sheila Keenan, *Scholastic Encyclopedia of Women in the United States* (New York, Scholastic Inc., 1996, 31).
Page 223: Adapted from Sheila Keenan, *Scholastic Encyclopedia of Women in the United States* (New York, Scholastic Inc., 1996, 31).
Page 225: Adapted from Jodine Mayberry, *Business Leaders Who Built Financial Empires* (Steck-Vaughn Company, 1995, 34).
Page 226: *Social Security: Your Number,* (Social Security Administration, SSA Publication No. 05-10002, U.S. Government Printing Office, April 1996, 5).
Page 232: Barbara James, *Waste and Recycling* (Steck-Vaughn Company, 1990, 6).
Page 234: Adapted from Lionel Bender, *Understanding Communication and Control* (Silver Burdett Company, 1984, 34-36).
Page 237: Adapted from Sigmund Kalina, *How to Sharpen Your Study Skills* (New York, Lothrop, Lee and Shepard Company, A Division of William Morrow & Company, Inc., 1975, 32-33). © 1975 by Sigmund Kalina. Reproduced by permission.
Page 244: (top) Adapted from "Preventive Medicine—Senses," *The Marshall Cavendish Encyclopedia of Health* (New York, Marshall Cavendish Corpora-tion, 1995, 607); (middle) Adapted from Eve B. Feldman, *Benjamin Franklin: Scientist and Inventor* (New York: Franklin Watts, 1990, 14-15); (bottom) Joy M. Reid, Editor, *Learning Styles in the ESL/EFL Classroom* (Boston: Heinle & Heinle Publishers, 1995). Reproduced by permission.
Page 245: Adapted from H. Leon Abrams, Jr., *Inquiry into Anthropology* (Globe Fearon, Simon & Schuster Education Group, 1987, 4-5). Reproduced by permission of Globe Fearon.
Page 249: Adapted from *Sleep Problems in Children: A Parent's Guide,* American Sleep Disorders Association, 1990, 1996, 8-10. Reproduced by permission.
Page 256: (top) *Getting Online: A Friendly Guide for Teachers, Students, and Parents* (U.S. Dept. of Education, ERIC 96-5029 R); (middle) Karen Bornemann Spies, *Our Money* (The Millbrook Press, 1992, 5); (bottom) *How to Study for and Take College Tests* (ACCESS ERIC, Office of Educational Research and Improvement, U.S. Dept. of Education, NLE 97-2527).
Page 261: (top) *Tips for Finding the Right Job* (U.S. Dept. of Labor, Employment and Training Administration, 1996, 1); (bottom) *Social Security: Your Number,* (Social Security Administration, SSA Publication No. 05-10002, U.S. Government Printing Office, April 1996, 5).

Index

Adjective clauses (see Relative clauses)
Adjectives, 139, 262
Adverbials, 262
Adverbs, 263
Adverbs of frequency, 37, 42, 247
Also, 69
And, 50
Appositives, 138, 219
Articles, 263 (also see Generic articles)
Auxiliary verbs, 264 (also see Modal aux-
    iliaries)

Bar graphs (see Graphs)
Basic sentence structure, 7, 210
Blue jeans (see Strauss, Levi)
Both, 69
Budgets, 66, 71
But, 50, 67

Car buying, 86, 95
Categorizing nouns, 108, 240
Charts, 16, 46, 48, 156
Chronological organizers, 131, 223
Cities, 168, 169
Classification sentences, 158, 161
Classifying, 152, 154 (also see
    Classification sentences)

Clauses, 269 (also see Relative clauses,
    Non-restrictive relative clauses)
Cohesion devices, 65 (also see Logical
    organizers)
Collecting, 32, 33, 34, 38
Colons, 161
Comma splices, 264
Commas, 161
Comparatives, 83, 214 (also see
    Comparing)
Comparing, 60, 62, 67, 69, 73, 75, 83, 212
Complements, 265
Complete sentences (see Basic sentence
    structure)
Complex noun phrases, 160, 227
Conditional sentences, 81, 254
Conjunctions, 265
Consumer behavior, 180, 183
Consumer housing (see Housing)
Contrasting, 60, 62, 67, 76 (also see
    Comparing)
Culture, 32, 35
Customs, 35

Data, 198, 202
Defining, 98, 100, 104, 105, 106, 108, 110,
    112, 118, 238, 242

Definition structures, 104, 112, 242 (also see Defining)

Description, 139

Determiners, 263

Developing, 126, 128, 134, 139, 145, 146, 163

Different forms of a word (see Cohesion devices)

Discovering, 180, 182

Discussions, 10

Dreams, 98, 101, 112

E-mail messages, 92, 93

Economics, 64 (also see Personal economics)

Example structures, 21, 146, 147, 165

Exams (see Tests)

Expressions of quantity, 37, 42, 252

Extended comparisons, 73, 75, 77 (also see Comparing)

Extended definitions, 118 (also see Defining)

For Example, 21, 165

For Instance, 21, 165

Formal definitions, 104, 105, 238 (also see Defining)

Fragments, 53, 266

Generalizations, 37, 246

Generic articles, 106, 229, 239

Generic nouns, 106, 229, 239

Geography, 152, 155, 159, 163

Graphs, 46, 47

Housing, 79, 81, 83

However, 67

Immigrating (see Migration)

In Contrast, 67

Informational writing, 7, 34, 62, 155, 160, 165, 183, 226 (also see Past informational writing)

Insomnia (see sleep problems)

Interactive communication in writing, 34, 54, 183, 185, 255

Interviewing, 52

Jeans (see Strauss, Levi)

Learner's notebook, 6

Learning styles, 13, 16, 25

Letter (see Personal letter)

Levi (see Strauss, Levi)

Like, 165

Listing, 38, 39, 56

Logical organizers, 21, 50, 57, 65, 68, 70, 77, 165, 167, 212, 213, 230

Memorandum, 22 , 29

Message (see E-mail messages)

Migration, 135, 172, 177

Modal auxiliaries, 37, 42, 250

Nightmare (see Sleep problems)

Non-restrictive relative clauses, 138, 219

Noun phrases, 267 (also see Complex noun phrases)

Nouns, 267 (also see Generic nouns, Proper nouns)

Objects, 268

On the other hand, 67

Opinion structures, 37, 246

Organizing ideas, 21, 56, 74, 156

Outlines, 157

Parallelism, 170

Passive sentences, 165, 232, 272

Past informational writing, 155, 183

Past tense verbs, 132, 221

Past time narrative writing, 128, 131, 132, 144, 221

Personal budgets (see Budgets)

Personal economics, 60, 63
Personal experience, 145
Personal letter, 90
Personal pronouns, 144 , 185, 224, 259
Persuasive writing, 34, 37, 42, 62, 81, 100,
    246
Phrases, 269 (also see Complex noun
    phrases, Prepositional phrases)
Pie charts (see Charts)
Prepositional phrases, 160, 215, 269
Prepositions, 269
Present tense verbs, 105, 233, 239
Presentations, 200
Pronouns, 65, 259, 269 (also see Personal
    pronouns)
Proper nouns, 144, 224

Questions, 52, 193, 256

Relative clauses, 110, 217, 241 (also see
    Non-restrictive relative clauses)
Repetition of key words and phrases (see
    Cohesion devices)

Sentence adverbials, 271
Sentences, 270 (also see Basic sentence
    structure)
Sleep, 98, 101, 112
Sleep problems, 118, 120, 121, 122
Sleepwalking (see Sleep problems)

Snoring (see Sleep problems)
So, 50
Spoken English, 52, 194
Stereotypes, 40
Strauss, Levi, 126, 129, 135, 142
Study techniques, 16, 25
Subculture, 55
Subjects, 272
Subject-verb agreement, 235
Such as, 165
Surveys, 9, 25, 190, 192

Tables, 187
Tally sheets, 198
Tests, 116
Textbook features, 15
Too, 69
Traditions, 35
Typical consumer, 187

Verbs, 272, 273, 274

Words of difference, 67, 212 (also see
    Comparing, Contrasting)
Words of similarity, 69, 213 (also see
    Comparing)
Written definitions (see Defining)

Youth, 44, 52